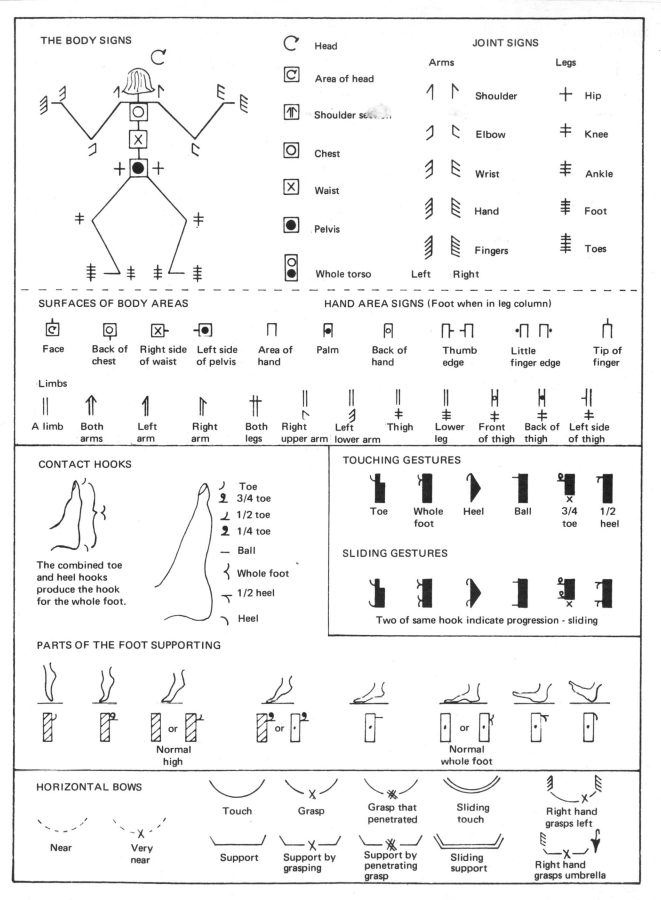

THE BODY SIGNS

Head
Area of head
Shoulder section
Chest
Waist
Pelvis
Whole torso

JOINT SIGNS

	Arms		Legs	
Shoulder			Hip	
Elbow			Knee	
Wrist			Ankle	
Hand			Foot	
Fingers			Toes	
	Left	Right		

SURFACES OF BODY AREAS

Face | Back of chest | Right side of waist | Left side of pelvis | Area of hand | Palm | Back of hand | Thumb edge | Little finger edge | Tip of finger

HAND AREA SIGNS (Foot when in leg column)

Limbs

A limb | Both arms | Left arm | Right arm | Both legs | Right upper arm | Left lower arm | Thigh | Lower leg | Front of thigh | Back of thigh | Left side of thigh

CONTACT HOOKS

The combined toe and heel hooks produce the hook for the whole foot.

Toe
3/4 toe
1/2 toe
1/4 toe
Ball
Whole foot
1/2 heel
Heel

TOUCHING GESTURES

Toe | Whole foot | Heel | Ball | 3/4 toe | 1/2 heel

SLIDING GESTURES

Two of same hook indicate progression - sliding

PARTS OF THE FOOT SUPPORTING

Normal high | or | | or | | | Normal whole foot | or | |

HORIZONTAL BOWS

Near | Very near

Touch | Grasp | Grasp that penetrated | Sliding touch | Right hand grasps left

Support | Support by grasping | Support by penetrating grasp | Sliding support | Right hand grasps umbrella

modern dance fundamentals

Nona Schurman

Sharon Leigh Clark

The Macmillan Company, New York
Collier-Macmillan Limited, London

Copyright © 1972, The Macmillan Company

Printed in the United States of America

The Macmillan Company
866 Third Avenue, New York, New York 10022

Collier-Macmillan Canada, Ltd., Toronto, Ontario

Library of Congress catalog card number: 79–151693

First Printing

DEDICATION

To

Doris Humphrey

and

Charles Weidman,

to whom I owe so much,

this book

is lovingly dedicated

Nona Schurman

To

my teachers

and to

my students

Sharon Leigh Clark

Notation by

Susie Watts Margolin

Orthography by

Irene Politis

Notation Checked by

Lucy Venable

preface

This book attempts to do three things: (1) to present simple, basic exercises in dance form for the beginner student or teacher; (2) to introduce these exercises with Labanotation; (3) to suggest the possible use of this material in a university or school situation in planning a well-balanced technique class or a class in improvisation.

The book is divided into three parts. Part I introduces the Laban system of movement writing and explains how to read it. In Part II, the main body of the book, the notated exercises will be found. These exercises have been arranged in anatomical order. Chapter 1 deals with the back, Chapter 2 with the feet and legs, Chapter 3 the arms, head, and shoulders. Chapter 4 is movement through space (the application of the technique in the space phrase). In order to help the reader in the first chapters, word notes and stick figures have been placed beside the notation. Chapter 5 contains the advanced material. This material is really beyond the technical reach of the beginner but it has been included to give him something to look forward to in developing physical skill and to show choreographic development. Part III contains suggestions for using these exercises as a basis for improvisation or for planning the technique class. In both cases the suggestions are for the inexperienced teacher, and are the result of many years' experience with students from pre-school age to university graduates. They have been tested and changed, tried again and revised. They work, they are enjoyable, and they are practical for the realities of public school teaching. Improvisation gives the beginning dance teacher a vision of what lies beyond the physical skill. However, it is wise to start from a reasonably secure technical base.

It has been obvious for some time that the traditional tools for recording movement—word notes, stick figures, drawings, and recently photographs and movies—leave much to be desired. Because of their very nature they can do only one thing describe the design the body makes in space. In other words, they stop the action. Word notes are at best a clumsy translation of lyric expression into pedestrian prose. Such tools therefore cannot describe the elements of speed, duration, accent, flow of energy, and so forth, which are such an important part of all movement. In order to suggest the elements of time, music notation is sometimes placed beside the drawings or word notes. The pictures (space design) and the music (time design) must of necessity be presented separately. In movement these two elements are inseparable. Movement is the subtle and simultaneous interweaving of various elements of time and space. The varying proportion of each of these elements within a specific movement is what gives that movement its character and identity. In order to dance it is not enough to know *how* or *where,* you must know *when* and *how fast* and *how long.*

The moving picture, although far superior to the other devices as a means of describing movement, stands in relationship to dance as recording does to live music. The moving picture does not describe, it records. In a recording the style and personality of the performer comes between the viewer and what is being performed. If this happens too early in his training the student tends to imitate. If this happens after the student has had some experience, it could be a lesson interpretation. In developing the artist the object is to train him to do things his way. For this to happen there must be some objective source available for him to study. Musicians can always return to the scores. It would help the dancer if he could do the same.

Dancers have never had the luxury of an efficient notation system. They have had to use the old methods of recording movement which, in turn, has kept alive the old methods of teaching movement, demonstration and imitation—the mouth to foot technique. There are few textbooks of the elementary exercises, and the ones available use the old notation system of stick figures. It is difficult to make a dance phrase from a series of stick figures just as it was difficult to make a sentence from the old picture writing. Without the use of notation, dance, after all these centuries, is still in the cuneiform period, complete with scribes.

Happily within the past twenty-five years a very efficient system of movement writing called *Labanotation* has been developed.[1] The time-space problem has been solved; and now duration, position, and movement can be described by a single symbol. Any movement made by the human body can be written with this system. Many dances have already been recorded in Labanotation and performed successfully and accurately without the composers' having to be present during the rehearsals. The problem is that the dancers cannot read the scores without taking a special course, so a notator must be present during the rehearsals to read and teach the dance. Musicians are never in this position. They have been trained to read music from their first lesson. Their first lesson introduces them to their instrument and to the notation. Musicians learn music by reading music, not by imitating. With the new system of movement writing, dancers can do the same.

Although there are complete dances recorded in Labanotation, up to now there have been no textbooks for the beginning dance student. If you want to develop a literate dance student, you must start at the beginning—with the first lesson. If the dance student learns to read his first exercises as he learns to perform them, he should be able to read quite complicated dance scores at the end of four years of training. This book hopes to do for the dancer what the music books do for the musician—with the first lesson introduce the dancer to his instrument and to the notation. This book, therefore, is a collection of basic fundamentals for the dancer, similar in scope to what would be five-finger exercises and scales for the musician. There are no full dances included, but the simple exercises are built into dance phrases which should give the student some feeling of what a phrase is before he has to compose or perform one. Dance notation can never replace a teacher, of course, any more than the music score replaces the music teacher, but with the notation the dancer will not be so dependent on the classroom situation. He will be able to study the mechanical and musical basis of the exercises out of class. Tempo, rhythm, phrase length, counts, body direction, and timing could be pre-

---

[1] See Ann Hutchinson, *Labanotation,* Second edition. New York: Dance Notation Bureau. 1970. Chap. 2.

pared before class thereby allowing more in-class time for the study of style and performance. This will change teaching procedures somewhat.

It is the good fortune of every writer to have an opportunity to express appreciation for those who have given support along the way. This type of book cannot be made by one person. It cannot be made by two people. It takes a team. Our most enthusiastic thanks goes to the technical half of "the team": Susie Watts Margolin and Irene Politis.

Susie Margolin, of the Dance Notation Bureau in New York, was responsible for notating the exercises. She was, in a sense, our Scribe. She analysed the movement, translated it into the symbols, and made neat copies for the orthographer—a time-consuming process with which she was more than generous. But before anything is put on paper the dancer's intention must be made clear. Sometimes this involved explaining a whole philosophy of movement. Mrs. Margolin's probing questions allowed our point of view also to appear on the staff, thus making an invaluable contribution to the book.

Irene Politis, a student of Miss Schurman's and a fine dancer in her own right, was responsible for the orthography. But beyond that, her intimate knowledge of the exercises, combined with her understanding of Labanotation and her incredible organizational skill, really brought this book to completion. She became the heart of the team, planning the whole working process from the copying of the first rough notation sketches to the final paste-up. Her tireless optimism and boundless energy were phenomenal. We are tremendously indebted to her.

Lucy Venable, formerly President of the Dance Notation Bureau in New York and now Director of its Extension Division at Ohio State University, checked the notation for accuracy. Her many constructive suggestions and words of encouragement are gratefully acknowledged.

It is one thing to write down what one thinks, but it is quite another to have it understood by one's colleagues. The authors express their deep thanks to S. Jane Dakak for her work on the class plans and her general enthusiasm for the project. To readers Edie Resnick, Katherine Terhune, Hope Wixson, Robert Myers, and especially Claudia Moore Read, who replaced Miss Schurman in the Humphrey-Weidman Company, our special thanks for their valuable suggestions.

The authors could never give enough credit to Lloyd Chilton of The Macmillan Company, our main sustaining force, for his courage in tackling the formidable task of the putting together the first book of this nature. We value his humor and kindness and are most appreciative of his special qualities.

We are indebted to Miss Lisa Ullman, Director of The Laban Art of Movement Center, Addlestone, Surry, England, for her waiving of the usual royalties for use of the basic vocabulary—a kind and generous gesture. We would also like to thank Ann Hutchinson, first for writing the textbook on Labanotation and also for permitting us to incorporate some of the sketches from it in Part I of this book.

To all these fine people our heartfelt thanks.

N. S.
S. L. C.

brief table of contents

detailed table of contents

part I
introduction to labanotation

The exercises in this book are in Labanotation. This system of movement writing, also known as *Kinetography Laban,* is a concise and precise way of describing with symbols any movement made by the human body. The system was invented by Rudolf Laban, a well-known teacher and choreographer, who taught in Germany for many years. When Hitler came to power, Laban moved to England where his work was already established at the Jooss-Leeder Dance School. It was at this school that Ann Hutchinson studied what Laban called *Script-dance*—"written dance," the emphasis being on writing the movement rather than position. With the outbreak of World War II, Miss Hutchinson returned to her native New York where she found others using the Laban system. Feeling the need of a central clearing house and information center, with three colleagues she founded the Dance Notation Bureau in New York. Contact with Laban and specialists in other countries was impossible during the war. However, the New York group concentrated on the practical application of the system, preparing the teaching materials and correspondence courses that culminated in Ann Hutchinson's first text book, called *Labanotation.*

After the war when contact was finally re-established, notators in different countries found they had developed some different writing rules as well as different uses for some of the symbols. In order to iron out the differences and develop a truly international system of movement writing, these specialists from all over the world formed the International Council of Kinetography Laban (ICKL). This unique organization meets every two years to standardize and develop this system of movement writing. Many modern dance and ballet choreographers have had their works successfully performed from the Labanotated scores. Governments of many countries are having their folk dances notated in Labanotation to preserve them before they disappear with the encroachment of urbanization. This is true of Hungary, Ghana, and many more. In a few years, if you can read notation, the dances of the world will be as close to you as your local library.

This book has been planned with the inexperienced reader of notation in mind. In essence, Labanotation is a new language. In learning any language, the student must become

1

familiar with the terminology. The difference inherent in learning the language of dance through notation is the opportunity it gives to act out the language of the body.

The design of the book is intended to make learning notation relevant to "doing" dance. The main glossary for the symbols will be found in the end papers. As you progress through the book any new symbols used in an exercise will be found in a page legend.

The purpose of this section is to give you, the reader, a complete picture of Labanotation. Read it through carefully, but do not become discouraged. Word notes and stick figures are included beside the notation in Chapter 1. In Chapter 2, word notes and stick figures have been reduced to only those exercises which begin a related series. Chapter 3 and 4 do not contain graphic aids, and in Chapter 5, the advanced material, there is only notation. By the time you get there we cheerfully hope you will be able to read and comprehend the exercises and perform them with confidence.

FUNDAMENTALS OF LABANOTATION

    A. Labanotation is the detailed analysis of movement of the human body in objective terms according to the elements of space, time, energy, and the part of the body moving.

    B. It uses symbols to describe these elements.

    C. These symbols describe movement in terms of

        1. Visual results in space
        2. Part of the body moving
        3. Direction
        4. Path
        5. Placement of the center of weight
        6. Timing—when to start, when to stop, how fast, how long
        7. Amount of energy
        8. Relationship—to the surrounding space, to other performers.

    D. One symbol states by its shape, the direction of the movement; by its shading, the level; by its length, the duration; by its placement on a staff, the part of the body moving.

SYMBOLS

Labanotation provides a sufficient number of symbols to describe very complicated movement, but because the exercises in this book are simple the reader need only be concerned with the simple symbols necessary to describe them. For convenience we will call the symbols *Primary* and *Secondary*. Also for convenience and clarity of analysis we will present separately the symbols used to describe the Spacial aspects of movement and the Time aspects of movement.

Space Symbols

Primary

Direction

The basic symbol, the rectangle ☐ indicates place *center* from which the directions are taken. Like a note in music or a letter of the alphabet it says little until it is used in a specific context. The principal directions are Forward, Sideward, Backward, and Diagonal. These directions are clearly indicated by modifying the shape of the basic symbol.

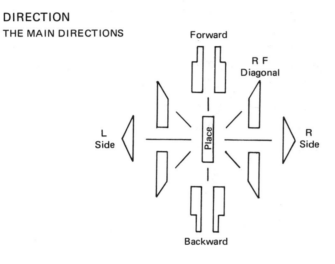

DIRECTION
THE MAIN DIRECTIONS

Forward

R F Diagonal

L Side

Place

R Side

Backward

Rotation

Left   Right

This symbol, a modification of the basic rectangle, is used for the whole body turning on its axis or to indicate rotation of a part of the body.

Level

To indicate level the basic symbol is shaded. The principal levels are high, middle, low.

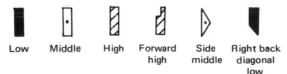

Low   Middle   High   Forward high   Side middle   Right back diagonal low

1. Level of Support. Normally we stand at middle level. Low is with bent knees; high is on the toes.

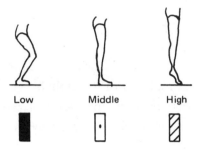

2. Level of Gestures. Movement of a limb which does not carry weight is a gesture.

Arm levels: Normally the arm hangs down by the side of the body when we are standing; place low the starting position. Middle level is horizontal with the shoulder. High is above shoulder level; low is below shoulder level. Because the whole arm moves from the shoulder joint, direction and level are taken from that joint.

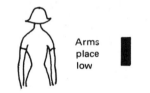

Levels for the Arms. Examples shown are for the right arm.

Forward low	Forward middle	Forward high	Place high
Side low	Side middle	Side high	Place high

Leg levels: Normally the legs are under the hips when we are standing, this is place low, the starting position. Middle level is horizontal with the hip; high above the hip. Because the leg moves from the hip, direction and level are taken from that joint.

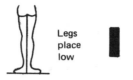

Legs place low

Levels for Legs. Examples shown are for the right leg.

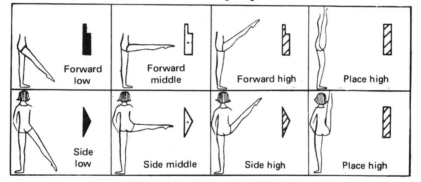

| Forward low | Forward middle | Forward high | Place high |
| Side low | Side middle | Side high | Place high |

Parts of the Body

Each part of·the body has its own sign and starting position. One of these signs placed before a direction symbol indicates movement for that part of the body.

The arms and legs are normally below the point of attachment: the head, chest, and whole torso are normally above the point of attachment from which they move, i.e.

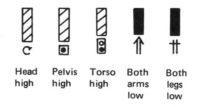

Head high   Pelvis high   Torso high   Both arms low   Both legs low

5

PARTS OF BODY

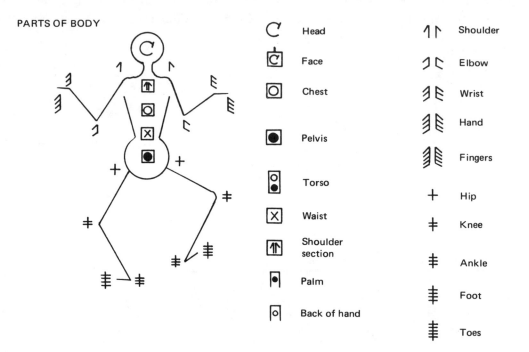

Head	Shoulder
Face	Elbow
Chest	Wrist
Pelvis	Hand
	Fingers
Torso	Hip
Waist	Knee
Shoulder section	Ankle
Palm	Foot
Back of hand	Toes

Flexion (contraction and curving or folding)

There are two forms of flexion: contraction and curving (folding).

1. In contracting the limb, the extremity approaches the base on a straight line. The center bulges and is displaced in space. A contraction sign placed before the required direction symbol modifies it.

The six degrees of contraction

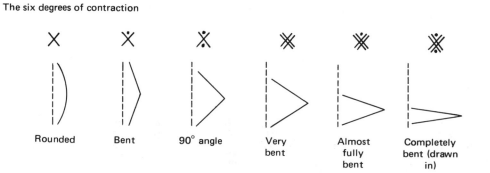

Rounded   Bent   90° angle   Very bent   Almost fully bent   Completely bent (drawn in)

Contracting the arm: Normally the arm is held with a soft elbow and a relaxed (but not limp) wrist. When the arm is contracted the hand and the shoulder approach each other on a straight line, the center joint, the elbow, bends and is displaced in space.

6

Contraction in the forward direction, middle level: Elbow moves side.

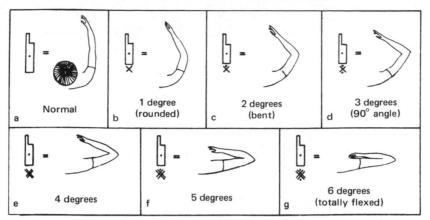

a Normal
b 1 degree (rounded)
c 2 degrees (bent)
d 3 degrees (90° angle)
e 4 degrees
f 5 degrees
g 6 degrees (totally flexed)

If the contraction starts with the arm rotated outward, (palm facing up), the degrees of flexing will be the same but the elbow will move downward instead of side.

Contraction of arm, rotate outward. Elbow moves down.

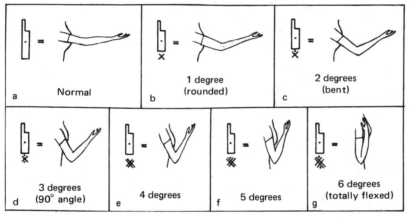

a Normal
b 1 degree (rounded)
c 2 degrees (bent)
d 3 degrees (90° angle)
e 4 degrees
f 5 degrees
g 6 degrees (totally flexed)

Contracting the leg: When contracting the leg, the hip and foot approach each other on a straight line, the center joint, the knee, bends and is displaced in space.

Contraction for leg, turned out. (Outward rotation.)

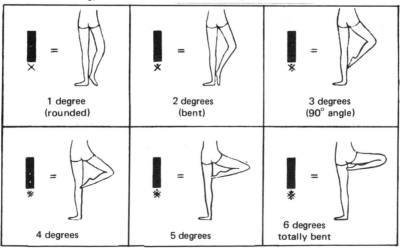

1 degree (rounded)
2 degrees (bent)
3 degrees (90° angle)
4 degrees
5 degrees
6 degrees totally bent

2. *Curving (folding).* In curving (folding), the extremity approaches the base on a curved line. The base joint is not affected and does not move.

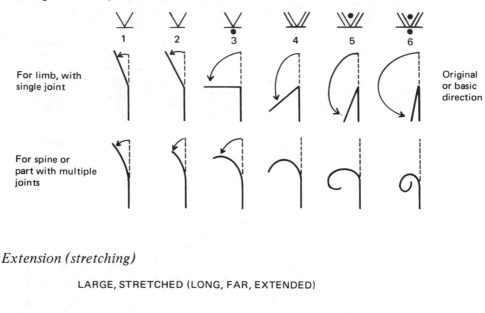

Six degrees of folding, or bending

For limb, with single joint

For spine or part with multiple joints

Original or basic direction

Extension (stretching)

LARGE, STRETCHED (LONG, FAR, EXTENDED)

Large, side, stretched (straightened)

Very large, very side, very stretched, extended, pulled out

Extension of the arm: A stretched arm gesture means that the arm is straight; the elbow, wrist, and hand are in a straight line. The fingers are straightened as part of the hand but are not especially taut or extended.

Extension of the leg: A stretched leg gesture means that the knee is taut, and the foot is pointed.

These symbols can be used to indicate length of stride or steps that are wider or longer than normal.

Center of Weight

The center of weight (center of gravity) is in the pelvis and is indicated by a large black dot ●. The progression of the center of weight that occurs in movement through space, such as walking and leaping is taken for granted. However, it is sometimes important to indicate whether the center of weight preceeds or follows the action. In big body movements such as back bends the center of weight shifts although there is no movement through space.

Details of Body Signs

1. Body Areas.

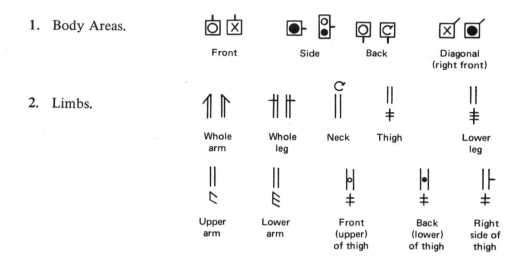

2. Limbs.

3. Contact hooks for parts of the foot: Hooks attached to a movement symbol indicate which part of the foot is in contact with the floor either touching or supporting weight.

Toe ⌐ and heel ⌐ hooks combined produce the symbol for the whole foot ⟨.

Key to parts of the foot: Note the different uses of the ball of the foot. In addition to the normal ½ toe there is the higher ¾ toe (high arch) and a lower use with the heel closer to the floor. The small circles indicating these differences are white for the higher and black for the lower.

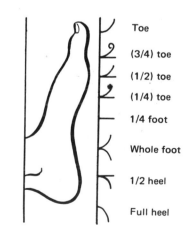

Relationship, Relative Position, or Displacement

1. The black pins indicate the relationship of one part to another, i.e., ⬇ in front, ⬆ behind. They state which foot or hand or arm is in front of or behind the other. The point of the pin is the indicator. Placed inside the rotation symbol they show the degree of turn.

2. Degree of turn.

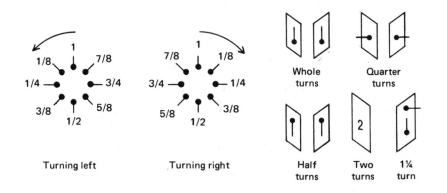

Front Signs

The sign for an area is a square. □ A flat ⊥ pin placed in this square shows what part of the area, studio or on stage, the dancer is facing. Eight main directions are indicated in this way.

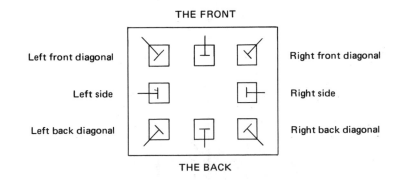

Path Signs ▮

As the body moves through space, (walking, running, turning), it creates a path. Normally we move forward on a reasonably straight path. Modifications of this path are indicated by combining several symbols. A direction sign placed in the path sign specifies the direction of travelling.

1. *Straight path.*　　　　　　　　　　　　　　　**2.** *Circular path.*

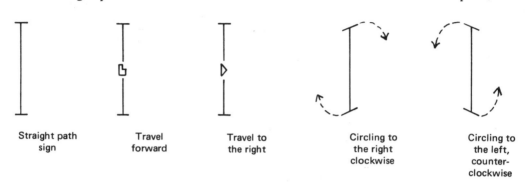

| Straight path sign | Travel forward | Travel to the right | Circling to the right clockwise | Circling to the left, counter-clockwise |

Black pins placed within the broken vertical line show the amount of circling and the degree of change of front.

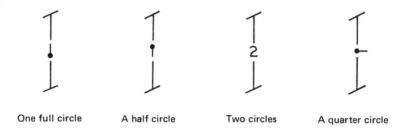

| One full circle | A half circle | Two circles | A quarter circle |

Retention Signs

1. Body Hold. **O** This sign is used to indicate a pause or stopping of movement of a particular part of the body.

2. Space hold. **◇** The sign is used to show that one part of the body holds its position in space although the rest of the body moves.

Cross of the Body Axis ⊢◇⊣

This sign indicates that direction is judged from the structure of the body. This means that "up" is always toward the head and "down" is always toward the feet, even if you are lying on your back, are upside down, or in some other position.

11

Time Symbols

Primary

The passage of time is indicated by the length of the movement symbol written on the paper.

The Time Line

A vertical line indicates the passage of time. Regularly occuring beats are indicated by placing small horizontal strokes at regular intervals across the vertical time line.

Duration Line

A lighter vertical stroke is used in a more specific context. When combined with an action symbol it states how long an action is to last.

Length of Symbols

The length of the movement symbol determines its time value—its duration.

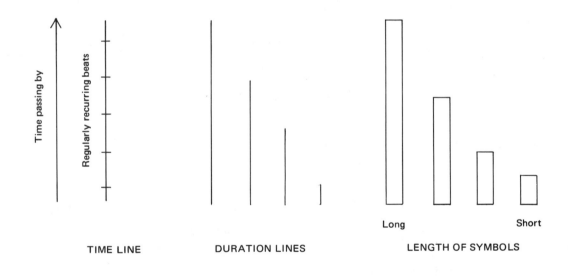

TIME LINE   DURATION LINES   LENGTH OF SYMBOLS

The Measure

As in music, beats are organized into groups called measures. Music measures are separated by the vertical bar lines. The labanotation bar line is horizontal, cutting the time line at right angles.

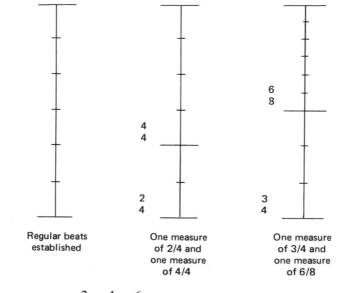

| Regular beats established | One measure of 2/4 and one measure of 4/4 | One measure of 3/4 and one measure of 6/8 |

Time Signatures, Meter. $\frac{3}{4}$, $\frac{4}{4}$, $\frac{6}{8}$

Two numbers written vertically at the beginning of the notation. The upper number represents the number of beats in a measure, the lower number indicates the note value of those beats. The 4 on the bottom represents a quarter note (♩) the 8 an eighth note (♪).

Tempo Markings

The Italian word *tempo* simply means *how fast,* at what rate of speed the beats are occurring. For this we use the regular musical terms as well as metronomic markings. These symbols and indications (e.g. Lento ♩ = 60) will be found at the beginning of most exercises, under the notation.

Dynamic Markings

The degree of force used for a movement, and the presence of accents are indicated with the following signs:

13

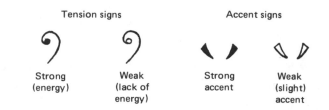

Tension signs

Strong
(energy)

Weak
(lack of
energy)

Accent signs

Strong
accent

Weak
(slight)
accent

Note: The accent sign points in to the symbol it describes.

Repeats and Second Endings

Repeat signs ÷, ≑ , indicate how many times an exercise or phrase should be repeated.

The concluding movement or position, after all the repeats have been made, is found in the second ending.

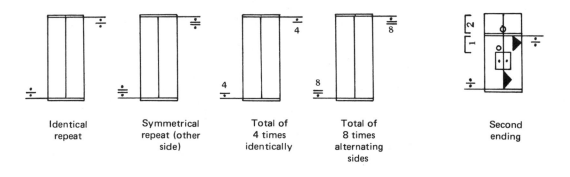

Identical
repeat

Symmetrical
repeat (other
side)

Total of
4 times
identically

Total of
8 times
alternating
sides

Second
ending

HOW TO READ NOTATION

The Staff

The symbols by themselves describe isolated movement but they are like pieces of a jig-saw puzzle—only when they are organized and placed in their proper relationships can the full picture be seen. The organizing agent for the symbols is the staff. This staff is similar to the five line music staff but is turned on the vertical and read from the bottom up. The main staff consists of three lines. The middle line, representing the center line of the body, serves as the time line and also divides the staff into right and left. Movement for the right side of the body is written on the right side of the staff, movement for the left side of the body on the left side. The beat lines cut across the center line, the bar lines across the full staff. The spaces between the lines become columns, each reserved for the action of a particular part of the body. By placing the symbols in their respective columns and giving them specific time values we get a complete picture of what the body is doing. The elements of time and space have been fused and the result can be read back as movement.

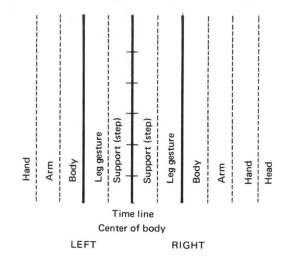

The Columns: The columns close to the center line are for the supports—usually the feet. However if any part of the body is actively supporting the body weight that sign is placed in the support column. Next to the support columns are the leg gesture columns used for action of the legs when they are not carrying weight. Outside the main staff are the body columns. The one on the left is used for the pelvis and whole torso; the one on the right for the rib cage and shoulder girdle. Adjacent to the body columns are the ones for the arms and beyond these on the right side of the staff is the column for the head. In writing action for the limbs the column is sometimes divided for clarity and ease of reading. (see diagram).

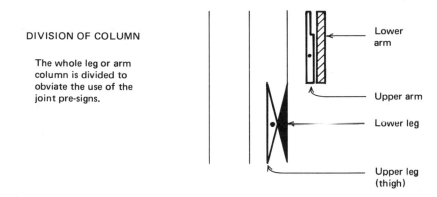

DIVISION OF COLUMN

The whole leg or arm column is divided to obviate the use of the joint pre-signs.

General note: Movement of the feet and legs is found inside the staff; movement of the torso, arms, and head is found outside the staff.

Timing: Rhythm and Duration.

The space between the beat lines represents the duration of a beat. If a movement is to last for one beat the movement symbol will occupy the space between the beat marks. If a movement is to last a full measure the movement symbol will fill the space between the bar lines. The space for the beat can be subdivided into various lengths to represent specific rhythms. Usually the beat is divided according to music note values (i.e. eighth notes, sixteenth notes, triplets, etc.). The shorter the time value the shorter the symbol. It is the length of the symbol which determines the duration of the movement.

Note: In reading notation we see the total movement which includes its time and space values. When learning to dance there are times when one aspect of the movement is emphasized at the expense of another depending on what the student finds difficult. The same procedure can be used here. If there is a timing problem just clap the rhythm until it is familiar. If there is a movement problem ignore the beat for a while and find out what the body is doing. Or, work on the supports and then add the other parts of the body. After it is understood slowly put it all together. Just because it is all written down does not mean it has to be performed that way the first time around. Again like the puzzle—once the pieces are in place you have the picture.

Supports

1. Two feet.

1st position   2nd position   Parallel 1st

2. One foot.

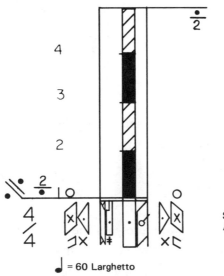

Starting Position:
As in Ex. 85

♩ = 60 Larghetto

16

3. Different parts of the Body: (Sitting, lying, kneeling, rt. hand support, transfer of weight.)

| Standing | Sitting on both hips | Lying on back | Kneeling on both knees | Supporting on both hands |

Use of full staff: **Whole body**

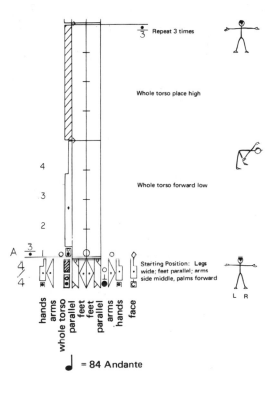

If the starting position for an exercise is from the normal upright standing position the symbol for the whole torso is not included, it is assumed that if we are standing the whole torso will be place high 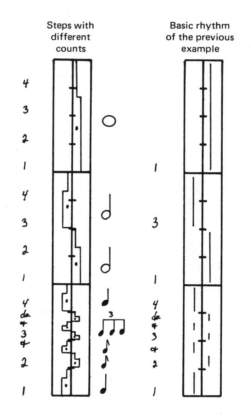. However, in the example the standing positions for all parts of the body have been included to show how the columns are used, but do not expect to find the body position included in the starting position unless it is a deviation from the normal.

Timing and Rythmn:

Note: Dancers' counts are on the left, music notes are on the right to show the relationship.

Elevation and Leg Gestures

It is important to remember the simple rule—the absence of a symbol in the support column means absence of support—you are in the air, or elevated.

There are five basic forms of elevation.

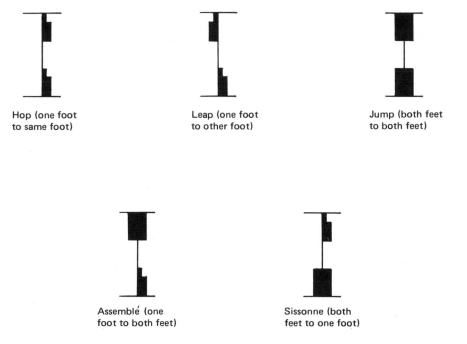

Hop (one foot
to same foot)

Leap (one foot
to other foot)

Jump (both feet
to both feet)

Assemblé (one
foot to both feet)

Sissonne (both
feet to one foot)

Movement

The timing of movements may be either sequential or simultaneous. Indications written one after the other are performed sequentially in time. Indications written side by side occur simultaneously.

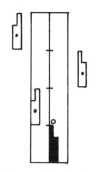

Sequential actions

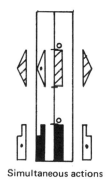

Simultaneous actions

The Duration Line

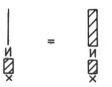

A duration line is used to indicate the time value for flexing or extending when there is no change in direction.

Circular Path

   The diagram represents a path walked with forward steps. This path can be broken up into portions of circling: 1/4 circle clockwise; 1/2 circle counterclockwise; straight for a few steps; 1/4 circle counterclockwise; 3/4 circle clockwise.

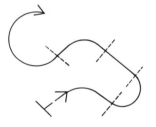

The notation for this path in space is as follows:

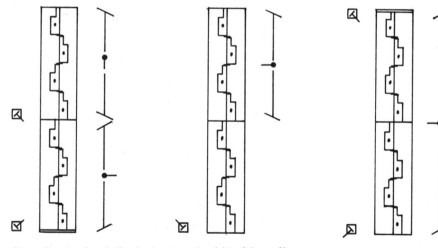

Note. The sign for circling is placed on the right of the staff.

   The front signs, on the left, indicate where the dancer is facing at certain points during the circling.

20

Steps

Use of parts of the foot

For Gestures

A hook indicating contact is drawn from the leg gesture symbol into the support column, (representing the floor). The different parts of the foot are represented by different hooks.

 =

A low leg gesture
to the side

 =

A side gesture
touching the floor

For Supports

By placing the hook on the support symbol, the specific part of the foot contacting the floor can be indicated.

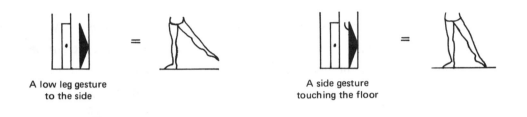

Normal walk, using
the flexibility of
the foot

A flat-footed
walk

Walking on
the heels

Low walk on
the ball of
the foot

Sliding Supports

The usc of two of the same hooks indicates a sliding support.

Steps sliding on
the whole foot

Steps sliding
on the heel

No slide; step on heel,
then whole foot

In these examples, the foot does not leave the floor between steps. The sliding occurs as the weight is transferred.

a   b

A distinction must be made between a *sliding gesture* and a *sliding support*. Where a gesture is used, the weight of the body remains in place (Figure a). In a step the weight begins to travel at once toward the direction stated (Figure b).

Turns

Turns can be made on one foot, on two feet, or in the air.

Turns on One Foot

The appropriate turn symbol is placed in the appropriate column, right or left.

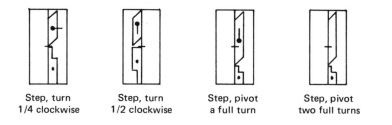

| Step, turn 1/4 clockwise | Step, turn 1/2 clockwise | Step, pivot a full turn | Step, pivot two full turns |

The turn sign does not indicate level. A turn is performed in the same level as the previous step or support.

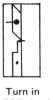

Turn in middle level   Turn in low level   Turn in high level

The turn sign is drawn across both support columns. For clarity, the positions in which you finish have been indicated in the first three examples.

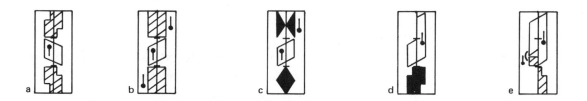

Notice the black pins beside the symbols in Figures b and c. They indicate the position of the feet. In b the left foot is in front to start. When the turn is completed the right foot is in front. In Figure c the turn is completed with the right foot in front. Figure d shows a turn starting on both feet and finishing on the right foot. In Figure e the reverse occurs; the turn starts on the right foot then the left is placed on the floor, and the turn continues on both feet. Figures a, b, and c can be done in the air.

Combinations of Step Turns

Turn as a Preparation for a Step

Turn on the left foot, step forward with the right. (See Figure A.)

Step as a Preparation for a Turn

Here the step is less important, the main action is that of turning. The turn is made on the same foot that takes the step. Step forward on the right foot, turn to the right. (See Figure B.)

Step and Turn Simultaneously

The two symbols for step and turn tied together with a bow shows that the two actions happen at the same time. As you take the step you are also turning.

          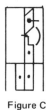

Figure A   Figure B   Figure C

Musical References

To understand the musical side of the notation the reader is urged to avail himself of a small music dictionary and a metronome. The authors have included all the information necessary to read the notation. However, readers may have musical questions that either are not answered in this book or are beyond its scope and which a music dictionary could handily answer.

The metronome, a device used by musicians for measuring rates of speed, is absolutely essential. The speed of the exercise is the key to its character and determines its technical value. At the beginning of the exercise there are two kinds of tempo markings. One is the metronomic marking, with the quarter note as the unit of time. The ♩ = 54 means there are 54 beats of the metronome per minute. The second indication of the speed is the musical term. The 54 beats per minute is Largo, which means slow. The reason for two indications is that there can be slight fluctuations of tempo depending on the size or character of the class, the degree of fatigue, and so on. The ♩ = 54 sets the speed precisely, whereas Largo can mean any speed between 40 and 60. The broad band of Largo gives the student and teacher some leeway in setting the tempo for the class.

There are several types of metronomes on the market. Probably a used wind-up type could be picked up somewhere, for very little expense. Such metronomes tend to slow up as the spring unwinds and are not very reliable. New, small, portable wind-ups are available which are very accurate and which have the Italian terms on the face. Electric metronomes are expensive but useful because of the flashing light attachment which can replace the click, an advantage when recording. However, they depend on the current of electricity and are not always accurate. If the reader cannot obtain a metronome, he might try taking his own pulse and checking it against his watch, then try to get relative speeds from that reading. Be sure to check the pulse before starting the exercise, not after.

Conclusion

In learning to read notation, the first thing to look at carefully is the total starting position. This is very important. If a starting position is clearly understood, the movements that follow will occur logically. Proceed slowly at first, ignoring all tempo markings until the movements of the exercise are understood; then attempts should be made to perform it at the given tempo. Good luck!

part II
the exercises

The exercises presented in this book were developed during my years of teaching at the 92nd. St. Y in New York, the New Dance Group Studio, and my own Studio. In this free studio atmosphere with virtually no technical, artistic, or administrative restrictions, I was free to explore and experiment with my material. The time between the experiment and the result was often very short. If things got dull the students dropped the class. If they didn't like what I did they said so. If they injured themselves I risked being sued. Most of them, however, kept coming back year in and year out, worked like professionals, and seemed to enjoy being guinea pigs. So the material presented here has been well tested in the open market, and I can honestly say it is teachable, enjoyable, builds strong bodies with good technique, and does so with a minimum of injuries. And, most important of all, it develops a love of and an understanding of dance.

Most of the exercises are mine, but all of them are based solidly on the technical principles I learned while studying with Doris Humphrey and Charles Weidman. Doris Humphrey's artistic application of the basic principles of body movement—fall and recovery, succession and opposition—plus her concept of the two types of rhythm—metric, or foot, rhythm—and breath rhythm—were revolutionary. Charles Weidman, with his musical sensitivity and wonderful sense of form, used these principles to design technical studies of breath-taking interest and vitality. Charles makes principles dance. From both of them I am indebted for their clear statements of the elements of dance composition without which it would have been impossible to develop my own material and keep myself fresh as a teacher. Their technique classes, so full of choreographic invention and provocative ideas on many subjects were a joy to take. I am grateful to them for encouraging us to develop our own studies based on these principles, thus starting me on a long voyage of discovery which is still going on.

But the greatest teacher of all is the human body, that remarkable and fascinating instrument. I want to thank all my students for giving me the opportunity of observing so many bodies in such detail and for being so patient with my experimenting. Teaching the body how to move well is an art of staggering complexity. There are more questions than there are answers, and in the end it is the body that teaches the teacher. Learning how to stand up straight becomes a philosophy and the craft supersedes the art. The craft of the dancer is all about the joys of simple things and that is what this section is about.

Nona Schurman

chapter 1
the back

If there is anything modern dancers of different technical persuasions could agree on, it might be the importance of the back as the source of all movement. For the modern dancer, this technical point of view has many artistic and choreographic implications. The concentrating of energy in the back and middle body gives importance to every movement the dancer makes and adds the rich emotional overtones so characteristic of this style of dance. This way of moving permits the choreographer to make (in movement terms) major social and philosophical statements that would look pretentious without this technical foundation.

This centralizing of movement in the deep muscles of the torso—particularly those surrounding the spine—has great anatomical validity; in designing exercises to develop the student's awareness of his back, it is wise to consider the characteristics and function of the spine.

Considered from a practical point of view, the spine could be thought of as a suspension bridge on which is hung the weight of the body. In four-legged animals, this analogy is very obvious.

The human animal stands upright with the heaviest weight of the body on top, but this vertical position has not changed the ancient function of that remarkable and flexible string of bones in his back. Man is still hung from his spine.

Although the principal function of the spine is to support the weight of the body, its outstanding characteristic is its snake-like ability to fold and unfold along its entire length. It can also rotate on its axis to some degree. Add to this the ability of the pelvis to tip on the legs, and we find the human animal—compared to our four-legged friends—has an enormous movement range. This range plus the vertical posture have increased the demands made on the muscles and ligaments surrounding the spine. The back must be strong enough to support and move the weights of the body without that strength in any way limiting the native flexibility of the spine. Modern dancers have been intuitive in their artistic application of these physical principles.

With the upright stance, man has virtually suspended himself in air. He is also suspended by air. The buoyancy and bounce of man's movement through space is at least partly the result of the lungs—the two balloons of air situated on either side of the top of the spine and which help to keep it in a vertical position, much like a child's balloon on a string. Protecting the lungs is the bony, airy rib cage, stable yet flexible, on which rests the shoulder girdle with the arm appendages. Thus protected, these balloons serve as air cushions helping to support the weight of the head and arms and absorbing the shock of lifting heavy objects by lightening the action. Without breath in the lungs, the human walk would be ponderous and level; as it is, man bounces from foot to foot as he moves about. The removal of the bounce is what gives the military goose-step its ominous quality.

The symbols used in this chapter are nothing more than a graphic way of describing what the body does naturally. The folding and unfolding of the back is called *successional movement.* When the action starts from the head and moves in toward the middle of the body, it is called an *inward succession* (a folding in of the torso) and is written this way: $\wedge$. When the action starts in the center of the body and moves out, it is called an *outward succession* (an unfolding of the torso) and is written like this: $\vee$. These terms are usually associated with the action of the back, but the arms and legs can and do move this way too. Practically every move man makes is successional. It is with difficulty that this basic action is inhibited.

The following exercises emphasize the successional action of the spine and are designed to increase the flexibility and strength of the back and middle body. The question of alignment will be discussed in Chapter 2. This chapter is mostly for movement.

* * * * *

A basic principle of body activity is opposition. There are many kinds of oppositional activity; the most obvious one is the mechanical opposition of the arms and the legs in the normal human walk. This could be described as the weights of the *opposite sides* of the body moving in the *same direction* at the *same time.* For instance, the *right arm* moves forward as the *left leg* moves forward. Or it could be thought of as the weights of the *same side* of the body moving in *opposite directions* at the *same time*—the right leg moving forward as the right arm moves backward.

A different kind of opposition is the take off and landing for elevation. First comes the plié (the going down) before the spring into the air. After the height of the jump, the legs again bend to catch the weight. If the legs are not strong enough to support the weight on the landing, the body will collapse. On landings from jumps, there is an automatic lifting up of the torso to maintain stability. In the simple relevé, the shoulders should press down as the heels come off the floor; otherwise the rib-cage tends to shift around.

Another type of opposition is the counter weight in movements like the back bend. If the head and chest are moved backward, the pelvis must move forward if balance is to be maintained.

28

The bending and extending of all the joints of the body involve the double action of the contraction of one set of muscles as the opposing set stretches. In all our movements, there is a resistance some place in the body to any motivated action of the human being. It is this built-in resistance which gives us our stability. Even the inhale and exhale is a form of opposition, and, of course gravity is our constant companion. Our vertical posture opposes its downward pull.

The study of opposition within the body is a tremendously exciting subject. The more you look, the more you find.

* * * * *

Reading the Stick Figures: The figures have been drawn to illustrate the notation. The figure has his back to you therefore *his* right side is *your* right side and the symbols for the action will be found on the right side of the staff, or the direction symbols will indicate "to the right." Do not look for the teacher-student relationship known as "mirror image." However, because of the problem of perspective it has sometimes been necessary to turn the figure around in order to make very complicated positions clear.

WARM-UP IN STANDING POSITION

1   Forward Succession from Standing

The forward succession from standing is an excellent body warm-up. It teaches the student how the back folds and unfolds, inward and outward succession.

Starting Position: The feet, in the support column, are either side of center ⟨⬧⟩ and parallel ⫿ . The arms are place low █ relaxed ⟩ at the sides.

In Measure 1, the inward successional symbol ∧ and the bow (indicate that the successional movement is lead by the head 𝒸 . The long black symbol █ indicates that it takes four counts to complete the succession, smoothly rolling each part of the body all the way down. (See Ex. 2 for detailed breakdown). In Measure 2, the outward succession ∨ starts up from the hips and the movement takes four counts to reverse the order of succession and return to the starting position ⫿ . Repeat four times ⌐⁄₄ . To increase skill and add excitement, the same movements are then done in two counts. The musical tempo does not change, but the body tempo does—it is twice as fast. Repeat four times ⌐⁄₄ . When the movement is done in one count, it must be started on the "and" or "up beat" so that it is finished on the "down beat." The music tempo retards in this but the body tempo again speeds up.

The quality of this exercise is a relaxed folding and unfolding. The feeling is of falling on the head. This may be somewhat frightening at first, but developing courage is part of, and one of, the great values of dance training.

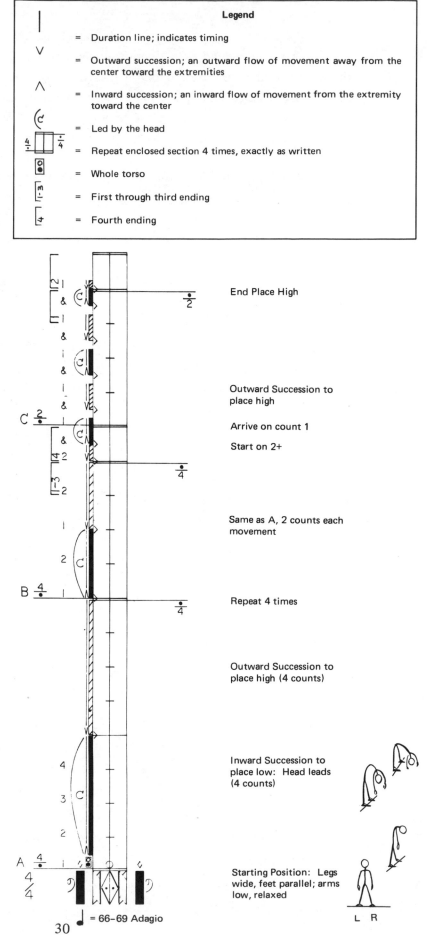

Legend

❘	=	Duration line; indicates timing
∨	=	Outward succession; an outward flow of movement away from the center toward the extremities
∧	=	Inward succession; an inward flow of movement from the extremity toward the center
(𝒸	=	Led by the head
⁴₁ □ ⁻⁄₄	=	Repeat enclosed section 4 times, exactly as written
⦾	=	Whole torso
⌐₁₋₃	=	First through third ending
⌐₄	=	Fourth ending

End Place High

Outward Succession to place high

Arrive on count 1

Start on 2+

Same as A, 2 counts each movement

Repeat 4 times

Outward Succession to place high (4 counts)

Inward Succession to place low: Head leads (4 counts)

Starting Position: Legs wide, feet parallel; arms low, relaxed

♩ = 66–69 Adagio

L   R

30

2 Breakdown of Forward Succession from Standing

This is a detailed breakdown of inward ∧ and outward ∨ succession, a simple folding and unfolding of the body in the forward direction.

Notice the notation symbols: ℂ -head; ▣ rib cage; ⊠ waist; and ⦿ pelvis. Each part of the body follows smoothly in succession, taking four counts to lower and four counts to reverse the order and recover to the starting position.

No other movement is indicated on the staff; therefore no other part of the body moves.

Note: A space hold ◊ is indicated for the arms. They remain hanging down with gravity (see stick figure drawings).

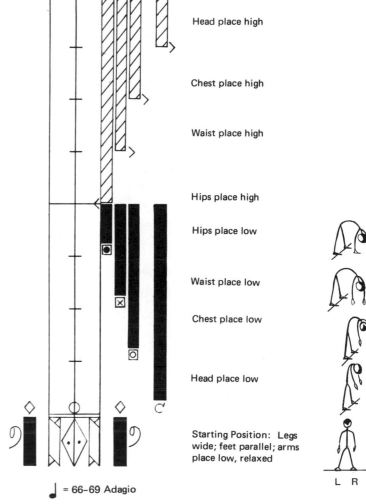

Head place high

Chest place high

Waist place high

Hips place high

Hips place low

Waist place low

Chest place low

Head place low

Starting Position: Legs wide; feet parallel; arms place low, relaxed

4

3

2

4/4

♩ = 66–69 Adagio

L   R

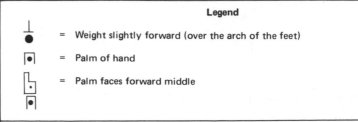
3 Forward Body Tip with Straight Back and Body Drop and Lift

A dancer not only must be able to move well, he must be able to stop moving at any time and hold given positions with strength and elegance. By holding or stopping the action, strength is built up around the joints, thereby greatly increasing control. For movement to be clear, the starting and ending positions must be precise and clearly performed.

In this exercise, the natural successional activity of the spine is inhibited. With the arms to the side ◁ ▷ , shoulder level, the whole torso tips forward smoothly in one piece from the hips to a position parallel to the floor forward middle. The back does not bend; the face does, however, maintain its spatial relationship to the front causing a slight backward bending of the neck. The arms stay in their starting position ○ .

Still maintaining the straight spine, the whole torso comes back to place high. There are four counts for each movement—four counts down, four counts up. The fourth time the torso is held in the forward tilt position for two counts. Then activity starts again in section B.

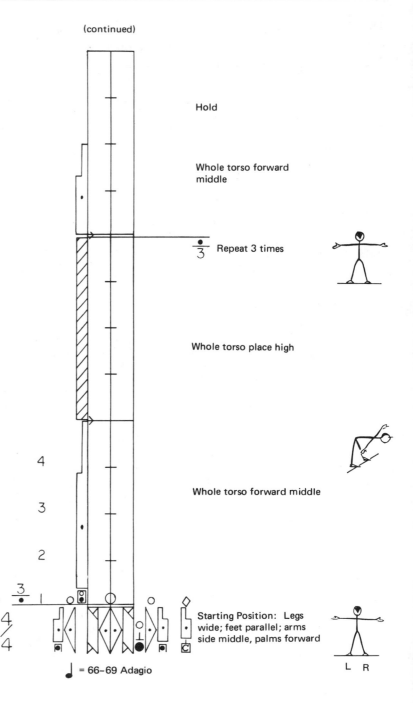

(continued)

Hold

Whole torso forward middle

Repeat 3 times

Whole torso place high

Whole torso forward middle

Starting Position: Legs wide; feet parallel; arms side middle, palms forward

♩ = 66–69 Adagio

L R

32

There is a quick release, the rib cage drops to place low ▮ ; a slight bounce occurs as the hands grasp the elbows, arms over the head; then the rib cage is swung up again to the horizontal position, arms side. This is repeated eight times. At the end of the eighth repeat, the whole torso is lifted to its normal standing position, which is place high. This takes two counts to perform. The arms take two counts to lower to their normal position, place low ▮ .

Note 1: On the drop of the rib cage there is a stretch of the muscles of the lower back followed by a sudden contraction and holding on the lift. Be sure the abdominals are pulled in on the lift to support the back. Make sure the knees are not hyperextended and the weight is forward over the arch.

Note 2: For a position to be clear, the body must be properly aligned. In notation the normal starting position of the whole torso is place high above the supports of the legs. The parts of the whole torso, the chest, pelvis, and head, are also properly aligned directly over the supports. Imagining these parts of the body as blocks, from the side the position would look like this. However, many people stand with the body poorly aligned, like this. Starting from this position the forward tilt would look like this, whereas what is asked for is this.

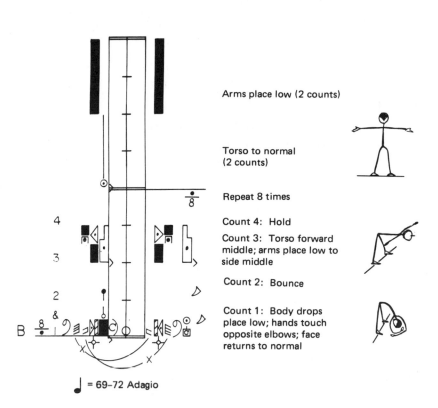

Arms place low (2 counts)

Torso to normal (2 counts)

Repeat 8 times

Count 4: Hold

Count 3: Torso forward middle; arms place low to side middle

Count 2: Bounce

Count 1: Body drops place low; hands touch opposite elbows; face returns to normal

B

4

3

2

&

♩ = 69–72 Adagio

33

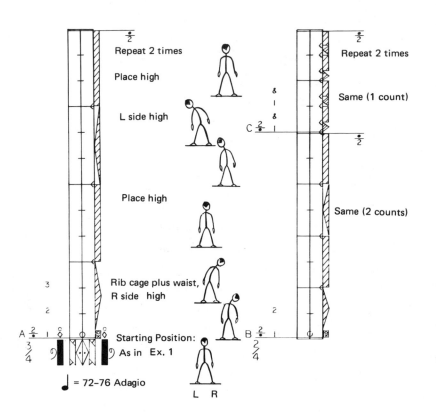
4   Side Bend of Rib Cage and Head

The body is capable of movement in any direction. This sequence introduces movement to the side, giving a tremendous stretch in the waist in the side away from the direction of the bend. The feet are in parallel second position   . The body is upright   . The arms are place low.

Starting Position: The same as in Ex. 1.

On count 1, the whole upper torso   tilts to the side, while the pelvis and center of weight are held steady, facing front. Neither the head nor the shoulder girdle should fall forward high   . The action is   , side high.

Note: As the movement changes from one side to the other, the body starts through center   on count 1, without stopping. Increasing speed adds excitement, as in Ex. 1, and shows how a change in tempo can alter the character of a movement. Avoid bending the knee or falling forward.

34

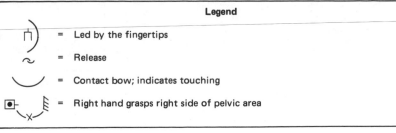
5 Side Bounce with One Arm

This is a variation of Ex. 4. The body does the same thing but now the weight of one arm over the head has been added. This results in a stronger, deeper stretch.

Starting Position: Same as Ex. 4, except the L arm is above the shoulder, making it place high , L palm facing front . The R hand is on the R hip, . The elbow is to the side.

There is a small pushing down —•— and a corresponding spring back —o— to create the bounce.

Note: There is a quick change of arms to the opposite side on the count "8 and." Repeat eight times .

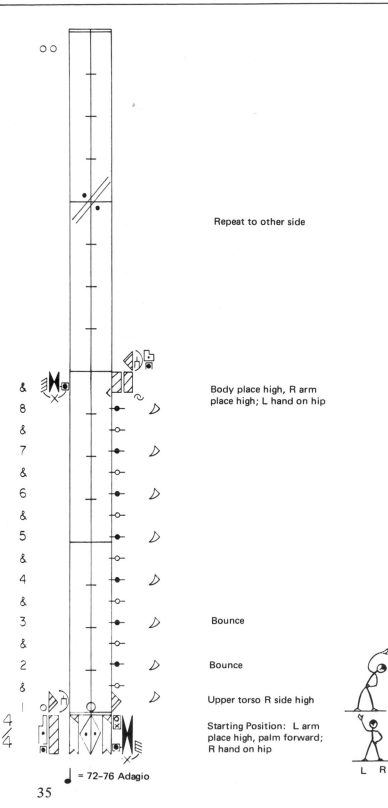

Repeat to other side

Body place high, R arm place high; L hand on hip

Bounce

Bounce

Upper torso R side high

Starting Position: L arm place high, palm forward; R hand on hip

L   R

♩ = 72–76 Adagio

35

Legend

○ = Body hold; used to indicate a part of the body maintains its relationship to the body even though the body is moving in space

6   Transition from Ex. 5 to Ex. 7

Transitions give a needed breath-pause after the effort of an exercise. At the same time they serve to keep a class moving by tying together a series of techniques. The manner and order of presentation, pacing, is as important as what is presented. This is what distinguishes a dance class from an exercise class.

After the bounces with one arm (Ex. 5), the right arm is lowered through the side ▷ to place low ▮ and both arms come up through side ◁ ▷ to place high ▨ , preparing for the side tilt.

7   Side Bend with Both Arms

Here is another variation of Ex. 4—the side tilt with both arms over the head. The added weight of both arms increases the stretch and control necessary to tilt the upper body cleanly into the side direction. Because this sequence uses the deep strong muscles of the middle body, it is deceptively difficult. The quality of the movement is smooth. The rib cage carries both arms in a wide arc over the head as it swings through center. Repeat twice for a total of eight counts.

Note 1: It is easy to see that Ex. 5 and Ex. 7 are very similar. There is, however, a dynamic and rhythmic change. Watch for the hold ○ on the arms as they remain overhead. A common error is for the arms to move to ▷ on the body tilt.

Note 2: An inhale on the lift to center is a tremendous help.

8   Coda for Ex. 7

At the end of Ex. 7 both arms are slowly lowered through side ◁ ▷ to place low ▮ .

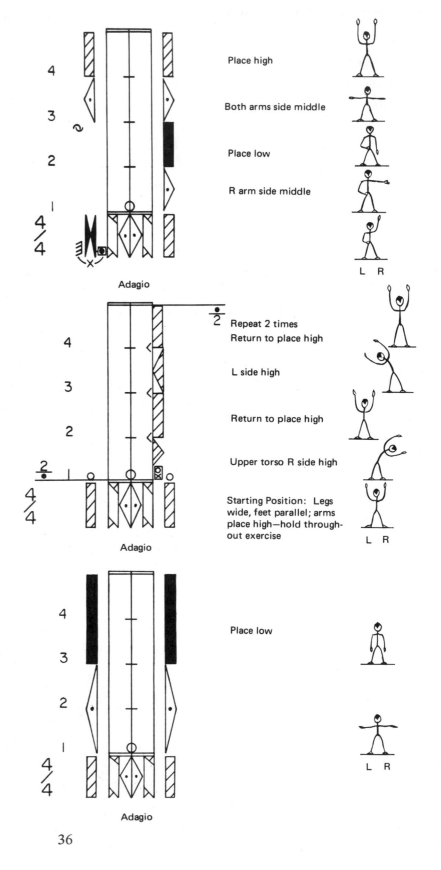

Place high

Both arms side middle

Place low

R arm side middle

L R

Adagio

Repeat 2 times
Return to place high

L side high

Return to place high

Upper torso R side high

Starting Position: Legs wide, feet parallel; arms place high—hold throughout exercise

L R

Adagio

Place low

L R

Adagio

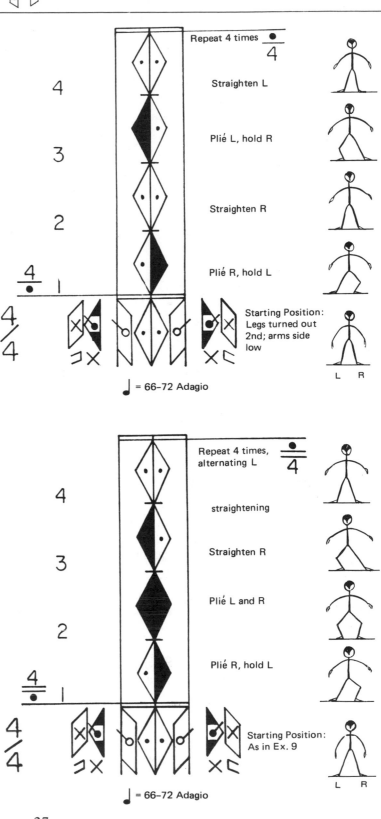
= Right arm is side low, flexed one degree and slightly forward diagonal elbow is rotated inward slightly

= Repeat enclosed section 4 times, alternating sides

= Legs rotated out so that feet form a 45° angle

9 Leg Action for Side Bend

Chapter 2 will deal more thoroughly with the action of the legs. However, students must learn to relate the body to the legs as soon as possible. It is difficult to keep the body moving without some involvment of the legs. This weight shift is introduced as a contrasting yet related activity.

Starting Position: The legs are slightly turned out. The right knee bends while the left leg holds its position. The center of weight ● shifts toward the bending leg. When the R leg straightens, the center of weight returns to normal ⊙ . This is repeated to the other side.

Note: The basic leg alignment, knee bending over the center of the foot, should be maintained (see Chapter 2).

Repeat 4 times

Straighten L

Plié L, hold R

Straighten R

Plié R, hold L

Starting Position: Legs turned out 2nd; arms side low

♩ = 66–72 Adagio

10 Leg Action for Body Circle

The start is the same—R knee bends carrying the center of weight with it. Then the L knee bends, but the R knee holds its bend. The center of weight shifts to the center between the feet, but stays low. The L knee holds its bend while the R knee straightens, forcing the center of weight to the L. Then the L knee straightens and there is a return to the starting position. This is repeated, starting to the opposite side.

Repeat 4 times, alternating L

straightening

Straighten R

Plié L and R

Plié R, hold L

Starting Position: As in Ex. 9

♩ = 66–72 Adagio

11 Leg Action for Side Bend and Body Circle

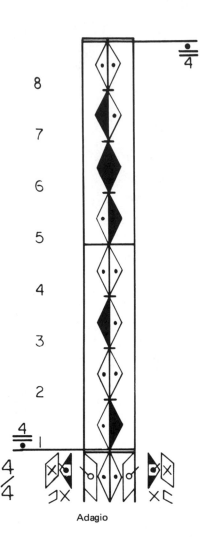

Starting Position: As in Ex. 9

Adagio

12 Side Bends with Both Arm and Leg Action

Now when the arms are added again, there is the satisfaction of a return to familiar material, but in a new context. The intellectual pleasure is obvious and clearly visible in the increased energy output.

The starting position is as in Ex. 7 except for the turn-out of the legs. Ex. 7 and Ex. 9 are put together. The arms swing in a wide arc over the head with the weight shift in the legs, increasing the range.

Note: Some breath support is helpful. Be sure to keep the shoulders down (see Chapter 3).

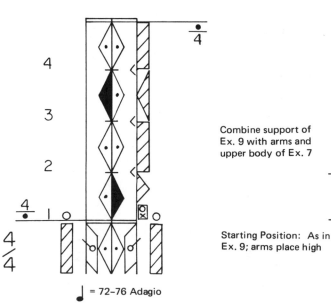

♩ = 72–76 Adagio

Combine support of Ex. 9 with arms and upper body of Ex. 7

Starting Position: As in Ex. 9; arms place high

L   R

38

13 Body Circle with Leg Action

Each individual exercise has a quality of its own. Combining them is sometimes difficult and surprising, but the satisfaction of bringing a whole sequence to a conclusion is an exciting moment, definitely worth the risk of possible technical errors.

Starting position is as in Ex. 12. The body bends side R as in Ex. 12. Then it swings into a forward low bend, only now both knees are bent with the body hanging between them. To complete the circle the body rolls into a side bend to the L and from there returns to the center starting position. This is repeated to the other side.

The most common error is to start the circle with a diagonal bend to the R and come up on the L with the same kind of position. The diagonal does not provide a full stretch and lacks the contrasting facings of the body. The full circle must go through side high on the start and on the finish of the circle. Although the emphasis here is on the action of the rib cage, it is obvious the hips *must* move back as the upper body drops forward and move forward again as the upper body moves into the side bend.

Legend

$\underline{x}$	=	One degree contraction toward the front of the limb or body part
и	=	Stretch
x	=	Flex one degree
|	=	Duration line indicates timing
|x	=	Flex one degree in one count
|и	=	Take one count to stretch
	=	Whole torso rounded forward low

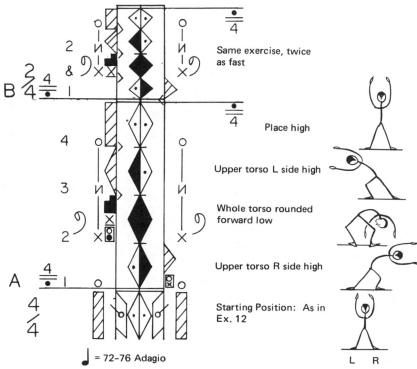

Same exercise, twice as fast

Place high

Upper torso L side high

Whole torso rounded forward low

Upper torso R side high

Starting Position: As in Ex. 12

L   R

♩ = 72–76 Adagio

14 Half Circle of Body with Leg Action

This is the most demanding section of this sequence and may be used late in the term as a form of review with a fresh challenge. It is an extreme stretch even for the advanced dancer. The stress is on the reach И from the center and remaining in the side bend instead of coming up to the center. Performed this way there is no chance of even the slight breath-pause that normally occurs on the center position—it is one continuous stretch.

Starting Position: The same as in Ex. 12. The change is in count 3 on the L side—there is a hold of one count in the side bend—then the swing forward again and the side bend on the R with the hold. This is repeated four times.

In the two-count variation, the movement is exactly the same, but the stretch and release of the big muscle groups is very fast. If the class is up to it, it is good to do four of the four-count circles followed by eight of the two-count circles. This is difficult but very exciting.

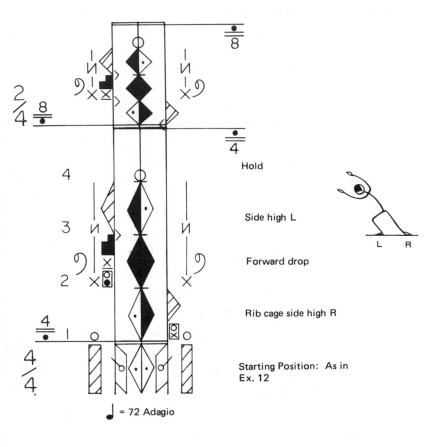

Hold

Side high L

Forward drop

Rib cage side high R

Starting Position: As in Ex. 12

♩ = 72 Adagio

15 Coda for Ex. 9 Through Ex. 13

To finish, come to center from the R side and lower the arms to place low ▮ as in the transition for Ex. 5 to Ex. 7.

Note: Codas, cadences, and transitions are important parts of dance exercises. People like to know when things are finished. There is a release of tensions, however slight—the resolution of one thought—that allows for the next one to start. Aside from the emotional satisfaction of having concluded something, cadences are physiologically sound. The body needs a break.

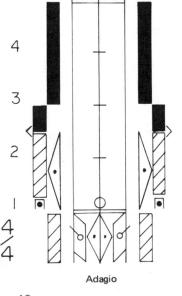

Adagio

Arms place low

Palms down

Arms side middle, palms up

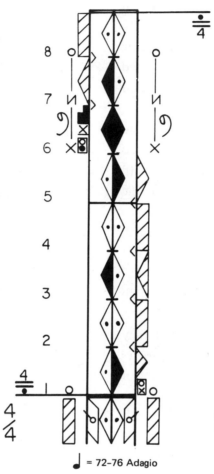

Starting position: As in
Ex. 12

♩ = 72–76 Adagio

17 Back Succession from Standing

This is the inversion of the forward succession (Ex. 1). This exercise is very hard on the back, and should *never* be given at the beginning of the training.

Starting Position: The only thing new is the position of the hands. They are placed on the back of the thighs, carrying some of the weight—elbows slightly bent.

Action: The $\wedge$ starts to the back lead by the head, as in the forward succession. To keep from falling the hips must move forward and the knees bend to counterbalance the back bend.

The return is lead up by the hips as usual, with the head the last thing to come to $\odot$.

Note: Be sure the body is "lifted" during the back arching and the abdominals do not bulge. The knees do swing slightly forward of the feet when they bend, but they must be kept parallel with them. The arches must be pulled up strongly. The control of the legs is in the top near the hips.

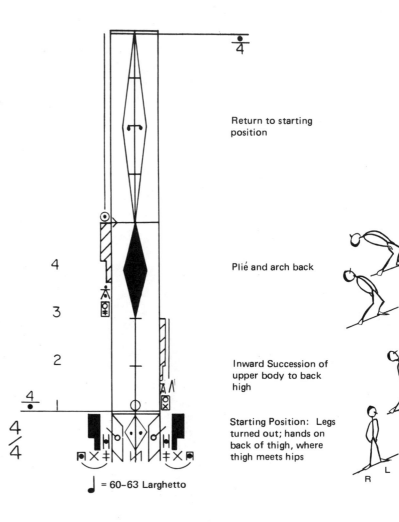

Return to starting position

Plié and arch back

Inward Succession of upper body to back high

Starting Position: Legs turned out; hands on back of thigh, where thigh meets hips

♩ = 60–63 Larghetto

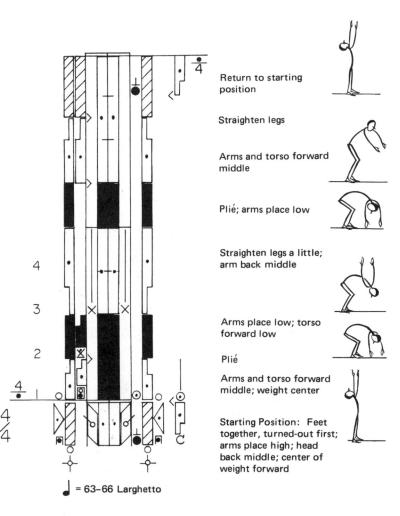
18 Preparation for Body Swings: Up and Down

The big body circles demand tremendous energy output and concentration. These little up-and-down swings add the legs to the forward bending of the body and include the arms; in other words, total body involvement in a slightly formalized action. The quality is free-flow. Because of its simplicity, energy is released; this action almost rests the body without its becoming static or standing still. The slow up-and-down action is intended only for the first few classes. Beginners soon discover the coordination and the fast swings become a happy easy interlude, a boost to their egos.

Starting Position: The legs are under the center of weight, heels together, slightly turned out. The body is upright with the arms over the shoulders.

Action: The whole body folds forward with the arms reaching out in front before they swing up and over the back to a back middle position, as the head drops.

To start the recovery, the arms swing forward and up followed by rest of the body in a succession to return to the starting position.

Note: Watch for the center of weight symbol ● pressing forward—at the end of the up swing. The arms go ▱ but the head is back ⬚ . Do not let the body sag at the end of the up swing. It should be well lifted above the legs.

Return to starting position

Straighten legs

Arms and torso forward middle

Plié; arms place low

Straighten legs a little; arm back middle

Arms place low; torso forward low

Plié

Arms and torso forward middle; weight center

Starting Position: Feet together, turned-out first; arms place high; head back middle; center of weight forward

♩ = 63–66 Larghetto

43

19   Body Swings: Up and Down

Watch for change in meter, 6/4, and the addition of accents.

Tempo is important for swings. If they are too slow they become bound-flow and lose the character of swing. If they are too fast, they become bound again and look frantic. Swinging movement is natural for all of us. It is an easy-going free flowing, almost aimless movement, but very important for students to experience.

The starting position is the same as Ex. 18. The counts are a fast six, which gives the feeling of a fall and a rebound.

Note: There is always a slight breath-pause at the end of each part of the swing. This is characteristic of swing movement. The counts are therefore not a strict six. Many musicians find this kind of movement difficult to accompany.

This exercise is the end of the beginners' warm-up.

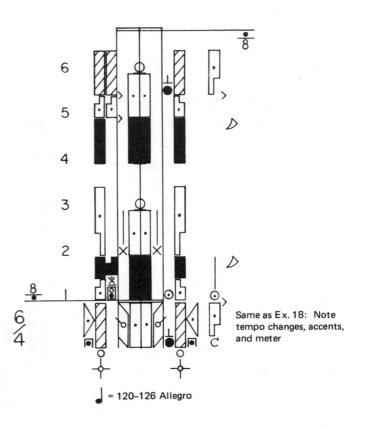

Same as Ex. 18: Note tempo changes, accents, and meter

♩ = 120–126 Allegro

44

Legend

) = Ad lib. timing

= Key indicating that the directions should be read as if there were no rotation

= Rotate, twist, or pivot to the right

= Rotate, twist, or pivot to the left

= Rotate to the right until you return to normal; unrotated state

= Rotate to the left until you return to normal; unrotated state

20   Rib Cage Rotation

This exercise combines a hamstring stretch with a relaxation of the neck and back. The slight rotation of the rib cage causes some students to experience motion discomfort. It will not, however, last for long.

Starting Position: A wide, parallel second [symbols]. The whole torso [symbol] hangs [symbol], arms folded over the head. Rotate the rib cage slightly to the L, let it drop center and repeat to the R. The timing is ad lib.) . It is the drop to the center that is important. Watch for the rotation symbols on the rib cage as it moves from side to side.

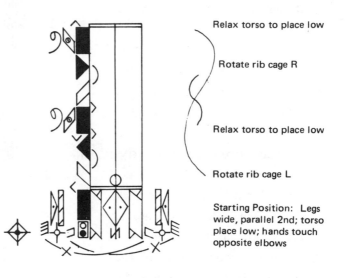

Relax torso to place low

Rotate rib cage R

Relax torso to place low

Rotate rib cage L

Starting Position: Legs wide, parallel 2nd; torso place low; hands touch opposite elbows

21   Head Rotation

Starting Position: The same as Ex. 20, except the head rotates. Obviously, the head must include the neck, otherwise it could hardly move at all. The student is really upside down on this one. The face must face the back.

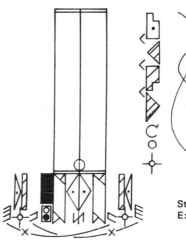

Forward middle

L side high

Back high

Head R side high

Starting Position: As in Ex. 20

45

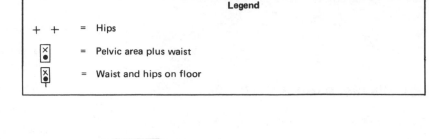
EXERCISES FOR THE BACK ON THE FLOOR

22 Pelvic Tilt to the Back from Sitting Position

This sequence is specifically for the abdominals and the lower back.

Starting Position: Sitting on the floor with the legs straight in front, whole torso place high.

Note: The hip symbol in the support column ₊|₊; the legs in the leg-gesture column—forward middle and turned parallel , feet pointed. The palms are resting on the thighs; face facing front.

Action: The pelvis tips backward, carrying the upper body with it in an outward succession ∨ (see Ex. 2) until the middle back is on the floor . This takes two counts. On the next two counts, starting again from the pelvis, the body is brought back to the starting position, pelvis is center. Notice the space hold ◇ on the face. Repeat this four times ÷/4. This can also be done faster—one count for each movement. The fast action gives a snap to the recovery thereby greatly increasing the abdominal control.

Caution: Some students experience uncomfortable pressure on the coccyx and sacrum. If this occurs, they should put a pad under the hips to prevent bone bruise during this exercise.

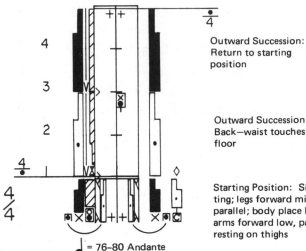

♩ = 76–80 Andante

Outward Succession: Return to starting position

Outward Succession: Back—waist touches floor

Starting Position: Sitting; legs forward middle parallel; body place high; arms forward low, palms resting on thighs

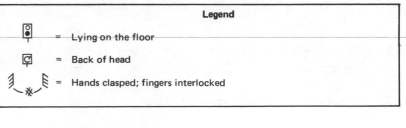

23 Body Curl from Lying Position

This exercise, a reverse of Ex. 22, is excellent as a back stretch but even better for strengthening the abdominals.

Starting Position: Whole body lying on the back on the floor. The inward succession starts from the head, as Ex. 1. The rib cage lifts off the floor leaving the pelvis and waist on the floor. This takes three counts. There is a hold for three counts and a return to the starting position, three counts—nine counts in all or three Measures of 3/4.

Note: The middle back remains in contact with the floor at all times.

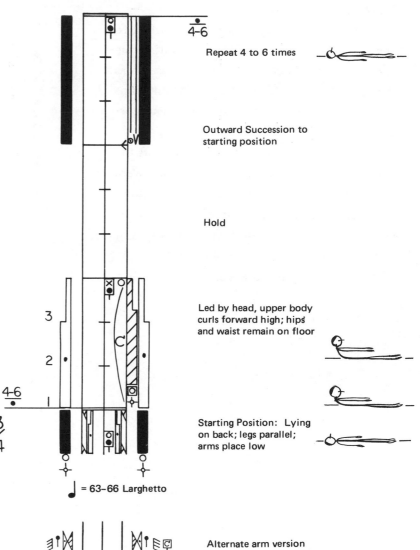

Repeat 4 to 6 times

Outward Succession to starting position

Hold

Led by head, upper body curls forward high; hips and waist remain on floor

Starting Position: Lying on back; legs parallel; arms place low

♩ = 63–66 Larghetto

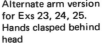

Alternate arm version for Exs 23, 24, 25. Hands clasped behind head

47

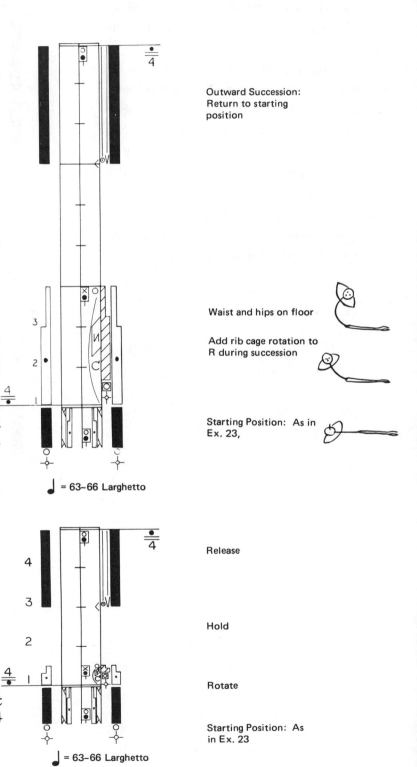
24 Body Curl with Rotation of Rib Cage

Starting Position: As in Ex. 23.

Notice the rotation symbol attached to the direction symbol. It says: During the chest lift, the upper torso rotates as far as possible to the R . The waist and hips remain in contact with the floor (support column).

This variation stretches and contracts the deep inner muscles of the torso that were missed on the simpler forward and back action. Gymnastic as it is, it is important both for strengthening the middle body and as a point of reference for more advanced work.

Note: The phrasing is as in Ex. 23.

Outward Succession:
Return to starting
position

Waist and hips on floor

Add rib cage rotation to
R during succession

Starting Position: As in
Ex. 23,

♩ = 63–66 Larghetto

25 Dynamic Variation of Body Curl with Rotation of Rib Cage

As can easily be seen, this is simply a rhythmic variation of Ex. 23. There is a sharp attack on the first count, a hold, and a release, alternating sides. It allows the student to throw the weight thereby getting up farther than with the slow lift. This dynamic change is exciting and takes away the feeling of gymnastics. The arms can be used with one hand back of the head to take some of the weight with the other arm at the side or both hands may be clasped back of the head. Elbows may come forward on the lift.

Release

Hold

Rotate

Starting Position: As
in Ex. 23

♩ = 63–66 Larghetto

48

26 Inward Succession from Lying Position

Here is a full body succession from a lying position, commonly called a "sit-up." Notice the similarity between this and Ex. 1. Starting position as in Ex. 23: Inward succession ∧ to a sitting position, hips in the support column +|+; arms have a space hold ◇. Outward succession ∨ back to starting position.

   Note: This exercise is not done with a straight back, as is sometimes seen in gymnastic classes, but, rather, with a rounded back. The succession signs, ∧ and ∨ are what make the difference.

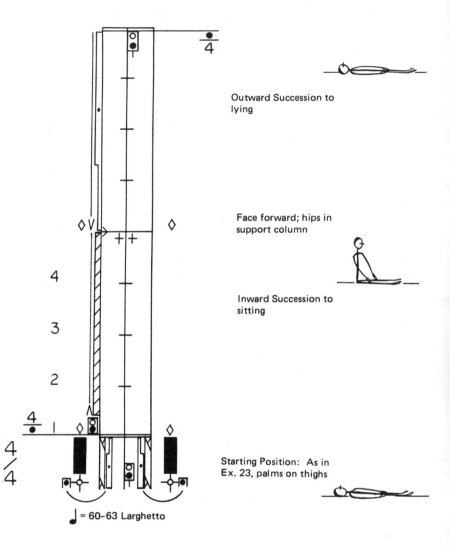

Outward Succession to lying

Face forward; hips in support column

Inward Succession to sitting

Starting Position: As in Ex. 23, palms on thighs

♩ = 60–63 Larghetto

49

27 Body Bends from Sitting Position: Side

Body bends from a sitting position can be useful. There is no problem of balance and many
students will risk the extra stretch that they
were afraid of while standing. In this series,
the hand and lower arm are used as support.

Starting Position: Sitting on the floor,
body high [symbol]. The R leg is bent in front as
can be seen by the notation in the right leg-
gesture column—the R thigh is on a forward
diagonal [symbol], the lower leg to the left side [symbol].
The L leg is also bent, but the lower leg is on a
back diagonal [symbol]. The weight is resting on
the outside of the R thigh. Both hips need
not be on the floor. The R arm is bent across
the body, the L arm is to the side [symbol]. Palms
face down [symbol].

Action: The lower body holds as the R
arm moves, on the upbeat to [symbol]. The R hand
touches the floor to take the weight as the
upper torso tilts to the side [symbol]. The L arm
moves to a position over the head. This takes
two counts. To come back to normal the L
arm moves to its starting position pulling the
upper torso with it for the return. This series
is repeated four times [symbol].

Note: The rib cage plus waist symbol
[symbol] in the right body column; the contact bow
with the lower arm on the floor [symbol]; and
the release sign [symbol] as the arm comes off
the floor on the return to normal. The "fourth
ending" shown on the right of the staff [symbol]
means that at the end of the fourth repeat
the position is held for the last count of the
measure.

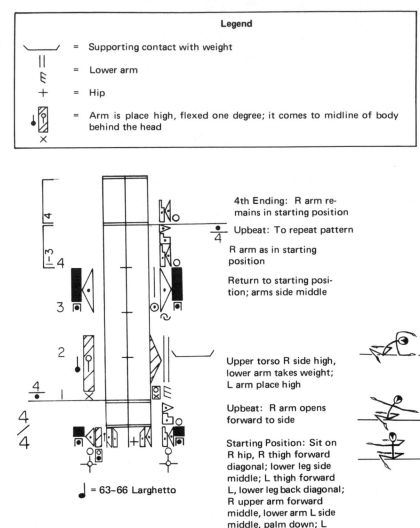

Legend

[symbol] = Supporting contact with weight

[symbol] = Lower arm

+ = Hip

[symbol] = Arm is place high, flexed one degree; it comes to midline of body behind the head

♩ = 63–66 Larghetto

4th Ending: R arm re-
mains in starting position

Upbeat: To repeat pattern

R arm as in starting
position

Return to starting posi-
tion; arms side middle

Upper torso R side high,
lower arm takes weight;
L arm place high

Upbeat: R arm opens
forward to side

Starting Position: Sit on
R hip, R thigh forward
diagonal; lower leg side
middle; L thigh forward
L, lower leg back diagonal;
R upper arm forward
middle, lower arm L side
middle, palm down; L
arm side middle, palm
down

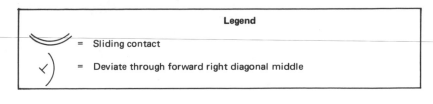
28   Body Bends from Sitting Position: Forward

Starting position is the same as in Exercise 27. Every part of the body holds its position but the whole torso—seen in the L hand body column ▯▯ —tips forward high ⧄ for two counts and returns to the starting position. Note the similarity to Ex. 3 when the whole torso goes to ⧄ with the back flat. Because of the sitting position, forward middle is impossible, so the whole torso goes as far as it can to ⧄.

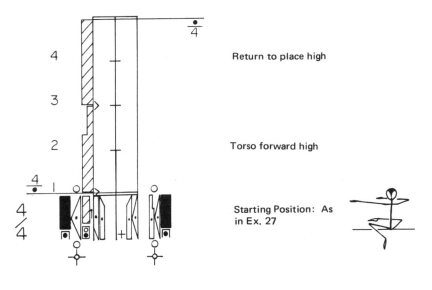

Return to place high

Torso forward high

Starting Position: As in Ex. 27

29   Body Bends from Sitting Position: Side and Forward (Ex. 27 & 28 combined.)

This starts as in Ex. 27, but the body swings forward over the thigh before returning to the starting position. There should be a strong accent ▶ on count 3 when the body begins the forward swing.

Note: The release symbol ᴖ on the R hand on count 3; the whole torso circles forward, passing through the diagonal ✓. The L arm is carried with the torso before going to the side.

The movement should all be done smoothly. Notice the fourth ending ⌐

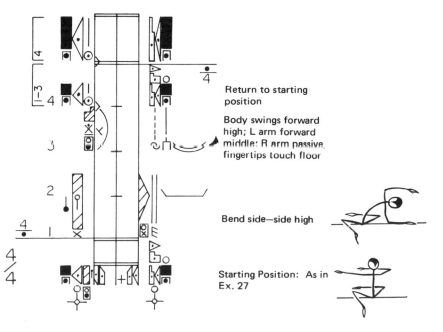

Return to starting position

Body swings forward high; L arm forward middle; R arm passive, fingertips touch floor

Bend side—side high

Starting Position: As in Ex. 27

51

30 Body Bends from Sitting Position: Forward and Side

Inversion of Ex. 29. Instead of starting with a side tilt, the action starts forward and swings to the side, followed by a return to the starting position.

Teaching Note for Ex. 27, 28, 29, 30: For drill repeats are important. However once patterns are learned it is interesting to combine them to make dance phrases. In this case doing Ex. 27, 28, 29, 30 each through once makes a four-measure phrase with a definite feeling of dance. It starts with little energy output but builds to quite strong movement at the end.

Repeat the whole phrase before changing sides. See Ex. 32 for transition.

31 Body Bends from Sitting Position with Slide to Floor

This is a much more complicated variation that takes the body down onto the floor. It starts with a forward bend as in Ex. 30, but after the hand touches the floor, the whole body slides onto the R side and then rolls onto the back, shoulders resting on the floor. The recovery starts with a roll to the R side. The rest is as counts 3 and 4 of Ex. 29.

Note: There is a tremendous and sometimes uncomfortable stretch in the thigh on the side away from the bend. Stretching the front of the body is always painful and difficult.

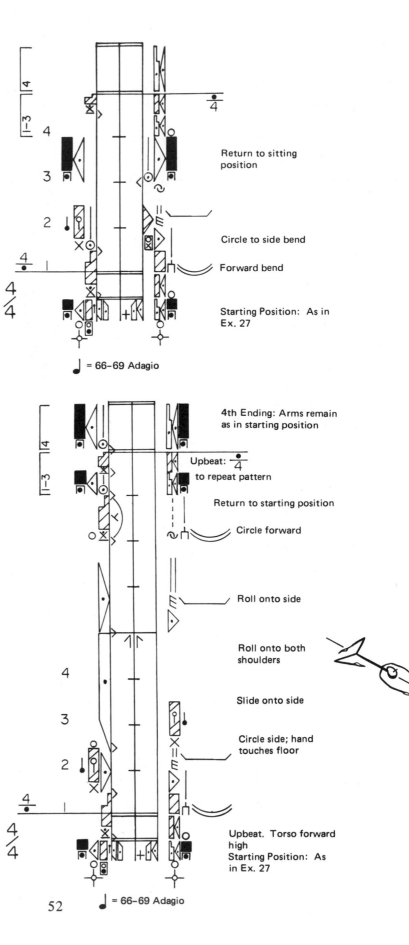

Return to sitting position

Circle to side bend

Forward bend

Starting Position: As in Ex. 27

♩ = 66–69 Adagio

4th Ending: Arms remain as in starting position

Upbeat: to repeat pattern

Return to starting position

Circle forward

Roll onto side

Roll onto both shoulders

Slide onto side

Circle side; hand touches floor

Upbeat. Torso forward high
Starting Position: As in Ex. 27

♩ = 66–69 Adagio

52

32 Transition to the Other Side for Body Bends Series (Ex. 27 through Ex. 32)

The weight comes center—sit on both hips $_+|_+$; the body is ⊘ ; arms go ▮ . Both legs straighten in front ⊟⊟ , the weight shifts to the new side and the legs bend into the starting position for the exercises.

Note: Be sure to watch for the symbols in the proper columns. It is not just the symbol but where it is placed on the staff that is important.

Teaching note: For the first few classes, it is wise to do each section four times on one side, then make the transition and repeat to the other side. This is an unfamiliar position for many people. Because of lack of stretch in the inside of the legs the outside leg muscles often cramp if they stay too long in this position.

On the swings it is good to think of the movement existing in a 1/4 arc of a circle ◷ . It makes the student begin to think spatially, not just muscularly.

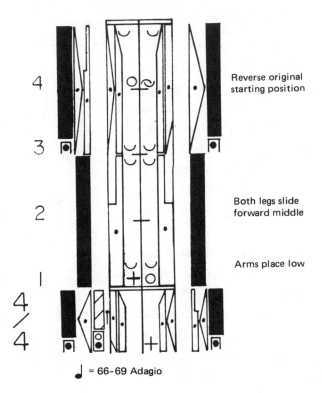

Reverse original starting position

Both legs slide forward middle

Arms place low

♩ = 66-69 Adagio

33 Back Study and Variations

Here is a study designed to be performed as shown, without a break. Although the exercises are similar to those in the body bend series, it is the arrangement which gives this sequence the feeling of a study rather than a collection of exercises.

Starting Position: The legs are the same as in Ex. 27. The body is folded and tipped to the back, quite relaxed. The hands are on the knees.

Section A: The whole torso takes two counts to stretch to ▨ and return to the starting position. Repeat ⋮⁄₄ .

Section B: Same as Section A, adding arms to the pattern. The arms are exactly as in Ex. 27 except that the elbow leads the action up (ᒉ. Keep the shoulders pressed down. Watch for the body repeat in the staff.

Section C: Same lift in the body and arms, but faster—one count—arms are held ○ as the whole torso tips forward on count two. On count three, the torso returns to ▨ ; on count four return to starting position.

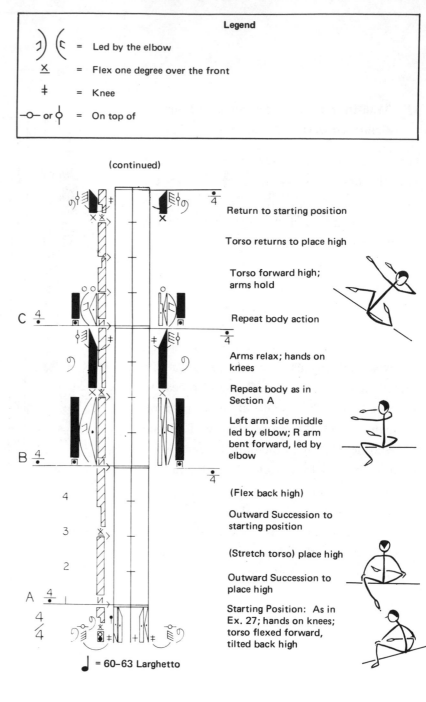

Legend

ᒉ) (ᒉ = Led by the elbow

X̲ = Flex one degree over the front

‡ = Knee

—○— or ○̸ = On top of

(continued)

Return to starting position

Torso returns to place high

Torso forward high; arms hold

Repeat body action

Arms relax; hands on knees

Repeat body as in Section A

Left arm side middle led by elbow; R arm bent forward, led by elbow

(Flex back high)

Outward Succession to starting position

(Stretch torso) place high

Outward Succession to place high

Starting Position: As in Ex. 27; hands on knees; torso flexed forward, tilted back high

♩ = 60–63 Larghetto

Legend		
T ⫽ ǂ	=	Knee presses back middle
⊥ ⫽ +	=	Hip presses forward middle

Section D: Note the change of meter (6/4). On count 3, the body folds forward as in Ex. 29. On count 4 the back straightens again. On count 5 come to center, and on count 6 return to starting position. Note the space hold symbol ◇ on the arms on count three. The head drops below them.

Section E: Is like Ex. 30 (counts 1 and 2) and 3 and 4 of Ex. 29. With the repetition there is a strong thrust forward from the starting position into the side swing. Watch for the dynamic markings on the R side ▶ (strong), and the breath-pause (on count "3 and") before the return.

Note: Once the sequence is learned, omit the repeats, except for Section E, which should be repeated once before repeating the whole phrase. There is a slight increase in tempo on the fifth measure of Section E.

Performance note: The whole phrase has a total of six Measures. There is a definite drop of energy to start the repeat. The quality is of an inhale and an exhale, increasing in strength as the energy builds. This back study starts as a whisper and ends as a shout.

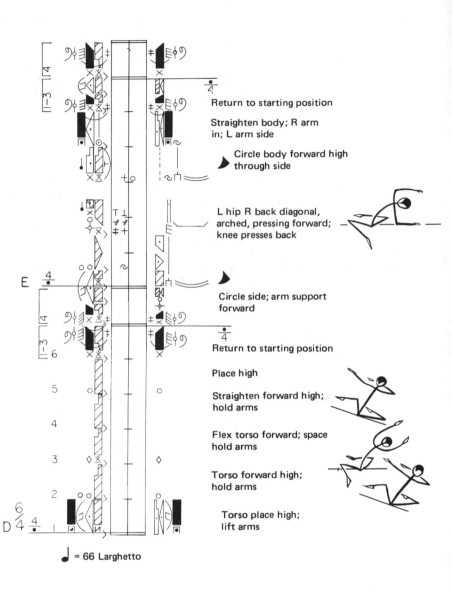

Return to starting position

Straighten body; R arm in; L arm side

Circle body forward high through side

L hip R back diagonal, arched, pressing forward; knee presses back

Circle side; arm support forward

Return to starting position

Place high

Straighten forward high; hold arms

Flex torso forward; space hold arms

Torso forward high; hold arms

Torso place high; lift arms

♩ = 66 Larghetto

TO33894

34 Variation I of Ex. 33 (Section E): Back Study

The only change is one of level. The hand, instead of the lower arm, is placed on the floor. The hips lift off the floor until the weight is supported on R knee . The lifted leg is to the side with the knee bent , the body strongly arched to the back with the head back.

On the return, notice that the toe of the lifted foot touches first, followed by the knee before the hips are brought back to their starting position. This variation is notated in 4/4, but if it is included in the previous study, it should be performed in 6/4.

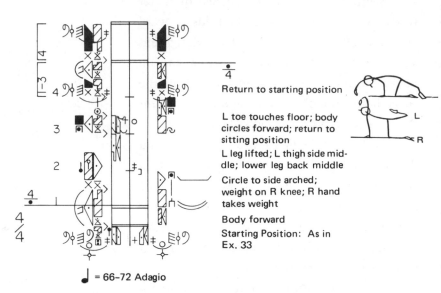

Return to starting position

L toe touches floor; body circles forward; return to sitting position

L leg lifted; L thigh side middle; lower leg back middle

Circle to side arched; weight on R knee; R hand takes weight

Body forward

Starting Position: As in Ex. 33

♩ = 66–72 Adagio

35 Variation II of Ex. 33 (Section E): Back Study

The change is in the lifted leg–on count 3, the leg straightens in the air and bends again on count 4. The rest is the same. In this Variation the body really lies out to the side in a very expansive movement.

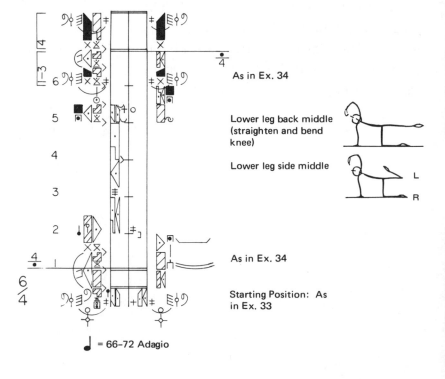

As in Ex. 34

Lower leg back middle (straighten and bend knee)

Lower leg side middle

As in Ex. 34

Starting Position: As in Ex. 33

♩ = 66–72 Adagio

36 Coda for Back Study

On counts 1 and 2, rise to the knee and hand as in Ex. 34. On count 3, the body comes to place high, left leg is brought forward with the knee still bent and the whole foot placed on the floor in front of the hip. The arms move to side middle. On count 4, shift the weight to the left foot and come to standing, ending in first position, arms place low.

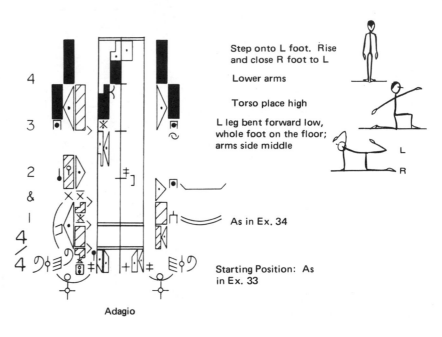

Step onto L foot. Rise and close R foot to L

Lower arms

Torso place high

L leg bent forward low, whole foot on the floor; arms side middle

As in Ex. 34

Starting Position: As in Ex. 33

Adagio

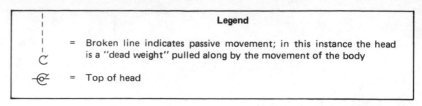
37 Rib Cage Lift from Lying Position

This is a preparation for the outward succession from a lying position.

Starting Position: Lying on the back, legs straight forward, parallel, arms ◁ ▷ , palms on the floor ⌣⊓ ⊓⌣.

Action: The whole torso lifts off the floor, led by the rib cage; arms are space held ◇. The head falls back until the face is to the back. The weight is carried by the hands, hips, and head. This takes two counts; the return to the floor takes two counts. Repeat ·⁄4.

Note: Be sure the abdominals do not bulge on the lift. The logical development of this is to come up to sitting, ending with a straight back (see Ex. 38, Measure 2).

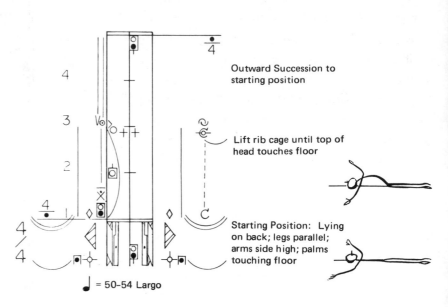

Outward Succession to starting position

Lift rib cage until top of head touches floor

Starting Position: Lying on back; legs parallel; arms side high; palms touching floor

♩ = 50-54 Largo

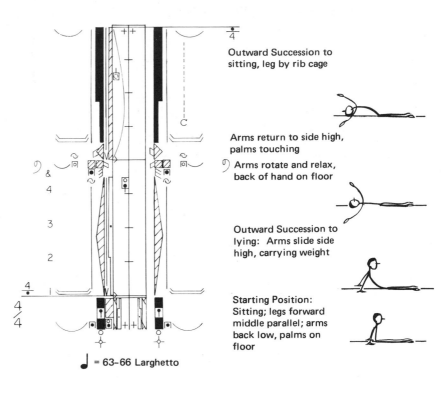
38 Outward Succession Down and Up from Sitting Position

Starting Position: The notation for the body and legs should be familiar by now. The arms are slightly back of the body, palms on the floor.

Action:

Measure 1 The ∨ starts from the hips, the arms slide out to the side as the torso reaches the floor.

On the "and" of the count 4, the arms and hands roll over (palms up), to release the tension in the shoulder.

Measure 2 On the recovery the arms rotate again, palms down, the rib cage lifts as in Ex. 37, and the ∨ starts back to ▱ led by the rib cage.

Note: Again be sure the abdominals pull in at all times during the exercise. The back stretches on the descent, contracts on the ascent. The arms and hands must be quite firm to carry the weight. On the backward succession, the shoulders roll forward as the head drops forward. On the forward succession, the shoulders roll back as the head drops back. There is quite a stretch across the pectorals.

Outward Succession to sitting, leg by rib cage

Arms return to side high, palms touching

Arms rotate and relax, back of hand on floor

Outward Succession to lying: Arms slide side high, carrying weight

Starting Position: Sitting; legs forward middle parallel; arms back low, palms on floor

♩ = 63–66 Larghetto

39 Inward Succession Arching Back from Sitting Position

This is an inversion of Ex. 38; same starting position.

Measure 1 The succession starts with the head leading back until it touches the floor (see Ex. 37). The arms slide diagonally back carrying the weight; the body is highly arched.

Measure 2 Come back to starting position, rib cage leading (see Ex. 38, Measure 2).

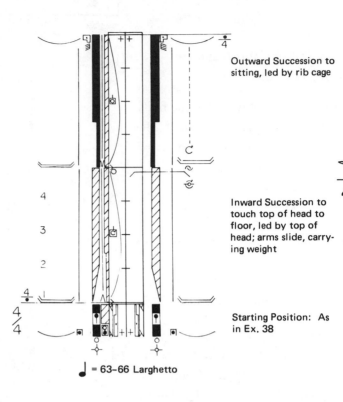

Outward Succession to sitting, led by rib cage

Inward Succession to touch top of head to floor, led by top of head; arms slide, carrying weight

Starting Position: As in Ex. 38

♩ = 63–66 Larghetto

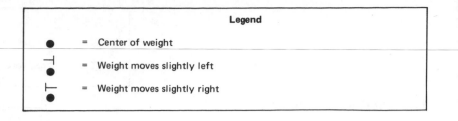

40   Hip Roll from Lying Position

Starting Position: Lying on the back, arms side high as in Ex. 37.

Action: With the heels, head, and shoulders on the floor, rotate the hips as far as possible to the R and repeat to the L. The work is done by the buttocks and abdominals. There is a very strong twist in the waist.

Note: The legs must be very straight with the thighs pulled together firmly; otherwise the exercise cannot be done at all. The buttocks also must be tight and the abdominals pulled in strongly. To give proper leverage, the heels, shoulders, and hands press into floor.

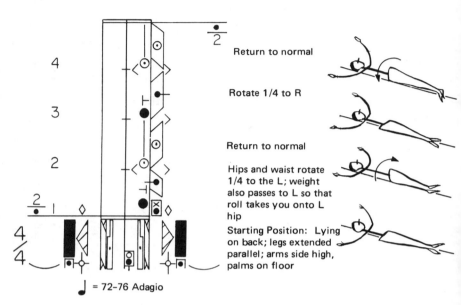

Return to normal

Rotate 1/4 to R

Return to normal

Hips and waist rotate 1/4 to the L; weight also passes to L so that roll takes you onto L hip

Starting Position: Lying on back; legs extended parallel; arms side high, palms on floor

♩ = 72–76 Adagio

41 Hip Roll and Recovery

Starting Position: As in Ex. 40.

Measure 1 Count 1: Starting with the hips, roll onto the L side, arms go place high ▱ , body arches; (2) bend the L knee to ♩ ; (3) sweep the R arm forward, ending side low as the body starts to fold forward over the bent knee. Notice the ◊ on the R leg. The inward succession continues forward carrying the bent leg with it, and ending with both legs forward middle, with the body folded over them; and (4) bring body up to place high ▱ , hands on floor back of hips.

Measure 2 This is identical to Measure 1, Ex. 38.

    Repeat, rolling to the other side.

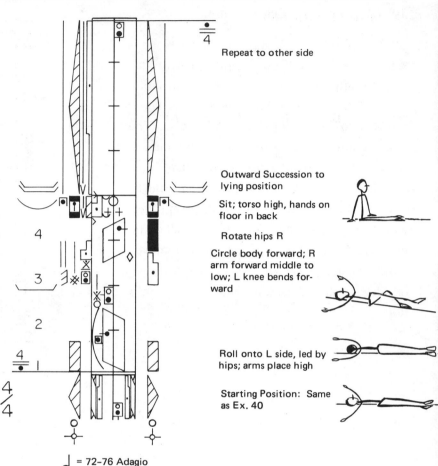

Repeat to other side

Outward Succession to lying position

Sit; torso high, hands on floor in back

Rotate hips R

Circle body forward; R arm forward middle to low; L knee bends forward

Roll onto L side, led by hips; arms place high

Starting Position: Same as Ex. 40

♩ = 72–76 Adagio

42 Dynamic Variation of Hip Roll and Recovery

Just like Ex. 41, except that the whole sequence is performed in four counts (i.e., twice as fast).

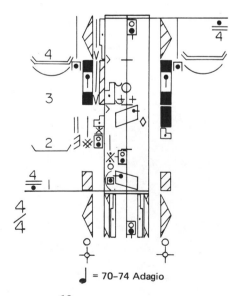

(*Note* count changes.)

Starting Position: As in Ex. 40

♩ = 70–74 Adagio

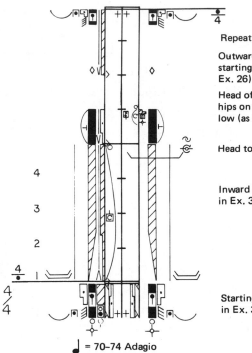
43　Inward Succession with Curl and Sit-up

This exercise is a combination of Ex. 39, Ex. 23, and Ex. 26.

Measure 1　Back arch (see Measure 1, Ex. 39) (four counts).

Measure 2　The position is reversed. The middle body is pressed into the floor ▦ ; the head lifts off, chin on chest; the arms are placed against the sides. This position is held for one count. The recovery is as in Ex. 26, Measure 1.

Note: Such a strong body change has to be started in the pelvis. Measure 2 is a very fast ∨ followed by a slower ∨ .

Repeat

Outward Succession to starting position (as in Ex. 26)

Head off floor; waist and hips on floor; arms place low (as in Ex. 23)

Head touches floor

Inward Succession: As in Ex. 39

Starting Position: As in Ex. 39

♩ = 70–74 Adagio

44 Inward Succession with Curl and Roll Over

Measure 1 Same as Ex. 43.

Measure 2 Count 1: Same as Ex. 43. On counts 3 and 4, the body rolls onto the L side 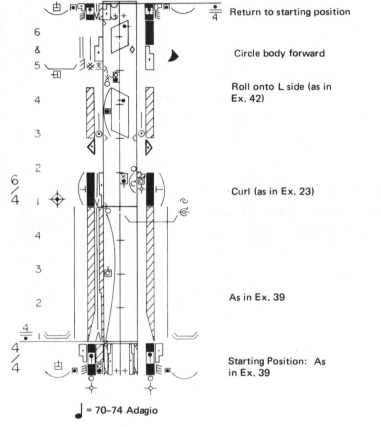, led by the hip, . The arms circle to . This is a strong arch as in Ex. 43.

The R arm moves thru to . There is also a strong accent in the R arm as the body begins the recovery through a forward fold over the L knee to the starting position.

Repeat this to the other side.

Note: This is a big, generous movement, full of all sorts of contrasts—big body changes from open to closed positions; dynamic changes from smooth to sharp; and changes in body facings. It is exciting.

Return to starting position

Circle body forward

Roll onto L side (as in Ex. 42)

Curl (as in Ex. 23)

As in Ex. 39

Starting Position: As in Ex. 39

♩ = 70–74 Adagio

64

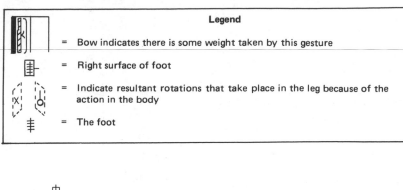

45 Short Version of Inward Succession with Curl and Roll Over

Identical to Ex. 44, except Measure 1 has been reduced to one count and the whole exercise is done in six counts (6/4): (1) arch back; (2) curl; (3) roll over; (4) hold; and (5 and 6) return to normal.

Coda: Repeat Ex. 45 four times. The last time, after the roll over, there is a rise on the bent knee, L, on count 5. On "5 and" the R leg is flexed in as the body lifts to ⬓ arms ◁ ▷ . On count 6, come to standing.

Note: During this sequence there is a change of facing. Watch for the facing pins on the L side of the staff. At this point in the sequences the exercises begin to make little dance phrases, with none of the basic training being abandoned.

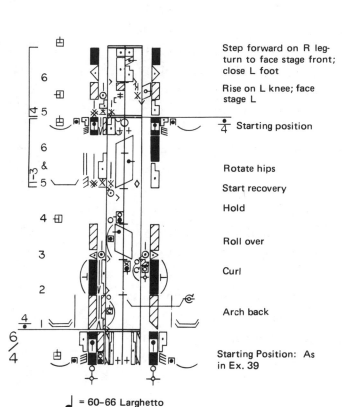

Step forward on R leg- turn to face stage front; close L foot

Rise on L knee; face stage L

Starting position

Rotate hips

Start recovery

Hold

Roll over

Curl

Arch back

Starting Position: As in Ex. 39

♩ = 60–66 Larghetto

65

46 Hip Lift from Sitting Position

This exercise is the last section of Doris Humphrey's opposition study. It is a wonderful exercise for the middle body. Large and expansive in feeling, it is tremendously satisfying to do. Doris always did it fast—one count for the lift, one count for the return. Here it is slowed up for technical accuracy—four counts for each section.

Starting Position: Sitting on R hip, R leg extended forward, not turned-out, R hand on the floor slightly back of hip. L leg bent, not turned-out, whole foot on the floor. L arm bent and inside of L leg, palm facing in ▷ . Body folded over forward, head below bent knee.

Action: The outward succession starts with the hips lifting—notice the center of weight symbol ● in the R-hand body column going ⊠ place high. As the hips lift, the L heel comes off the floor and the rib cage rotates a 1/4 turn to the R. The L arm reaches for the ceiling.

At the peak of the movement, the body is highly arched, head back, the weight carried by the R hand, R foot, and L foot which is under the center of weight forming sort of a tripod. For the return, the hips rotate a little to the L to return to normal, and the whole body folds into the starting position. Repeat ·/4 .

Note: This can be done with the two- and one-count reduction. A good combination is two patterns of the four-count version and four of the one-count. Of course the tempo for the one-count retards a little. An excellent combination is Ex. 38 and Ex. 46 (see Ex. 47).

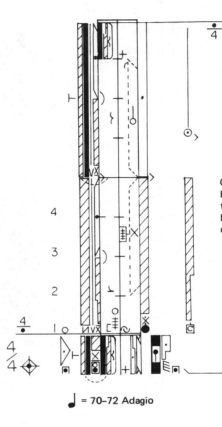

♩ = 70–72 Adagio

Return to starting position

Outward Succession to back high: Torso rotated to R; support on R arm, ball of L foot and outside of R foot; face to back

Starting Position: Sitting on R hip; R leg parallel forward middle; L thigh forward high; lower leg place low, whole foot on floor; body curled over front; R arm place low behind body, hand pointing back middle, palm taking weight; L upper arm place low, lower arm place high; whole arm inside L knee, palm facing R side middle

47 Back Succession with Hip Lift

Note: The change in the action of the leg on Measure 2 of Ex. 38 to get into the starting position for Ex. 46. Start with four counts and work up to one count retard (of course) from ♩ = 76 to ♩ = 72. This reduction of counts is fun, demanding, and exhilarating.

Teaching Note: It is wise to prepare for this exercise by splitting the class into two groups. Have group one do the four-count version four times, then rest as the second group works. Repeat to the other side.

Use the same system for the two-count version. For the one-count action, it is fun to repeat it four times, alternating sides.

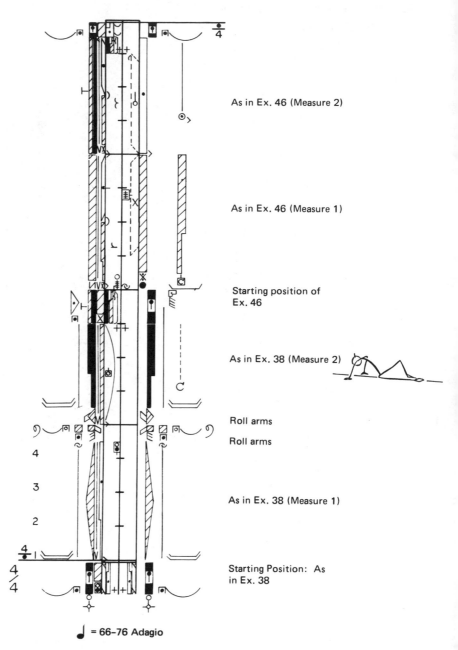

As in Ex. 46 (Measure 2)

As in Ex. 46 (Measure 1)

Starting position of Ex. 46

As in Ex. 38 (Measure 2)

Roll arms

Roll arms

As in Ex. 38 (Measure 1)

Starting Position: As in Ex. 38

♩ = 66–76 Adagio

48 Side Succession on the Floor
(Preparation for Side Fall from
Sitting Position)

Side action from a sitting position is difficult and hard on the arms. As Ex. 2 was a breakdown of the forward succession, this exercise does a similar service for the side succession at the floor level.

Starting Position: In all sitting exercises, the ∨ starts from the hips.

Measure 1 Count 1: The R hip lifts off the floor ⌒ . The Ꮯ and ▣ tip to the R ▷ in opposition to the thrust to the L by the hips; and (2) the fall (or succession) starts. The L hand is placed on the floor ⌣, ⊓ and the succession ends with the body lying on the side ꟷꞵ .

Note: Be sure to retain the right-angle in the hips.

Measure 2 Count 1: The R side of the rib cage leads the body up ▣). The head drops to the L. The L hand carries some of the weight but, as always, the middle body is doing most of the work.

Repeat to the other side.

Note: Try it as described (4/4). Reduce to 2/4, and, with the real fall, use one count for each movement. As in Ex. 2 the movement must start on the upbeat when it is done quickly. There is a definite suspension at this speed as the body carries through the center. The oppositional action in the head and rib cage now becomes very obvious.

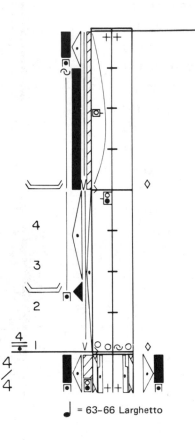

♩ = 63–66 Larghetto

Outward Succession to sitting position, led by R side of rib cage

Outward Succession to lying on L side: Slide on L hand as legs hold to body; release R hip

Starting Position: Sitting; legs forward middle, parallel; torso place high; arms side middle, palms down

68

49 Back Succession from One Knee
(Preparation for Back Fall)

This is more familiar than it would appear at first glance. Look at counts 3 and 4 of Measure 1 and counts 1 and 2 of Measure 2. They are Ex. 38. Count 4 of Measure 2 is the same at this starting position.

Starting Position: Kneeling on L knee ⬚ lower leg on ⬚ , R leg bent, ball of foot on floor, no weight. Arms ⬚ , body ⬚ .

Measure 1 Counts 1 and 2: The ⬚ folds ⬚ carrying the arms forward; and (3) the L hip touches the floor, the arms move to the back to help support the weight as it continues back and down. The ∨ starts ending with the ⬚ on the floor, R leg extended, on count 4. The arms rotate as Ex. 38.

Measure 2 Counts 1 and 2: Rib cage lifts as in Ex. 37. The R leg starts to bend preparing to return to its starting position. The hands slide along the floor carrying some of the weight but trailing the action; and (3) body folds up as on count 1, Measure 1. The whole body is folded up tight at this point, rib cage on thigh, hips on L heel, head below knee level; the hands come off the floor ∿; arms swing ⬚⬚; the weight shifts to the L knee; and the movement continues to return to the starting position.

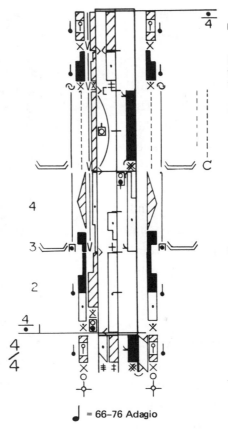

$\downarrow$ = 66–76 Adagio

Rise to starting position

Body and arms continue forward as weight shifts to L knee

Outward Succession to sitting, led by rib cage; R leg flexes in

Outward Succession to lying: R leg extends forward, L leg stays

Sit back on L hip

Body and arms forward as weight is lowered

Starting Position: Kneeling, place high on L knee; lower leg back R diagonal middle; R leg bent, ball of foot on floor beside L knee; arms place high behind head

69

50 Side Succession from One Knee
(Preparation for Side Fall)

This is very similar to Ex. 49. The difference is that the action is sideward. Notice the starting position is identical.

Measure 1 Counts 1 and 2: The hips shift side as the upper torso ⧆ bends ▷ . The arms are ⧆ ; and (3 and 4) the L hip touches the floor diagonally ⧆ to arrive at knee level. R arm goes ▷ . L arm bends across the body to ⧆ also. L arm continues across the body, palm touches the floor ⌇⌇⌐ , and the side succession ∨ starts to the L, ending with the body lying on the L side ⧆ . R leg is extended ▷ ; R arm bent in front ⧆ palm on floor ⌐⌇⌇ .

Measure 2 Counts 1, 2, and 3: The ⧆ lifts sidewards off the floor ◁ . The body folds ⧆ and shifts the weight onto the L knee. As the hips lift off the floor the R leg slides in ⧆ under the center of weight, ball of the foot on the floor; hands come off the floor. (Everything is all folded up at this point, as in Ex. 49,) and (4) return to starting position.

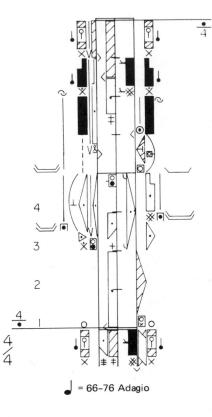

•/4 Rise on knee; return to starting position

R leg slides in bent place low

Body and arms forward, weight shift to L knee

Rib cage lift side

Outward Succession to lying on L side: R leg extends, R hand on floor, forward middle

Sit back L diagonal R arm side middle R

L arm crosses side middle R to touch floor side L

Upper torso R side high, as weight is lowered

Starting Position: As in Ex. 49

♩ = 66–76 Adagio

70

Note to Ex. 49, Ex. 50, and Ex. 51: As can be seen, these three exercises use a complete folding and unfolding of every joint in the body. This is the mechanical essence of Doris Humphrey's first series of falls—the body fully extended in one direction, a folding up, and an extension into a new direction.

51   Side Succession on the Floor (Side Fall Preparation from Lying Position)

Here is successional activity of the whole torso moving sidewards. In actuality it is the end of the floor section of Doris Humphrey's side fall (first series), as well as the recovery from that fall. In this sequence start lying on the right side 🬀, R leg bent underneath. The rib cage begins the movement with a lifting action that is taken over by the torso swung forward over the knee. At that point, the L leg is free to move in under the body to take the weight. The whole body is folded up with the hips over the L heel. From this position (really the center section of the fall) the weight (hips) shifts side, and the succession starts to the left, ending in the starting position, but on the other side.

Coda: This is the regular recovery from the side fall ending in a standing position. From the folded position, shift the weight to the forward foot and come to standing (see Ex. 27).

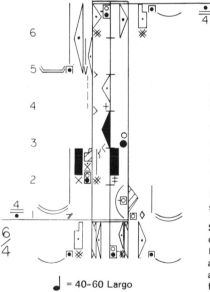

♩ = 40–60 Largo

Lying on L side

Outward Succession to L side

Sit on L hip (body passive—acts as counterbalance)

Without rising, weight shifts to L leg

Body forward, as weight shifts to R knee

Rib cage lift, led by L side of rib cage

Starting Position: Lying on R side; L leg extended; R leg bent underneath; R arm extended on floor above head; L arm bent forward middle, palm touching floor in front of rib cage

71

chapter 2
feet and legs

Important as the back is for supporting and carrying the weight of the torso, legs really make the dancer. So many brilliant and beautiful things that everyone associates with dance are done by the legs. In order to do these things, the legs and feet must be properly prepared. For this reason a large part of a dancer's training involves the legs and feet. Proper training of the legs gives the dancer the ease and strength needed to perform difficult movements with style and grace. Poor training results in poorly developed muscles, frequent injuries, and gaucheness.

Modern dance has borrowed many exercises for the feet and legs from ballet. The plié and relevé are examples of this. The timing and phrasing of these exercises, however, are typical of modern dance—uneven phrase lengths and free use of meter. Also, the exercises are arranged to be performed in the center of the studio, away from the barre. The modern dancer still trains in bare feet, and although shoes may be worn many times during performances, the bare foot is typical of the modern dance class.

Many studios in schools, colleges, or adult centers are either not equipped with barres, or the ones they have are poorly placed and constructed as well as being insufficient for a large class. It is good to know that much barre work can be successfully taught away from the barre. It is almost impossible, however, to teach body alignment without a mirror.

During the following exercises, great attention must be paid to the proper alignment of the whole body. From the very first class, the student must be made aware of the plumb-line, or gravity line, running through the body and of the *importance* of carrying the weight forward over the arch.

Looking at the human skeleton from the side, the gravity line should run from slightly back of the ear, through the center of the shoulder, the center of the hip, the forward part of the knee, and should strike the floor over the center of the arch. If a line is drawn from the toe to the heel and another across the arch, the body weight should be balanced where those lines cross (intersect). This is the correct anatomical position.

The head and neck should be placed with the feeling that the back of the neck supports the weight of the head. The rib cage should be carried slightly up and forward of the hips with the yoke of the shoulders resting comfortably on it. The shoulder blades should come in neatly in back. Since the rib cage is full of air, it can support the weight of the shoulders without the help of the shoulder muscles. The abdominals should be pulled in under the ribs and flattened, as it were, against the back, thus assisting the muscles of the back in the work of carrying the weight of the upper body. A good rule to remember is that the front and back of the middle body should be both flat and parallel.

The pelvis must be held on a perpendicular line and not allowed to tip forward

or backward.

In order to accomplish this, it is often necessary to slacken the knees somewhat. Most people have some degree of hyper-extension in the knees, commonly called "saber legs" or "swayback knees." This condition causes the pelvis to tip forward to compensate for the backward pressure from the legs. It is imperative, therefore, that the bones of the legs be properly aligned around the gravity line. Continuously pushing the knees back puts a tremendous strain on the ligaments and cartilage of the knee joint and thereby increases the possibility of knee injury.

Looking at the skeleton from the front, the gravity line runs down the center striking the floor between the feet. The various parts of the body should be balanced symmetrically on either side of the gravity line.

The head, shoulders, and hips should not be allowed to shift or tilt to one side. The weight should be supported evenly on both feet. The legs should be aligned so there is no suggestion of bow-legs, knock knees, or a "rolling arch." A "rolling arch," or flat foot, is often the result of a "rolled-in" knee. Both problems can frequently be corrected by rolling the whole leg out slightly from the hip, thus correcting the lateral alignment of the leg.[1] A great part of dance training is concerned with correcting postural faults. This is a contribution good teaching can make to any student whether or not he wants to perform.

Dance makes tremendous demands on the feet. Because the feet support the total weight of the body, we must be sure that they are well prepared to do this with a minimum of strain; therefore proper alignment of the bones of the foot is vital. All the big supporting bones of the foot—the big toe, the ball of the foot, and the heel—must be on the floor; however, the arch should be lifted. The rule is: The knees and feet must face the same way, whether the legs are turned out or parallel. If the knees cannot rotate outward as far as the

---

[1] For more detailed analysis of this problem, see Celia Sparger, *Ballet Physique*, New York, The Macmillan Co., 1958, p. 23,24,25.

feet, the feet should accommodate the knees and not turn out so far. The well-trained dancer turns out the legs from the hips, not just the feet from the ankle. The degree of outward rotation in the feet and legs must be equal and parallel.

During the plié, the knees must bend over the center of the foot. The weight, as always, should stay over the arch and should not shift back with the bend.

If the weight shifts back during the plié, no action will take place in the ankle. The action in the ankle stretches the heel tendon and is one of the chief reasons for doing the exercise in the first place. If the ankle does not bend, there is usually a break in the hips or middle back, resulting in no plié at all. If the pliés are poorly performed, the result will be unbalanced take-offs and landings for jumps, for which no amount of strength in the back or legs can make up.

In order to straighten the legs after the plié (the élevé), care must be taken to keep the weight over the arch. The knees should be brought back to the gravity line. They should not, however, be swayed out to the back or rolled in to a knock-kneed position. This is true of all positions of the legs, whether they be parallel or turned out, wide base or narrow. One of the most important tasks of the dancer is to get the legs under the center of weight. This demands a great amount of sensitivity and concentration.

On the relevé (rising to the ball of the foot, sometimes called the half toe or half point), again the weight must stay forward as the heels lift. The dancer must take care that he does not go so high that the instep comes forward of the toes, beyond the support. Aside from destroying the body balance, the arch will be stretched too much and the foot will be weakened. The weight should be on the center of the ball of the foot and not carried entirely on the big toe. The ankles should not bow out to the side. As the heels come down again to the floor, the weight center of the body must be kept forward, the knees must not be allowed to hyper-extend, and the arches must be kept up. It is good to remember that a relevé should go only up, not forward and up. When the plié and relevé are combined, this weight balance must be maintained, otherwise the legs do not develop the proper spring.

Pliés and relevés—or any combination of them—are not merely exercises; they are the beginning and ending of jumps, leaps, and of many turns. When a plié is properly performed, only three joints are moving; the ankle, the knee, and the hip. The quiet torso is held in its normal upright position, without tilting or bending in any direction. It is the understanding of this relationship between the three joints of the leg and the torso, along with his personal timing of this action, that is the basis of the dancer's technique. A dancer's style and fluency depends on how sensitive and elegant is his performance of this often misunderstood coordination.

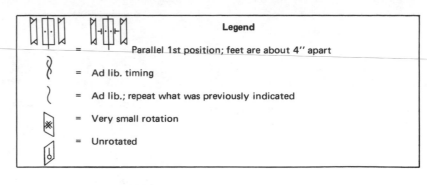

52 Leg Rotations: Parallel First Position

This exercise is a simple device to make sure the student knows what it means to "lift the arches."

Many people roll in on the inside of the foot causing a flat-footed look. This situation throws the entire leg out of alignment. In this exercise, the feet are held in a parallel first position about four inches apart, or just under the hips. The legs are then rotated outward slightly from the hip, bringing the knees parallel with the feet. Hold for a second and then relax. It is important to understand this alignment because in all basic training exercises for the legs, the knees *must* bend over the center of the feet and stay in that relationship as they straighten. They must not relax back into the rolled-in position.

Note: Many people with very low arches complain bitterly about pain in the arch when they perform this exercise. This is to be expected—the muscles of the feet are stretching. It will quickly subside as the strength and stretch develops. Also the increasing strength in the middle body will take much of the load off the feet (see Chapter 1).

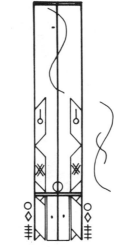

Ad lib. repeat; continue several times

Return to starting position

Rotate legs out

Starting Position: Feet parallel first, space hold on feet

L R

53 Leg Rotations: Turned-out First Position

Same as Ex. 52, except the feet are turned out slightly.

Note: The outward rotation of the legs should never be forced. A 45-degree angle is sufficient to start with (the skeletal turn-out). If the knees cannot bend over the center of the feet in that position, no greater turn-out should be attempted. Many dancers have been injured by the bad practice of forcing too wide a turn-out of the feet before the muscles of the legs are ready to control it. This forcing usually causes the pelvis to tip forward , the knees to sway back, and the arches to roll in. Only injury can result from such alignment.

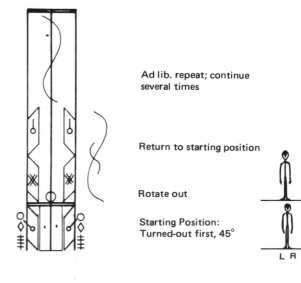

Ad lib. repeat; continue several times

Return to starting position

Rotate out

Starting Position: Turned-out first, 45°

L R

54   Half Plié: Turned-out First Position

This exercise is the very basis of the dancer's craft. It is the rock on which all his technique rests (see introductory comments to Chapter 2).

Starting Position: Standing straight, heels together, feet turned out at a 45-degree angle, arms slightly forward of side low, elbows slightly bent and lifted. The arms should have a smooth, unbroken line from the shoulders through the lifted elbow, a straight wrist and a curved but firm hand with the palms facing in toward the body (see Chapter 3).

Action:

Counts 1 and 2: Bend the knees

Counts 3 and 4: Straighten the
                         knees

Be sure the movement is sustained and firm throughout the entire action.

There is one continuous flow of energy with no breaks or accents. A well-performed plié demands the complete concentration and attention of the total personality.

Note 1: In all these exercises the center of weight must stay over the arch; the body is held erect, hips on a perpendicular, rib cage centered over the hips, shoulders resting comfortably on top of the rib cage, head back.

The proper balance of the weights around the plumb-line must be observed.

Note 2: The simple statement of the half plié seen in the notation is only the mechanical basis for what is in fact a very complicated and demanding action. The symbols notate the results in space of the movement. How to get those results is what good training is all about. Before the movement even begins there is a gathering together of the muscular tensions necessary to achieve the proper body

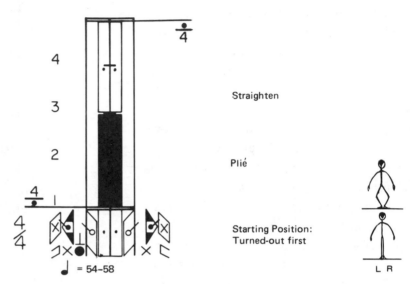

Straighten

Plié

Starting Position:
Turned-out first

L R

alignment of the starting position. As the legs rotate outward, all the great muscles of the pelvic region come into play. There is an enormous stretch across the lower abdominals from hipbone to hipbone as well as a tightening of the lower back muscles with the effort to keep the pelvis on the vertical and the weights of the rib cage and head correctly placed above it. This effort in the abdominals and lower back forces the rib cage to expand upward (away from the usual sagging position). The improved alignment of the rib cage creates the necessary firm foundation on which the shoulder girdle and arms can rest and allows the head to come back where it belongs over the plumb-line. The deeper inhale and exhale resulting from this situation adds buoyancy, increases energy, and allows the breath to assist the back in its work of supporting the great weight of the head and maintaining the perpendicular position. Once the position has been achieved the action can start.

During the plié the inside of the thighs are pressed open, forcing the knees to bend over the feet. The descending weight of the torso presses the feet into the floor causing a muscular resistance and tightening in the legs, especially in that area where the legs join the hips—over the groin in front and the "sit bones" in back. This resistance flows through the torso causing an oppositional lifting up of the upper body. The feeling is one of tremendous stability and power, of having finally achieved and comprehended the vertical posture, of intimately knowing one's bones.

In rising out of the plié the action in the legs is reversed. The thighs are pulled together, again from the inside, thereby straightening the knees, bringing the legs in to the plumb-line and pressing the weight upward.

Remember, when the legs are turned out, the bending action is sideward and involves no other direction. With the hips center, the knees open in a straight line *to* the side and close *from* the side. The action is very simple —it is center, side, center.

Perhaps it is worth noting that the words *command, power,* and *control* relate only to the dancer himself and his physical, emotional, and intellectual discipline.

Repeat this in turned out 2nd and parallel 1st .

55   Relevé: Turned-out First Position

Starting Position: Same as Exercise 54.

Action: Counts 1 and 2: Keeping the legs straight but not hyperextended, lift the heels off the floor and rise onto the balls of the feet; and (3 and 4) lower the heels to the floor keeping the legs straight.

Note 1: When the weight is carried on the balls of the feet, it should be center— halfway between the big toe and the little toe. All the toes should be on the floor and the ankles straight. Common errors are (1) carrying the weight entirely on the big toe and the bunion joint; (2) carrying the weight on the outside of the foot, on the little toe, and allowing the ankles to bow out to the side; (3) rising so high that the instep is hyperextended and moves forward of the supporting toes. This weakens the arch and often destroys the whole alignment of the leg (see introductory comments to Chapter 2). In all three cases there is inadequate support for the weight, and one part of the foot is overworked.*

Note 2: Review Note 2 for Exercise 54.

Note 3: The timing of this exercise is the same as Ex. 54, as is the slow, sustained quality and concentration. The weight now is being lifted, not lowered, and gravity is the resisting force. The tension created during the rise from the plié is continued upward and suspended on the narrow base of the half toe. It is like pressing the head against the ceiling. The buoyancy of the lifted rib cage combined with the precise balance of the body weights around the plumb-line gives an ecstatic sensation of flight—a control of the air space, in direct contrast to the commanding power of the earthy plié.

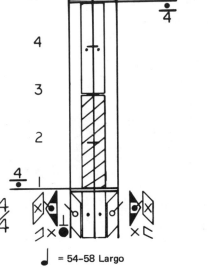

♩ = 54–58 Largo

Return to starting position

Relevé

Starting Position: Turned-out first

*For further discussion on this point see Sparger, *op. cit.*

56 Transition from Turned-out First Position to Turned-out Second Position

Holding the weight on the L, slide the R foot to the side, stretching the ankle and pointing the toes. Do not allow the big toe to curl under. It is the cushion under the toe that keeps the contact with the floor. When the ankle has been fully extended, shift the weight to that foot until it is centered between the feet. This is second position. The hooks on the side symbol mean the whole foot slides ending with the toe.

As the foot slides, be sure to keep the heel facing front.

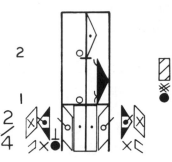

57 Transition from Turned-out Second Position to Parallel First Position

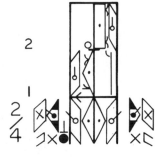

58 Plié and Relevé: Turned-out First Position

Combining the plié and the relevé prepares the legs for the spring of the leap and jump. Notice the action is from the low directly to the high 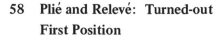. Going through the center position takes away the spring (although this action has other values) (see notes for plié and relevé, Ex. 54 and Ex. 55).

Note 1: Half Plié and Relevé in Turned-Out Second. Because of the wide position of the feet the half plié in second does not go down as far as in first position, nor does the relevé rise quite as high on the toes. It is also more difficult to maintain the center position of the pelvis.

Note 2: Half Plié and Relevé in Parallel First. In the parallel leg positions the weight is held farther forward than when the legs are turned out. This is because the forward-facing feet give greater support in that direction.

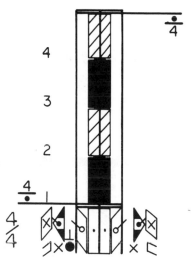

TRANSITIONS

Transitions are important; they relax the muscles and release tensions. They suggest that the next exercise is related to the previous one and must be performed in a similar way. They keep the class moving, the attention alive, and add a touch of importance and formality to simple exercises.

59 Basic Transition for Ex. 58

At the end of Ex. 56 finish in relevé, hold for four counts, then slowly lower the heels on counts 5 and 6. To complete the measure, take counts 7 and 8 to move into the next position.

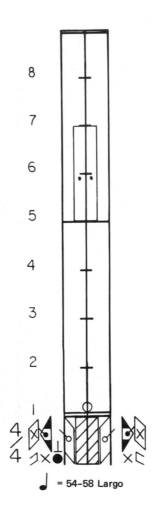

♩ = 54–58 Largo

60 Arms for Basic Transition

(For use of arms see Chapter III.)

Note: Transitions are usually performed at the same tempo as the preceding exercise. (Add arms to measure 1, Ex. 59.)

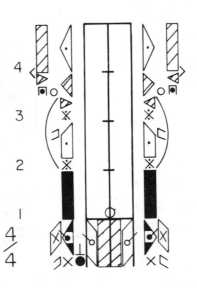

To side middle, palms up

Open side high

Go to side high

Cross forward diagonal

Arms place low

Legend	
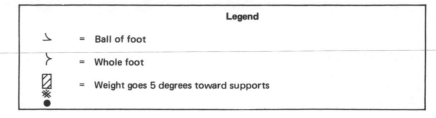	
⅃ = Ball of foot	
Ƴ = Whole foot	
= Weight goes 5 degrees toward supports	

61 Full Pliés: Turned-out First Position

In the full *plié*, the legs fold up. The center of weight—hips or pelvic area—moves down to a point level with the knees . It takes four slow counts to go down and four to come back up. Notice that the heels come off the floor on count "2 and" on the way down and return to the floor on count 2 on the way up on the second Measure.

The arms open to the side ◁ ▷ , palms facing down ▌.

The body is erect and travels up and down the plumb-line.

Turned-Out Second Position

This is a continuation of the half plié and is the only full plié performed *with the heels on the floor*. Care must be taken to keep the body erect as the center of weight is lowered to the knee level. *Do not go beyond that point.* Common errors are "sitting out" in the back or rolling in with the knees. If the student does not have the stretch in the hips to go the full way, he should go only as far as he can with the basic correct position maintained.

Repeat the full plié in parallel first position.

Note: The arms for parallel first position move side middle as in the other positions.

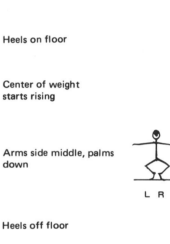

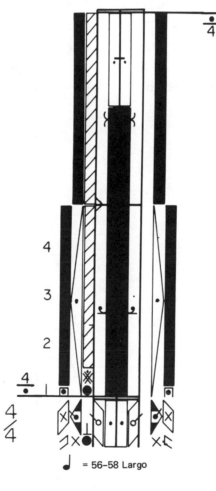

Return to starting position

Heels on floor

Center of weight starts rising

Arms side middle, palms down

Heels off floor

Lower center of weight

Starting Position: Turned-out first; center of weight forward; arms side low, elbows lifted

♩ = 56–58 Largo

81

62   Plié and Relevé Combination

This exercise is difficult for beginners as there is very little stretch in it. It should only be given as an occasional variation.

A second variation is the break in Measure 3, count "3 and." The heels lift off the floor while the legs are still bent ▮, holding on the ball of the foot the legs straighten ▨ and then the return to the beginning. The change here is in Measure 3, count 4, which is a return to the beginning. Repeat in all three foot positions; parallel first, turned-out first, and second.

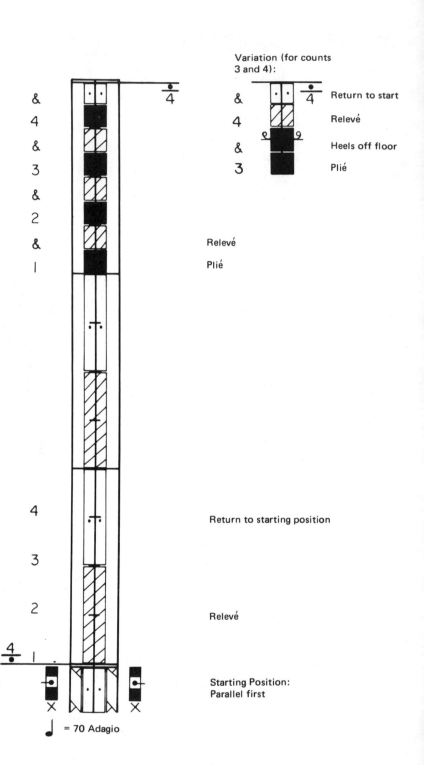

= 70 Adagio

63 Leg Swings Forward and Back

The hip is a ball-and-socket joint, and the leg should move freely in it. Unfortunately, most people of all ages seem unable to move that joint fully. A good way to learn to do this is with leg swings. As in the big body swings of the Chapter 1, this is free-flowing movement. It is an excellent preparation for leg action of all kinds—walking, running, and all the big air movements common to dance.

This is the student's first experience with using the leg without weight. This is called *leg gesture* (legs in the air) and is written in the leg-gesture column.

Notice the starting position: Standing on the turned-out left leg. The R knee is lifted parallel forward middle ⬚ (hip level), the lower leg dropping straight down from the knee, the foot relaxed ⬚ . Arms are side middle, elbows slightly bent ◁ ▷ , palms facing down ▮ . The pelvis must not be allowed to move ◇ .

Preparation: Two counts for each movement.

Note: If the pelvis moves with the leg swings, there is really no action in the hip socket and the directions ⬚ and ⬚ are not clear. The leg should swing forward and back of center. Therefore, the center (pelvis) must not move.

On count 1 the leg drops to place low with the whole foot brushing the floor. This means that the knee *must* straighten as the leg comes under the body. With this action, all three joints of the leg hip, knee, and ankle—are active. Very often this exercise is performed keeping the knee bent throughout. Then the hip joint only is working and the action becomes more bound.

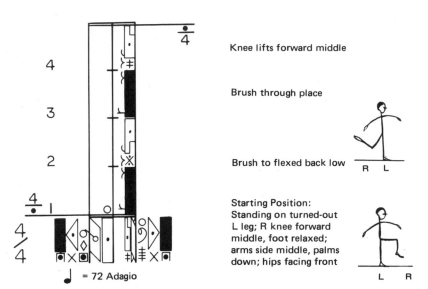

Knee lifts forward middle

Brush through place

Brush to flexed back low

R   L

Starting Position:
Standing on turned-out
L leg; R knee forward
middle, foot relaxed;
arms side middle, palms
down; hips facing front

L   R

♩ = 72 Adagio

64 Transition to the Other Side

Transition: Hold the R knee in the forward middle position for two counts. Then lower leg to place and lift the L leg. As the leg drops, lower the arms and bring them back up with the leg shift. Repeat on the other side.

65 Leg Swings Side

This exercise introduces the side direction for leg gestures and a rotation during the action. The leg turns *in* on the crossing and turns *out* as it lifts to the open diagonal ⬙ .

The starting position has the same support as Ex. 63. The working leg, the R, is to the side with the toe touching on the floor. Notice that the leg is rotated forward with the knee facing front.

On count 1 the leg moves in to place low as in Ex. 63. The knee moves across the body to ⬙ forward diagonal, hip level. Notice that the rotation occurs as the leg comes through place. There is a drop to place, the rotation occurs again but now the leg turns out, which means the knee faces the ceiling when the leg is out on the diagonal.

The pelvis again does not move. To keep the pelvis steady, there is an oppositional pressure outward in the left leg and hip to prevent it from swinging with the leg. Stability is increased when the shoulders are pressed down.

66 Transition to the Other Side

Transition to Side: Step to second, lower the arms to place low on counts 1 and 2. Shift the weight to the R and release the L on counts 3 and 4.

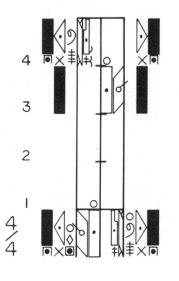

Starting Position: As in Ex. 63

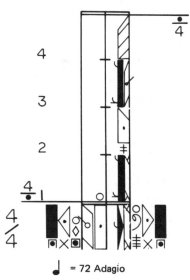

♩ = 72 Adagio

Starting Position: As in Ex. 63, except R leg side low, toe touching, knee front

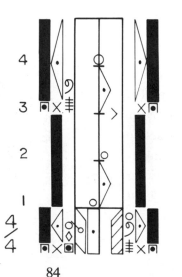

Arms side middle

Shift weight side

Arms to place low

67 Free Kicks Forward

This is a little more difficult and formal than the leg swings but still very free in the action. The difference is in the control of the leg as it swings straight rather than bent. There are, however, many similarities: (1) The whole foot touches the floor as it moves through place; (2) in the forward action the working leg is *not* turned out; (3) the arms are the same; and (4) body is place high. The center of weight must not move back and forth.

Starting Position: The ball of the working foot is on the floor, the supporting knee bent in plié. On the action the supporting leg straightens, giving an extra thrust to the kick.

Note: The kicks are in all three directions: forward, side, and back. To go into any of them, the preparation is from the opposite direction and level.

The working leg moves from back low to forward high . The supporting leg from bent to straight . As the leg is brought down the toe touches the floor first; then the whole foot slides to back low . This action in the ankle during kicks is standard dance procedure. It helps prepare the foot for landing from jumps and leaps. Many students are careless about it with the result they cannot bring the heels down on landings from elevation.

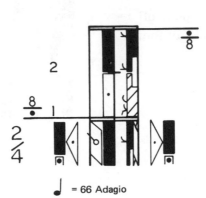

♩ = 66 Adagio

R leg brushes back low, L leg pliés

R leg brushes to forward high; L leg straightens

Starting Position: Standing on L leg, turned-out and in plié; R leg back low, ball of foot on floor, leg parallel; arms side middle, palms down

R   L

68 Transition to the Other Side

The transition should be easy to read. Step side R as the arms lower. Place L foot back with ball of foot on the floor. Bring arms up to side middle .

Remember—The pelvis does not move!

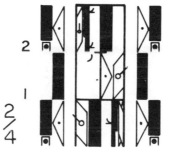

85

69 Transition to Side Kicks

Step to side with L, middle level, push off with R toe and cross R leg back, ball of foot on floor.

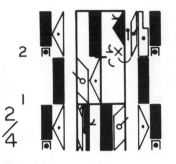

70 Free Kicks Side

With the same support, pelvis facing front, cross the R leg back, ball of foot on the floor, leg rotated out ⬗. Everything else is the same.

    The leg is kicked to the side, knee facing up, foot brushes the floor as it kicks, toe touches on the way down.

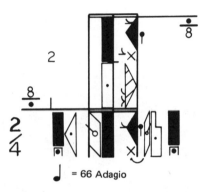

♩ = 66 Adagio

Starting Position: L leg plié, turned-out, knee bent; R leg, back, ball of foot on floor; L leg low; R arm forward middle; L arm side middle

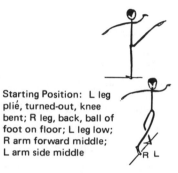

71 Transition to the Other Side

    Note: Ex. 70 to 75 the tempo remains the same throughout.

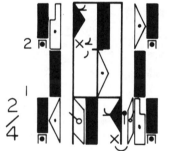

72 Transition to Back Kicks

Transition: From L side to R back.

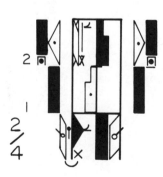

73 Free Kicks Back

In order to kick to the back, the leg must start forward. In this kick the weight shifts from the forward leg to the back leg, as the working leg travels beyond it to the back. There is a definite feeling of fall in this section. Also the working leg does not go as high and is turned out. It is more important to keep the pelvis center than to get the leg high.

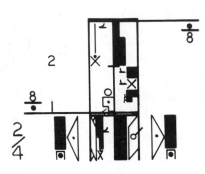

Starting Position: Standing on R, turned-out; L leg back low parallel, ball of foot on floor; arms side middle

74 Transition to the Other Side

Notice the transition from the R working leg to the L. There is a step back onto a straight leg, then a plié as the R slides to the back. With the L leg forward, it is now prepared to repeat the exercises on that side.

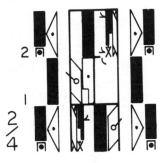

75 Coda for Free Kicks Series

Coda: To finish, step back into first position, make a half plié and straighten the legs.

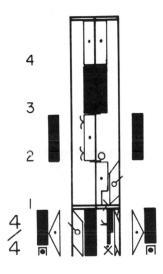

87

76 Brushes and Kicks Forward

This exercise is a more formal variation of the kicks but still maintains a swing quality.

The start is in first position. On count 1, the R foot slides forward until the toe touches then returns to the starting position. On count 2, the leg is swung up as high as possible forward without disturbing the body position and brought down again with the standard action—toe touch, whole foot, slide.

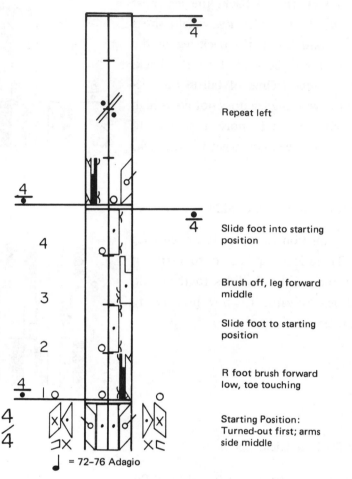

Repeat left

Slide foot into starting position

Brush off, leg forward middle

Slide foot to starting position

R foot brush forward low, toe touching

Starting Position: Turned-out first; arms side middle

♩ = 72–76 Adagio

77 Brushes and Kicks Side

Repeat to the side as in Ex. 70. Don't forget *the knees face up* on the side kick. Hips should not turn.

Note: Although the leg is written as moving into a side direction, it actually moves to the forward diagonal. The individual student should take the leg as far as possible to the side without disturbing the position of the hips. Naturally, this will be different for each student.

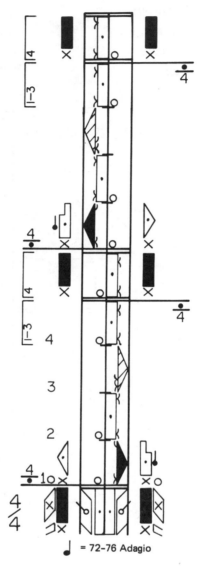

Starting Position: Same as in Ex. 76, except arms place low

♩ = 72–76 Adagio

78   Brushes and Kicks Back

Same to the back (as in Ex. 73). Turn out the working leg. The hips *must not tip* on the back kick. This exercise is to develop control in the abdominals and lower back.

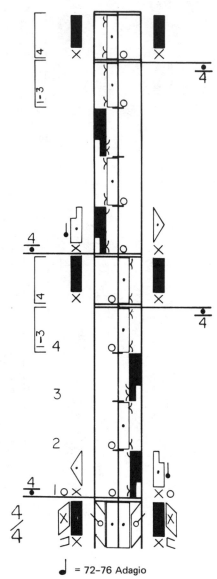

Starting Position:
Same as in Ex. 77

L   R

♩ = 72–76 Adagio

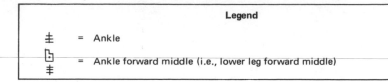

79 Leg Extensions Forward

This is a simple way to start extensions. Stand on the L, slightly turned out. Lift the R knee forward middle, at hip level and directly in front of it. Let the lower R leg drop straight down from the knee. Slide the R hand under the thigh on the outside of the leg to just above the knee, turn the elbow forward.

Note: This position serves several purposes: (1) It gives some support for the working leg; (2) helps to pull the R shoulder down; and (3) helps to keep the torso in its upright position.

Action:

Counts 1 and 2: Swing the lower leg up to knee level.

Counts 3 and 4: Lower the leg to its starting position. On the fourth Measure hold the leg in its extended position, release the hand and move the right arm to the side. Then slowly lower the whole leg to place low and repeat to the other side.

Note: Be sure that the shoulders stay level and the pelvis does not tip either forward or back.

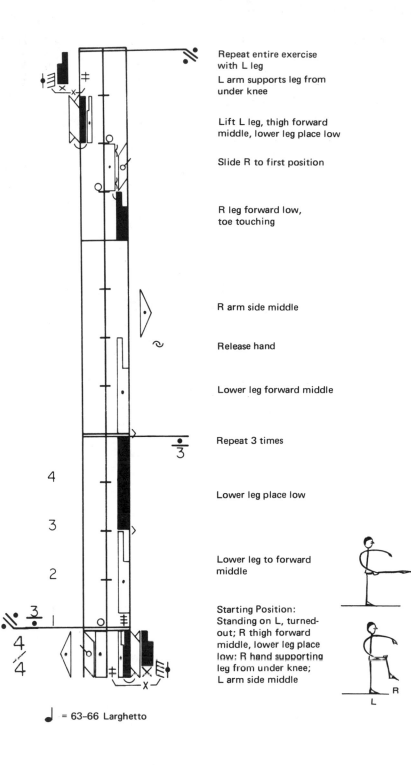

Repeat entire exercise with L leg

L arm supports leg from under knee

Lift L leg, thigh forward middle, lower leg place low

Slide R to first position

R leg forward low, toe touching

R arm side middle

Release hand

Lower leg forward middle

Repeat 3 times

Lower leg place low

Lower leg to forward middle

Starting Position: Standing on L, turnedout; R thigh forward middle, lower leg place low; R hand supporting leg from under knee; L arm side middle

♩ = 63–66 Larghetto

80 Leg Extensions Side

This is the same as Ex. 79 except that the leg is lifted to the side and the hand is on the inside of the R leg. Remember the important thing is to keep the pelvis and rib cage center, facing front. The tendency on side extensions is to turn the hips so that they face on a diagonal, thus destroying the line of the body.

The body is really not capable of performing a true side extension. Although the aim is side, the result is a diagonal of greater or lesser degree, depending on the individual's stretch and structure. Of course the *knee cap must face up to the ceiling.* Do not allow the leg to rotate in so that knee faces forward.

By rotating the leg outward, a higher extension is possible.

Note: The directions of the legs are taken from the pelvis—the center of weight. If the pelvis turns with the side extension, the movement becomes another forward extension. Only by establishing a clear front can there be clear directions in the movement.

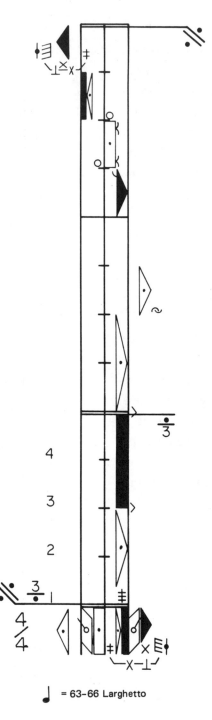

Starting Position: Same as in Ex. 79, but to the side; R hand approaches from front and grasps R leg beneath knee; both legs turned-out

♩ = 63–66 Larghetto

81 Leg Extensions Back

As always, the body is well centered. Hips stay center, facing front. The R leg is bent in the back similar to a ballet attitude; the thigh straight back; the lower leg bent at a right angle to it, the foot level with the knee. The R arm is [⬠] forward middle; L arm ◁ side middle; shoulders pressed down.

Action: The R knee straightens and bends. There should be no action at any joint except the knee.   The transition is through place low.

Note: As with the side directions of the legs the back directions are rarely performed as written. Actually the thigh is on a back diagonal slightly below hip level. The true back position is almost impossible for beginners.

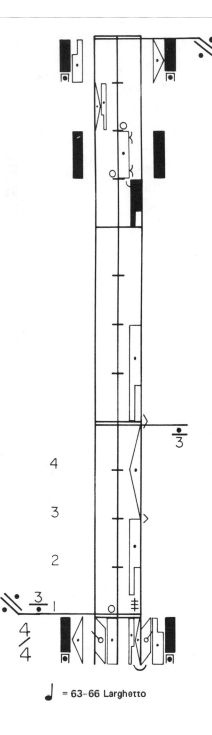

Starting Position: R leg bent in back; R arm forward middle

♩ = 63–66 Larghetto

93

82 Back Extension with Plié and Hip Tilt Forward

It is impossible to have a brilliant back extension of the leg unless the pelvis is involved in the action. By involving the pelvis, the back comes into play as well. In the following sequence, the total body is active and helps in a positive way to control the movement. The student will find mechanical similarity between the Ex. 81 sequences, the body successions of Chapter 1, Ex. 39, and the hip lifts Chapter 1, Ex. 46, as well as the 6/4 leg stretch of Ex. 136, Chapter 2.

Starting Position: Standing in turned-out first position, body well placed, arms place high.

Action:

Measure 1 Count 1: With a strong attack, shift the weight to the R and at the same time brush the L leg back low, turned-out, foot pointed. There is a feeling of locking the leg in the hip. From this point on there is *no action at all* in the L hip. The line from the hipbone to the knee does not change; (2) with a pressure down in front from the hands and up in back by the leg, start tipping the pelvis forward, carrying the lifted leg up in back as far as the stretch will allow; ("2 and") Start the plié and continue pressing the leg up in back, the arms down in front until the arms end under the shoulders, palms facing the floor. (At this point the arms feel like another pair of legs.) The face and rib cage stay facing the front. This causes the back to arch strongly. It is like being pulled from both ends like an archery bow with the greatest pressure in the pelvis and middle back. Continue the tipping through count 4.

Measure 2 Hold the position for the full measure.

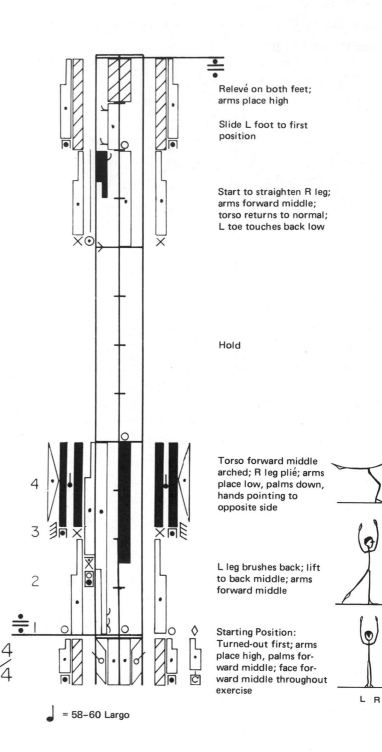

Relevé on both feet; arms place high

Slide L foot to first position

Start to straighten R leg; arms forward middle; torso returns to normal; L toe touches back low

Hold

Torso forward middle arched; R leg plié; arms place low, palms down, hands pointing to opposite side

L leg brushes back; lift to back middle; arms forward middle

Starting Position: Turned-out first; arms place high, palms forward middle; face forward middle throughout exercise

L R

♩ = 58–60 Largo

94

Measure 3 Counts 1 and 2: Start straightening the supporting leg, at the same time begin to bring the pelvis back to its perpendicular, carrying the lifted leg with it. The head and chest rise to their normal positions above it. The arms move forward and up to their starting positions over the head. This action reverses the pressures of Measure 1—it is now up in front, down in back; (3) the back should now be straight, the foot of the working leg slides in under the center of weight, and the return ends in a rising to relevé on both feet on count 4.

For the repeat, drop to the whole foot and brush the other leg back.

Note 1: When the leg is lifted to its full height in back, the pelvis must face the floor; do not allow it to face a diagonal. Also the working leg should stay turned-out, the knee facing side, heel pressed down. This exercise is like a see-saw, the body tilting on the supporting leg, one end goes up as the other end goes down. The only difference between this and a real see-saw is that the head and rib cage do not travel as far as the leg. There are various rates of speed for different parts of the body. Remember that the arching back controls the action and suspends the body on the supporting leg (see Chapter 1, suspension bridge). This exercise is an outward succession traveling in two directions, forward and back.

Note 2: The back starts straight, goes into an arch, and returns to the straight. Do not end with an arched back. The return to normal sign means just that. (See discussion on body alignment, in introductory comments, Chapter 2.)

83 Back Extension with Plié and Hip Tilt Forward with Bending and Straightening of Leg

This is exactly like Ex. 82 except for Measure 2. Here the knee bends for two counts and straightens for two counts. During this action nothing moves except the knee of the working leg. Because it is working in a turn-out, the foot, ankle, and hip are on the same plane—parallel to the floor—when the knee is bent. The feeling is of the heel moving toward the opposite buttock.

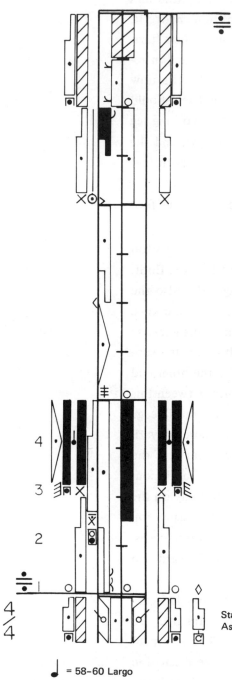

R   L

Starting Position:
As in Ex. 82

♩ = 58–60 Largo

**84 Back Extension with Plié and Hip Tilt
Forward Bending and Straightening of
Leg with Balance**

Measures 1 and 2 Similar to the two previous exercises but the final position and balance are more demanding. The change does not start until Measure 3.

Measure 3 The knee is bent a second time and held in that position for counts 3 and 4 of this Measure.

Measure 4 Is like Measure 3 of Ex. 82—the body returns to normal but the leg stays bent in back. Watch for the hold sign on the working leg.

Measure 5 Rise to the ball of the supporting foot and *hold through count 2 of Measure 6.*

Measure 6 To finish, lower the lifted leg to place high beside the supporting foot and bring both heels to the floor, the arms move through side middle to place low.

Note 1: Remember the pelvis leads the body up to the vertical position, and the line from the hipbone to the knee does not change. On the relevé press down in the shoulders. This oppositional pressure from the top against the pressure up from the relevé adds tremendously to the stability of the whole body during this rather difficult balance.

Note 2: Care must be taken to straighten the back as the body moves up to the vertical in Measure 4. The point is to return to the plumb-line although the leg is bent in back. The common error is to keep the back arched as the body rises. When this exercise is well done there is no pressure in the middle back. As in all vertical positions, the front and back should be flat and parallel. It is difficult to hold the lifted leg back of the hips. If the front of the thigh is not stretched enough, the muscles in the back of the leg are forced to work too hard to maintain the position. This results in muscle "cramp." (See note for leg extensions forward, Ex. 79.)

Ability to perform this exercise well is the result of the accumulation of much basic detail. Balance is surprisingly easy if the body is well placed with the weight over the arch of the supporting foot; the pelvis center facing front; the rib cage place high above the hips; and the shoulders, arms, and head in their proper relationship to the hips. It also helps to breathe with the up and down of the exercise.

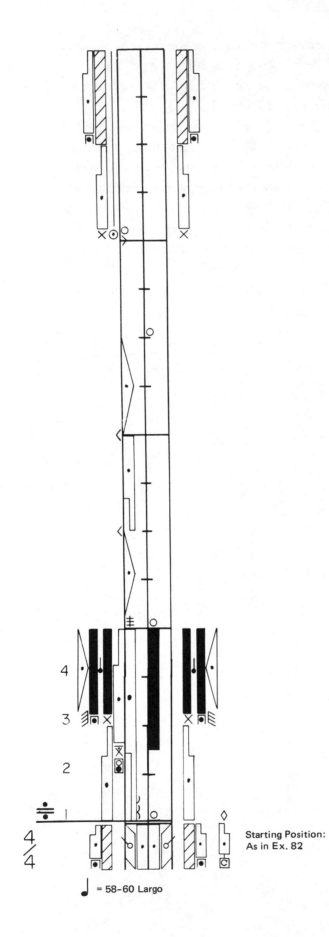

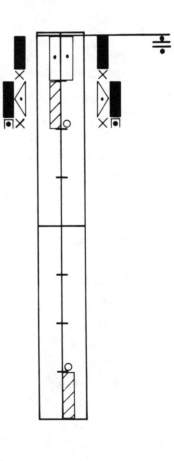

Starting Position:
As in Ex. 82

$\frac{4}{4}$

♩ = 58–60 Largo

85 Plié on One Leg

Starting Position: Similar to Ex. 79. Stand on the R, arms ◁ ▷ side middle, L leg bent forward middle .

Action: Simply bend the supporting knee for one count and straighten it again. Be sure the knee bends over the foot and does not roll in as it straightens.

Transition: Same as in leg extension series.

Note: To watch for body alignment, a student can perform this exercise facing sideways to the mirror or at the barre.

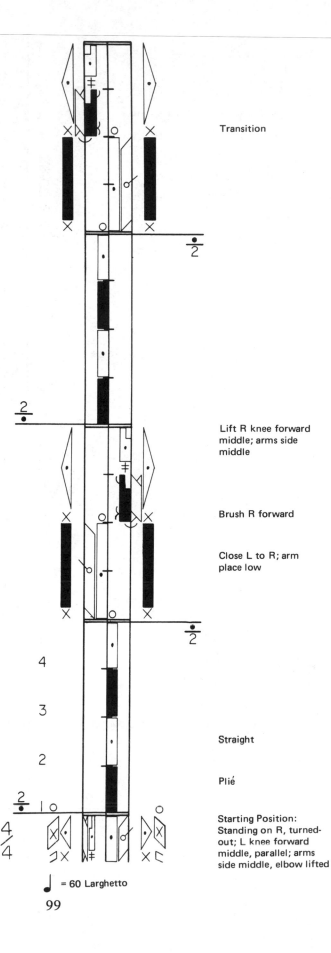

Transition

Lift R knee forward middle; arms side middle

Brush R forward

Close L to R; arm place low

Straight

Plié

Starting Position: Standing on R, turned-out; L knee forward middle, parallel; arms side middle, elbow lifted

♩ = 60 Larghetto

86 Relevé on One Leg

Same as Ex. 85 except there is a rise onto the ball of the foot. This is difficult but with the body well placed, the eyes focused on a point at eye level straight ahead, and the shoulders pressed down, it is remarkable what beginners can do. It helps to feel a quiet centering and concentration of energy around the spine.

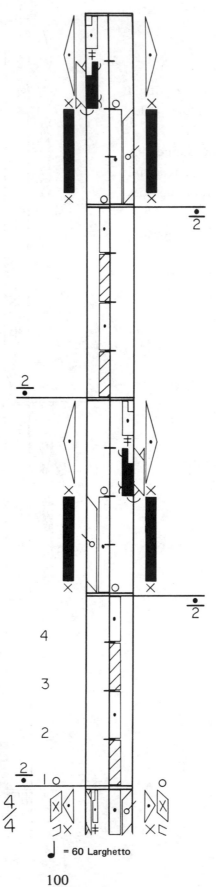

Starting Position:
As in Ex. 85

♩ = 60 Larghetto

87 Plié and Relevé on One Leg

Ex. 85 and Ex. 86 combined. This exercise requires the same concentration—quiet but firm; don't get frantic.

Note: It is a good idea to do these three exercises (Ex. 85, Ex. 86, and Ex. 87) dividing the class into two groups. This gives them a rest before the repeat to the other side.

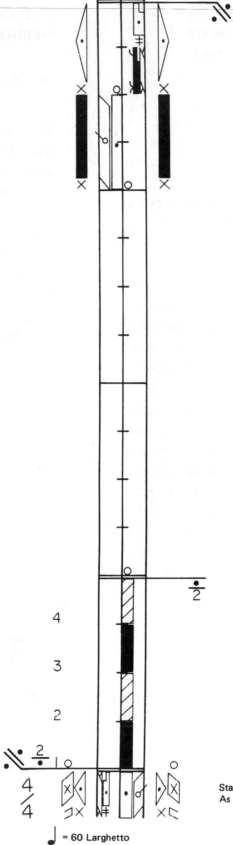

Starting Position:
As in Ex. 85

♩ = 60 Larghetto

101

INTRODUCTION TO FOOT PREPARATION SERIES: USE OF FEET FOR WEIGHT SHIFT AND ELEVATION

Dancers' feet take a terrible beating. If the student is to avoid injury, the feet must be properly prepared for the tremendous amount of hard labor required of them.

Most people think that dancers point their feet because it looks pretty. This is only partially correct—it really serves a function.

The human animal does not pull himself through space, he pushes himself from one foot to the other. For the dancer this push is emphasized and refined by stretching the ankle and toes. In other words, pointing the feet. On a jump, the last thing to leave the floor is the big toe. It is also the first thing to touch the floor on the landing. This is very difficult to do well and requires a great deal of patient drill. However, with a little choreographic invention, the drill can be varied and even become exciting. The following exercises include mechanical, rhythmic, and dynamic variety to help keep the interest alive. As always, the principal directions of the body are used—forward, side, and back.

EXERCISES FOR FEET WITH WEIGHT SHIFT

88 Exercise for the Feet with Weight Shift Forward

Brush the foot forward as far as it will go with the big toe in contact with the floor, knee straight. Without moving the toe from its position, shift the weight to that foot, bending the knee. Push off from the toe and slide the foot to place.

Note: Be sure the body alignment is maintained as the knee bends. Do not allow the hips or rib cage to shift back as the weight moves forward. Balance is improved if the shoulders are pressed down.

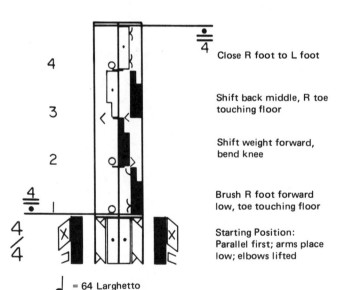

4

3

2

1

Close R foot to L foot

Shift back middle, R toe touching floor

Shift weight forward, bend knee

Brush R foot forward low, toe touching floor

Starting Position: Parallel first; arms place low; elbows lifted

♩ = 64 Larghetto

89 Exercise for the Feet with Weight Shift Side

This is like Ex. 88 except the shift is to the side. Keep the body upright and do not allow the pelvis or rib cage to tip.

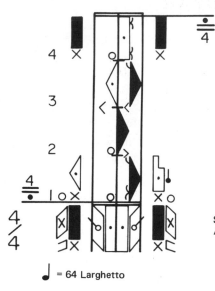

Starting Position:
As in Ex. 88

♩ = 64 Larghetto

90 Exercise for the Feet with Weight Shift Back

This one is difficult. Unusual demands are made on the heel tendon during the weight shift. It is like a plié on one leg. Be sure the pelvis stays center, facing front. A common error is to allow it to tip toward the working leg or rotate in that direction. The arms work in opposition. Right arm forward as the right leg moves back.

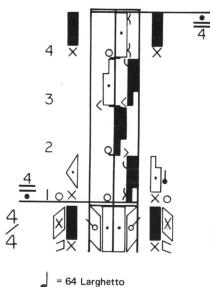

Starting Position:
As in Ex. 88

♩ = 64 Larghetto

91 Fast Push-offs Forward and Side

This is an inversion of the exercises for the feet with weight shift sequence. Start with the weight forward, knee bent.

Action: After a very fast push-off with the foot there is a fall into the starting position. The weight should not shift all the way to the back foot but stay suspended between the feet for a second before the return. This repeats in all directions, forward, side, and back. Watch for transitions.

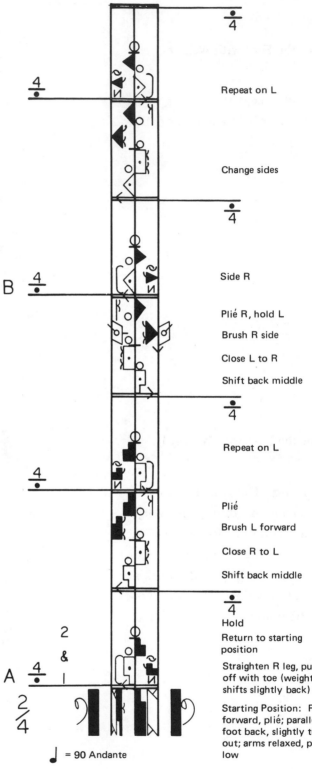

Repeat on L

Change sides

Side R

Plié R, hold L

Brush R side

Close L to R

Shift back middle

Repeat on L

Plié

Brush L forward

Close R to L

Shift back middle

Hold

Return to starting position

Straighten R leg, push off with toe (weight shifts slightly back)

Starting Position: R foot forward, plié; parallel, L foot back, slightly turned-out; arms relaxed, place low

♩ = 90 Andante

104

92 Weight Shift Forward and Back Changing Feet

Preparation for movement through space, forward and back. As in Ex. 91 the starting position is the same except the ball of the back foot is on the floor with the leg not turned-out. The weight is shifted entirely to the back foot in relevé. The feet close, then the weight falls forward onto the other leg.

    Note: Many students find it difficult to bend the knees when landing from leaps. This simple exercise prepares the legs to do this. Notice the arms, changing through ∎ place low and working in opposition.

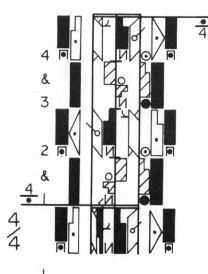

♩ = 78 Andante

Forward low on L; R ball of foot on floor; opposition arms

Close R to L
Arms place low
Shift back high
Starting Position: Plié R, L back low parallel, ball of foot on floor; R arm side middle; L arm forward middle, palms down

93 Weight Shift Side to Side Changing Feet

Same as Ex. 92 except the action is sideward. The suspension in the center seems more obvious. Don't forget to press the shoulders down as the arms lift. Body stays firm and well placed.

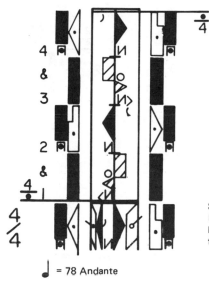

♩ = 78 Andante

Starting Position: Plié R turned-out; L side low turned-out, ball of foot on floor

105

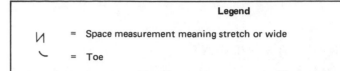
94   Weight Shift Forward, Back, and Side Changing Feet

This combines Ex. 92 and Ex. 93.   Forward action and side action.   Watch for the change of direction on counts 4 and 8.

Starting Position: R leg side, knee bent; arms in opposition.

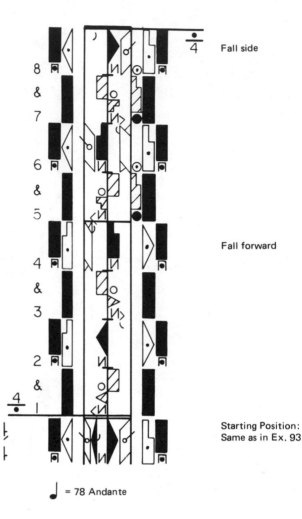

Fall side

Fall forward

Starting Position:
Same as in Ex. 93

♩ = 78 Andante

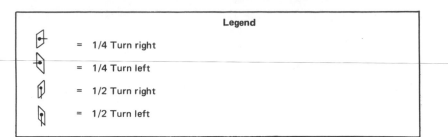
95 Weight Shift Forward, Back, and Side with Half and Quarter Turns

This is the same basic weight shift with a simple step or pivot turn. Watch for the rotation symbols.

As the weight shifts side, there is a half turn to the L. As the feet close make another half turn to the L, thus completing a full rotation. Follow with the fall away to the L.

On the repeat to the right, the rotations are the same (two half turns), but the fall away is forward.

From the forward position there are two quarter turns to the left (total—half turn) bringing the dancer to face the back of the studio. The repeat is to the right with the fall away to the side, the starting position. Watch for the facing pins on the left side of the staff 凸 早 .

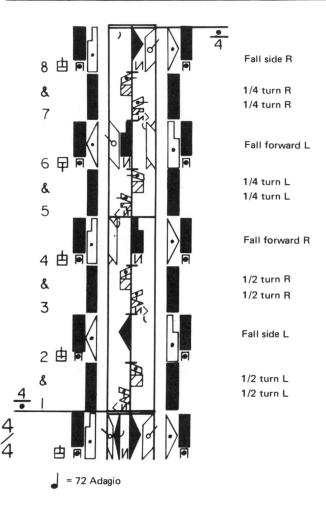

Fall side R

1/4 turn R
1/4 turn R

Fall forward L

1/4 turn L
1/4 turn L

Fall forward R

1/2 turn R
1/2 turn R

Fall side L

1/2 turn L
1/2 turn L

♩ = 72 Adagio

96 Weight Shift Forward, Back, and Side with Half Turns

This is the same as Ex. 95 except for the full turns on the second measure. These are divided into two half turns ending with the body facing the front. Notice the facing pins. This turn is not easy. It helps to turn the back foot out slightly before the weight shift and lift up well in body during the pivot.

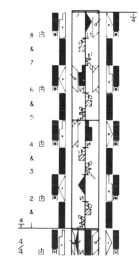

107

PREPARATION FOR VERTICAL ELEVATION

97   Ankle and Toe Isolation

Starting Position: Standing in parallel first.

Count 1: Lift the R heel, pushing down into the ball of the foot; (2) still pushing down, press the big toe down into the floor until the muscle under the toe nail touches the floor and the ankle is fully stretched; and (3) firmly bring the whole foot back to normal.

Repeat with other foot.

Note 1: The weight shifts to the left as the heel comes off the floor and stays there until the whole foot is brought down again to the floor.

Note 2: The toe *does not move* from its starting position. The common errors are to move the foot forward or pull the toe back as the toe points. The value of keeping the toe in place is that this prepares for the vertical take-off.

Note 3: If the feet are weak, the arch will "cramp" as the ankle stretches. Shake the feet and continue. Normally the cramping goes away as the muscles gain strength and the ankle stretches.

Repeat with other foot.

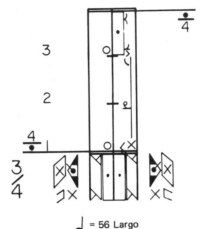

Return whole foot to floor

Continue lift until tip of toe is on floor

Lift heel and stretch ankle, ball of foot on floor

Starting Position: Parallel first; arms side low; elbows lifted

♩ = 56 Largo

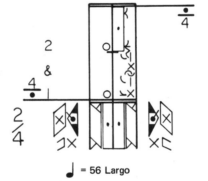

Return whole foot to floor

Toe touches floor

Fast push-off with foot until toe releases from floor

Starting Position: As in Ex. 97

♩ = 56 Largo

98   Quick Push-off

Similar to Ex. 97 except there is no pressure on the ball of the foot. There is a simple push-off from the toe; a release of contact as the foot points; a re-contact as the toe touches again and a quick return to the start.

Note 1: To do this, the knee must lift slightly but be sure it is the toe that pushes off; not the knee that lifts.

Note 2: Although it is important to perform this exercise with the "snap" of the push-off to develop the proper thrust for future elevation, it is often necessary to slow it down to half the normal speed until the release and contact are felt.

A nice sequence is four each of Ex. 97, then eight each of Ex. 98, first changing sides then all on one side.

108

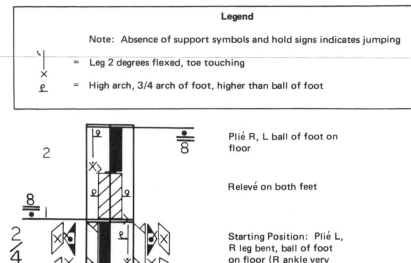

99 Preparation for Landings

Starting Position: Standing on the L in plié, R ankle stretched, ball of foot on floor, no weight.

Action: Shift the weight to the R, straighten L. Continue shifting to the R, ending in plié, L ankle stretched.

Note: Be sure the knee bends over the foot on the plié.

Plié R, L ball of foot on floor

Relevé on both feet

Starting Position: Plié L, R leg bent, ball of foot on floor (R ankle very stretched)

= 56 Largo

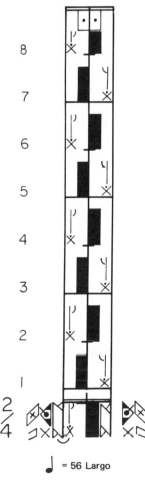

100 "Slow Treading": Spring from Foot to Foot

Starting Position: Plié right, left toe touching.

Action: With a slight spring, straightening the R knee, shift the weight to the L foot using the technique in Ex. 98, ending in plié on the L.

Note: This is too slow for real elevation and is very labored, but it is wonderful for finding out how to land.

"Fast Treading" For the real quality of elevation, pick up the tempo to = 88. This is really a run in place and is the exact tempo of the following jumps.

Land L

Spring

Land R

Spring
Land L in Plie, R toe touches floor
Little spring into the air
Starting Position: Plié R, L leg bent, toe on floor, legs parallel; arms side low, elbows lifted

= 56 Largo

VERTICAL ELEVATION

101   Little Jumps in Parallel First Position

Here is a very small jump. There is just a re-lease of pressure on the toe as Ex. 97. The knees must straighten in the air.

Note the slight plié before the push-off. Beginners often try to take-off without bend-ing the knees, just using the feet. This is next to impossible but somehow they try. If this action is repeated often enough, it can result in shin-splints. Proper elevation must have a plié *before* the elevation and *on* the landing.

Note: There is a similarity between this and Ex. 98. This exercise, however, is done in parallel first, turned-out first, and turned-out second.

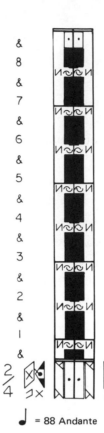

Land

Spring

Land in plié

Spring: Stretch legs in air; high enough to just release toes from floor
Plié

Starting Position:
Parallel first; arms low

♩ = 88 Andante

102   Little Jumps in Turned-out First Position

Same as Ex. 101, legs turned-out.

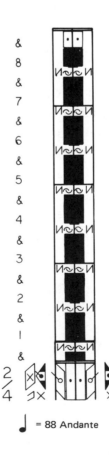

Starting Position:
Turned-out first

♩ = 88 Andante

110

103 Little Jumps in Turned-out Second Position

Just like Ex. 101 except the feet are in second position, turned-out.

Teaching note — Ex. 100 to 108:

No repeats have been included for these exercises. Eight jumps at one time is sufficient for beginners. To avoid sore calf muscles it is wise to divide the class into two groups. Let one group perform the exercises as written while the other group works, then repeat the exercises. For the first few classes only Ex. 100 to 104 with one repeat is recommended. The other variations can be added later as strength and endurance improves.

104 Jumps in Parallel First Position

This is really off the ground. The space between the support symbols indicates time in the air; the push-off and release are now taken for granted. In this exercise, the "air" space is on the upbeat, the landing on the downbeat. Also, notice the change in tempo ♩ = 70–72 to accommodate the greater height of the jump (the higher the jump, the slower the beat).

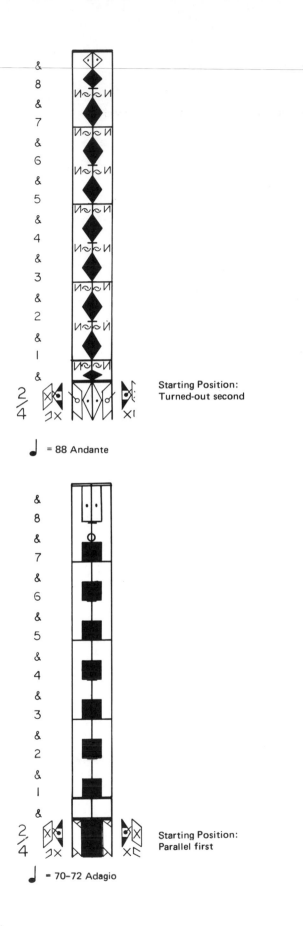

Starting Position: Turned-out second

♩ = 88 Andante

Starting Position: Parallel first

♩ = 70–72 Adagio

111

105 Jumps in Turned-out First Position

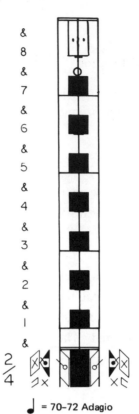

Starting Position:
Turned-out first

𝅘𝅥 = 70–72 Adagio

106 Jumps in Turned-out Second Position

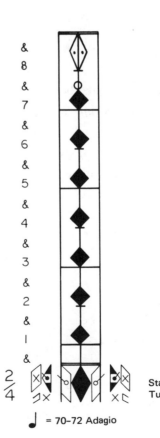

Starting Position:
Turned-out second

𝅘𝅥 = 70–72 Adagio

107 Jumps from First to Second Position

Jump from first to second, changing the leg position in the air.

108 Jumps with Leg Gestures

Jumping from second closing in first in the air and landing in second again.

Note 1: This one really goes up. The closing of the legs adds an extra lift. Remember, the *legs* come together, not just the feet. The action is from the inside of the thighs—the adductors—as in the plié-relevé sequence of Ex. 58 Chapter 2.

Note 2: The notation of all elevation looks very black on the page, whereas the feeling is light and the body is actually high—off the ground. The notation indicates the take-offs and landings, which are low—knees bent—in plié. It is surprising how many beginner students almost refuse to bend the knees on the landing. The action in Ex. 99 and 100 is correct; the whole foot comes to the floor. Jumping starts with the whole foot on the floor and ends that way.

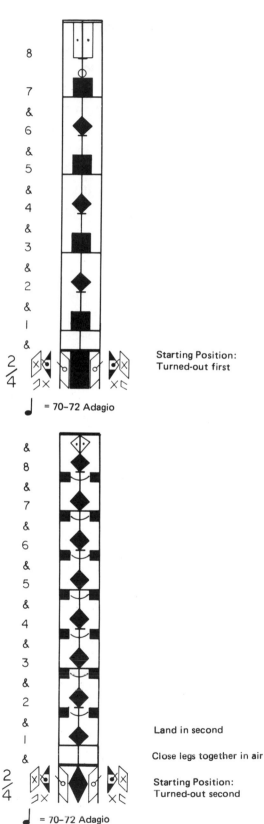

Starting Position: Turned-out first

♩ = 70–72 Adagio

Land in second

Close legs together in air

Starting Position: Turned-out second

♩ = 70–72 Adagio

FLOOR STRETCHES

The following series of exercises (109 through 118) is designed to stretch the legs. Typical of Modern Dance, most stretching is done sitting on the floor. This does several things: (1) Because the problem of balance has been eliminated, the body is more relaxed; thus allowing for easy, unforced stretching. (2) The floor area becomes a friendly place that the future dancer or choreographer can use freely as familiar rather than strange territory. (3) This series can be used as a change of pace during a class. Its exercises have many similarities. They all involve (a) the tipping of the pelvis on the legs; (b) the bending and straightening the legs in various positions; and (c) the torso-to-the-legs relationship, which can be applied to standing positions.

109 Single Leg Stretch

Starting Position: Sitting on the floor, back straight, R leg bent in front, L leg on a forward diagonal ♮ . Bend the body forward as far as possible without taking the hips off the floor.   Take four slow counts.   Return to starting position and drop over again. Repeat several times.   This is a simple outward and inward succession.

Note 1:   Some students have such tight backs or hamstrings they can only bend forward a very little way.   This is frustrating so they try to go farther by lifting the hips off the floor. This does no good. Part of the value of this stretch is to limber up the middle back.

As can be seen this is very similar to Ex. 1, Chapter 1. In this case the hips are static, also the legs.   Lowering the heavy weight of the head helps to stretch the middle back.

Repeat this on the other side.

Note 2:   Taken slowly, without a beat allows the students to become acquainted with the floor area and adjust to the many uncomfortable sensations they may be experiencing for the first time.   The teacher *must* remember that in our culture, we rarely sit on the floor.   When this is first done in a dance class, it is often a psychological as well as a physical shock. This little exercise gives students time to adjust.

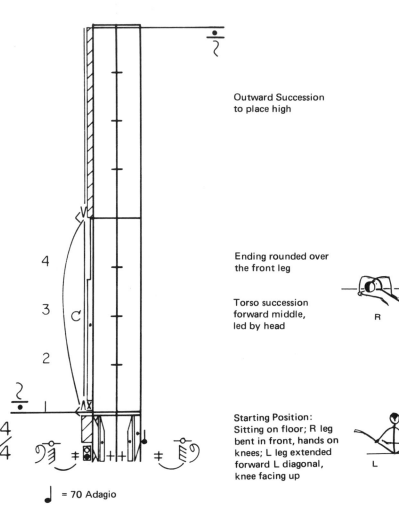

Outward Succession to place high

Ending rounded over the front leg

Torso succession forward middle, led by head

R   L

Starting Position: Sitting on floor; R leg bent in front, hands on knees; L leg extended forward L diagonal, knee facing up

L   R

♩ = 70 Adagio

115

110 Single Leg Stretch with Breath

Just like Ex. 109 except that an inhale and exhale is added as the body hangs forward.

Note: The inhale tightens the back muscles around the ribs; the exhale releases them allowing the hanging weight of the head to carry the body down. Recover to starting position and repeat. There really is no beat for this exercise but if it goes on too long, tension sets in again. The class atmosphere should be relaxed and unhurried.

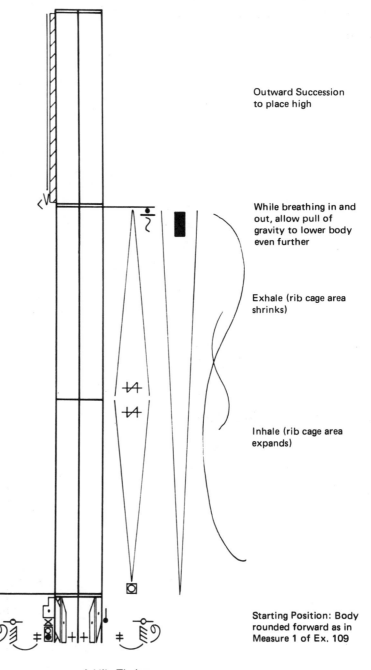

Outward Succession to place high

While breathing in and out, allow pull of gravity to lower body even further

Exhale (rib cage area shrinks)

Inhale (rib cage area expands)

Starting Position: Body rounded forward as in Measure 1 of Ex. 109

Ad lib. Timing

116

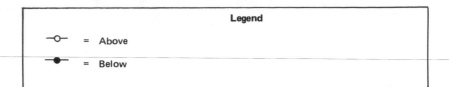
111 Single Leg Stretch with Body Bounces

Same position of the legs. Fold the body forward as far as possible with the hips on the floor. With a slight pressure from the hips, push the whole torso forward and down and let it spring back again. Repeat four times (16 counts) then change to the other side. (Remember Ex. 5, Chapter 1)

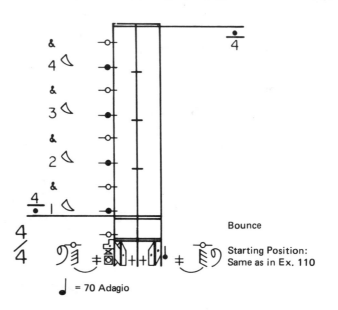

Bounce

Starting Position:
Same as in Ex. 110

♩ = 70 Adagio

112 Transition to Other Side

On the change, lift the body to its normal high ▧ position. Bring the legs together in front, then bend the L leg in front.

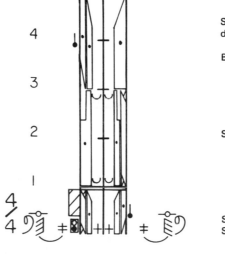

Slide R leg to forward diagonal

Bend L knee

Slide legs forward

Starting Position:
Same as in Ex. 109

117

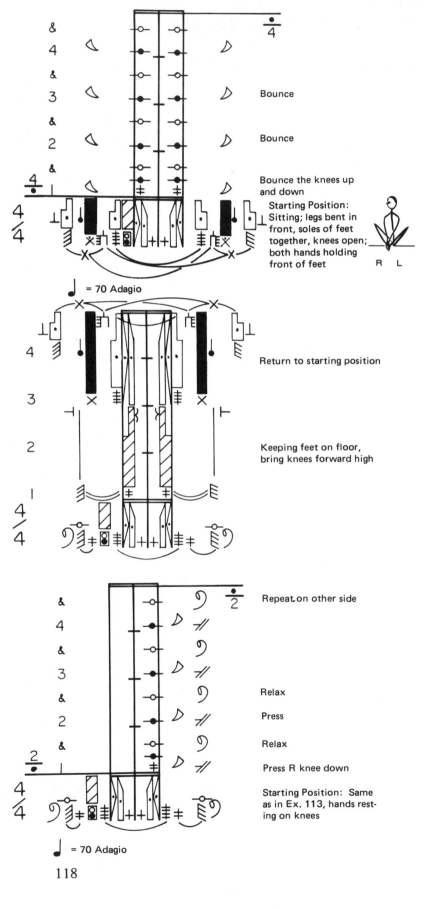
113 Double Leg Stretch: Bouncing Both Knees

Starting Position: Both legs bent in front, soles of the feet together, knees drop open, hands are holding the front of the feet.

Action: ⚬ . Just bounce the knees up and down 16 times, counting 1 and 2 and . . . etc. Do not force; this is uncomfortable.

114 Transition from Ex. 113 to Ex. 115

Transition: To rest the legs, bring the knees, still bent, together in front and let them drop open again to prepare for the next exercise.

115 Double Leg Stretch: Pressing One Knee

Place R hand on R knee. Gently push down and let it spring back eight times. Repeat to the other side.

Same transition as in Ex. 114.

118

116 Double Leg Stretch:
Pressing Both Knees

Hold the feet, tip the body forward until the elbows rest on the thighs just above the knees. Press down with both elbows at the same time. This is very uncomfortable; be careful.

117 Double Leg Stretch with Body Bounces

Still holding the feet, release the pressure from the elbows, fold the body forward as far as possible and (repeat the bounces as in Ex. 111) bringing the head as close to the feet as possible.

   Note: For the first few classes, it is wise to use the transition to rest the legs between each section. After a few classes however, the students can run through the whole sequence without a break, with little discomfort.

118 Transition from Ex. 117 to Ex. 119

Transition: Lift the body to place high ▨, slide the legs straight forward, and fold the body forward over the legs.

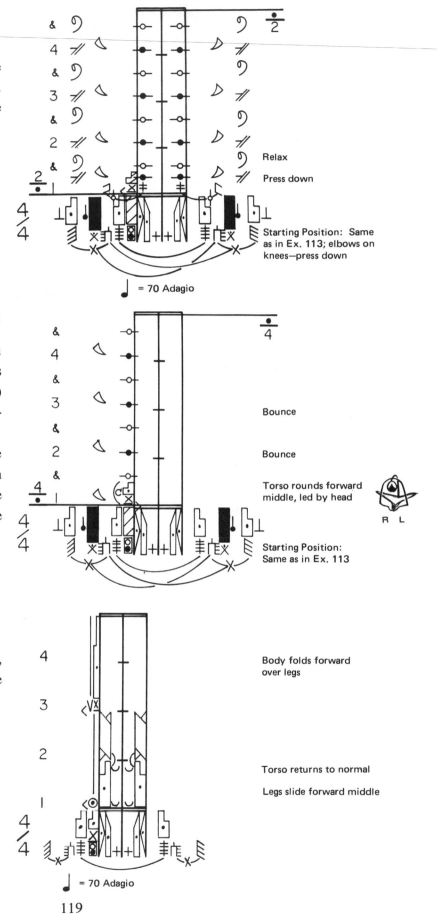

Relax

Press down

Starting Position: Same as in Ex. 113; elbows on knees—press down

♩ = 70 Adagio

Bounce

Bounce

Torso rounds forward middle, led by head

Starting Position: Same as in Ex. 113

R L

Body folds forward over legs

Torso returns to normal

Legs slide forward middle

♩ = 70 Adagio

119

119 Hamstring Stretch with Head Circles

This is by far the most difficult, uncomfortable, and important of all the leg stretches. It is difficult, particularly for men, because of their strength in the back of the legs. Very tight, strong muscles do not relax easily; and stretching is essentially relaxation. The hamstrings are particularly resistant because one of their chief functions is to hold the pelvis on the perpendicular. These muscles are, therefore, constantly in a state of static contraction. It is important to release this tension in the hamstrings in order to increase the movement range of the legs. A long stride depends on how much the muscles in the back of the legs are willing to give. The same is true of a wide leap or a high extension. Strength in the lifting muscles is not enough. If the muscular "antagonists" do not give, no amount of strength can compensate for that lack. Muscular elasticity is one of the goals of all dance training. Stretching helps to develop it.

Starting Position: Legs straight in front of the hips, body folded as far as it will go without bending the knees, hands resting on the floor, either side of the legs.

Note 1: Some students can do no more than lower the head. It is wise to have them just stay in this position for a few seconds. Add the inhale and exhale, lifting the body and dropping again with as little tension as possible. Rotating the head helps to relax the neck muscles. See Ex. 21, Chapter 1. Tempo is important. If the rotation is done too slowly the result is "bound flow"—no relaxation—too fast results in the same thing.

Note 2: The teacher must make every effort to encourage the student with any difficulty. No amount of scolding or pressuring will get results. Tension in the voice or manner of the teacher creates tension in the student. Stretching is to release tension, both physical and emotional.

Note 3: Do not allow the students to stay in any stretch position too long; too much time spent sitting in the same position builds up new tension in many people.

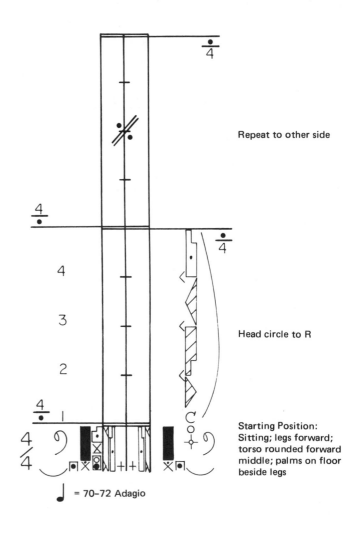

Repeat to other side

Head circle to R

Starting Position: Sitting; legs forward; torso rounded forward middle; palms on floor beside legs

♩ = 70–72 Adagio

120

120   Transition from Ex. 119 to Ex. 121

This exercise folds the body up—knees to the
chest, feet on the floor—before repeating.

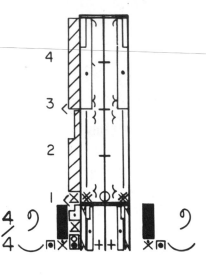

Slide legs forward,
torso place high

Fold legs in to body,
torso rounded forward
high

121   Hamstring Stretch with Bounces

Same position as Ex. 119. Notice the bounce
symbols and dynamic markings with a
light accent on the "down" of the bounce.

Note: The bounces (pressing down and
spring back) help develop elasticity.   (See
Ex. 111.)

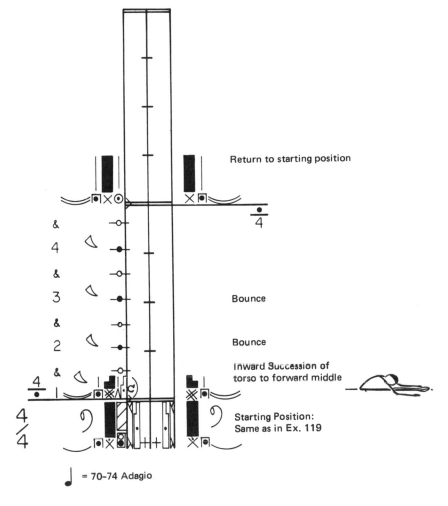

Return to starting position

Bounce

Bounce

Inward Succession of
torso to forward middle

Starting Position:
Same as in Ex. 119

= 70–74 Adagio

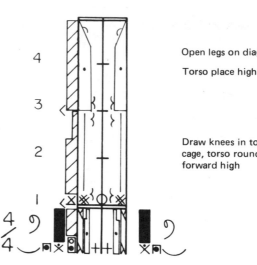
122   Transition from Ex. 121 to Ex. 123

Same as Ex. 118 (transition from Ex. 117 to Ex. 119). Fold the body up and bring the knees in to the rib cage. Slide the legs open to the diagonal. Be sure not to exaggerate the wide leg position. A good rule for the first few classes is to spread the legs as far as possible and then bring them in six inches.

Open legs on diagonal

Torso place high

Draw knees in to rib cage, torso rounded forward high

123   Pelvic Tilt

It is sometimes difficult to get into the starting position for the wide leg stretch especially for people with narrow hips. This little preparation helps.

With the hands on the floor to hold some of the weight, tip the pelvis back a bit and then rock it forward ending with the ischia—"sit bones"—on the floor. If the student is unable to sit on the "sit bones" with the legs wide, have him bring them closer together. If it is still impossible, have him stand in a comfortably wide leg position and repeat the hanging stretch as Ex. 20, Chapter 1. Let the student with this problem stretch this way until he is able to get some value out of the sitting stretch.

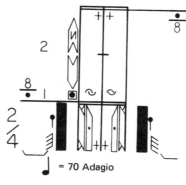

Tip forward—then sit again

Tip pelvis back; release hips from floor

Starting Position: Sitting; legs on diagonal; weight on hands

♩ = 70 Adagio

122

124 Wide Leg Stretch with Body Bounces

Starting Position: As in Ex. 123. Bounces.

Action: Rotate the rib cage to the right. Fold the body *forward* over the R leg, arms relaxed, hands on either side of the R leg. Bounce eight times. On the "and" of count eight, quickly bring the body to center, rotate to the L and repeat bounces over the L leg. On "and" of count eight repeat the bounces, folding the body forward between the legs. Hands *on the floor can take some of the weight* if necessary.

Note 1: This is a dangerous stretch. Forced too early, it can result in a permanent injury to the inner leg muscles. Here, it is designed to reduce that possibility—first bounce to the R, then to the L, *then* center.

Note 2: Remember, as in all these stretches the action is in the pelvis—it rocks, carrying the upper body with it. Everything is a little bit loose—head hangs, arms hang, feet are relaxed. This exercise is not for style.

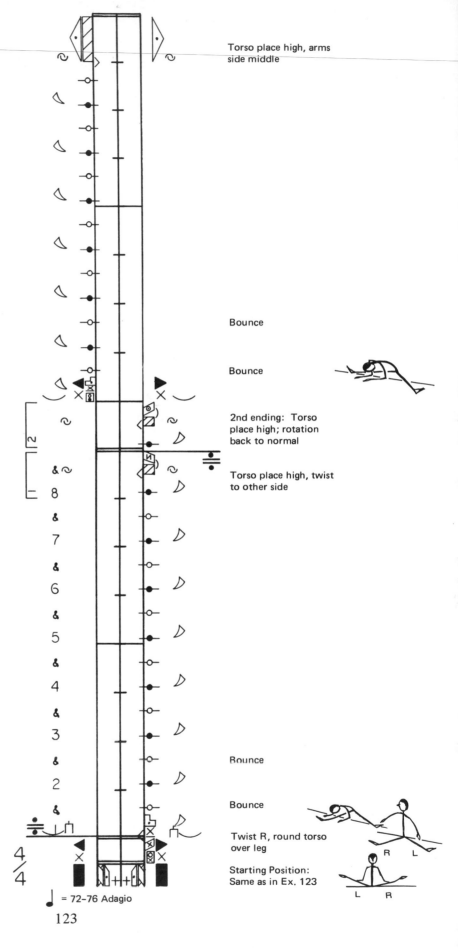

Torso place high, arms side middle

Bounce

Bounce

2nd ending: Torso place high; rotation back to normal

Torso place high, twist to other side

Bounce

Bounce

Twist R, round torso over leg

Starting Position: Same as in Ex. 123

♩ = 72–76 Adagio

123

125 Preparation for the Thigh Stretch

This stretch, or something similar, is common to all Modern Dance techniques. It is hard on the body and should be attempted only when the wide leg stretch of Ex. 124 is developed enough so the legs can roll freely in the hips when they are apart.

Starting Position: Sitting, facing the front R hand corner of the studio, body ▨ . The L leg is bent with the foot back of the knee; the R leg straight out from the hip on a forward diagonal, knee facing up, toes pointed. This is sometimes called "hurdle sitting." It is not necessary to sit on both "sit bones." If there is too much pressure on the bent knee, shift the weight slightly to the R.

Action: Bend forward over the extended leg as in Ex. 124, bounce eight times. Repeat with the body center, now going between the legs. Repeat bending over the L knee. On "and" of count four, bring the body center.

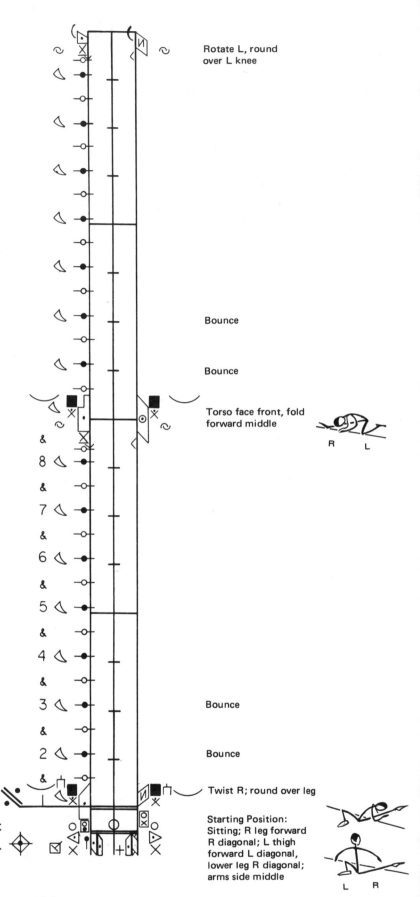

Rotate L, round over L knee

Bounce

Bounce

Torso face front, fold forward middle

Twist R; round over leg

Starting Position: Sitting; R leg forward R diagonal; L thigh forward L diagonal, lower leg R diagonal; arms side middle

Bounce

Bounce

126 Transition to the Other Side
(Beginners Transition)

Count 1: Straighten the L leg in front; (2) both legs come together in front, turn to face front; (3) shift weight to the L, bend the R knee, turn to face the front L hand corner of the studio; and (4) center the weight and prepare for the Repeat.

Ex. 125 & Ex. 126

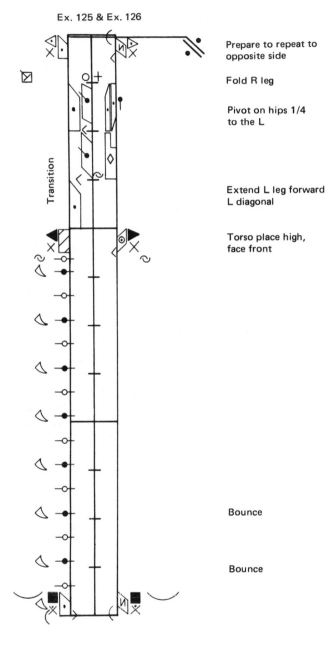

Prepare to repeat to opposite side

Fold R leg

Pivot on hips 1/4 to the L

Extend L leg forward L diagonal

Torso place high, face front

Bounce

Bounce

127 Thigh Stretch

Starting position same as Ex. 126, except for the arms. The L arm is side middle ◁ , palm down ∎ . The R arm is forward middle , with the elbow lifted, right toe pointed.

Action: Count 1: Fold the body forward center, the bent arm lifts slightly to clear the head; ("1 and") R arm cuts sharply to the side followed by the body; (2) R hand touches the floor carrying the weight of the body as it slides to a side position on the floor; and (3 and 4) roll onto the back bringing the L arm across the body to join the R.

For the recovery: Count 1: Roll over on to the R side, arms reach over the head, head drops back. The body is strongly arched; ("1 and") swing the L arm across the body to the L side, elbow slightly bent; (2) start pulling the body forward and up over the thigh (head back). The R arm follows, carrying some of the weight; (3) drop the body center and bring the R arm forward middle; (4) bring the arm to the starting position and lift the body to place high ▨ .

This movement is very expansive—generous in feeling and fun to do. The pull in the thigh is just as expansive and *not* fun for the strong-muscled types. If the knee cannot be kept on the floor during the roll onto the back, it is better not to roll over but to stay on the side for the fourth count. Sometimes, it is wise to prepare this by holding the position on the back for one measure before the return.

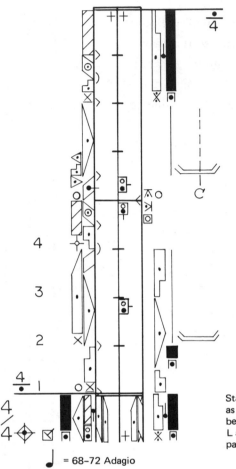

♩ = 68–72 Adagio

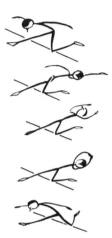

Starting Position: Sit as in Ex. 125, R arm bent forward middle; L arm side middle, palm down

R   L

128   Thigh Stretch with Hip Turn

This is really a variation of Ex. 127. It is much more formal and controlled with no swing or free-flow at all. Because it involves a hip rotation with a weight shift, it is prepared in detail in Ex. 129.

Starting Position: As Ex. 127. Arms are side middle, body center ▨ . Point the R foot strongly and tighten the R thigh to add a counterweight for the action.

Action: Shift the weight to the outside of the R thigh by rotating the hips to the R. This stretches the front of the L hip as the angle straightens and at the same time rotates the whole torso. The weight is balanced over the R hip socket.

Note: As the body turns, there is a strong side bend to the L to compensate for the thrust from the hips and to maintain balance. The abdominals pull in strongly; the shoulders press down; the face turns over the L shoulder, and the inside of the thighs (the adductors) almost squeeze together.

For the return, simply pull the L hip back and allow it to pull the upper body back to the starting position. This is not the relaxed position of Ex. 127. The tension in this exercise is very high; it is like sitting *off* the floor. This exercise involving a hip rotation and a weight shift is really a preparation for the full phrase of Ex. 129.

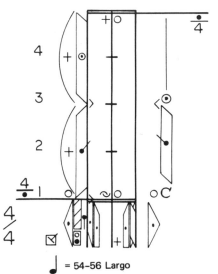

♩ = 54–56 Largo

Head turns L

L hip lifts off floor, rotates to R

Starting Position: As in Ex. 127, arms side middle

L   R

127

129 Hip Shift with Slide to Floor

Combines Ex. 127 and Ex. 128. Although this exercise has mechanical similarities to Ex. 127, there is a difference in its spatial and dynamic qualities. The free-flow has gone—along with the almost casual use of space. The energy is controlled and poured into a very formal, spatially restricted pattern.

Starting Position: As Ex. 128.

Action:

Measure 1 Counts 1 and 2: Repeat the hip shift; (3) turn the head over the R shoulder, R hand touches the floor taking weight; (4) whole torso slides onto the R side, both arms place high, hands touching the floor.

Measure 2 Counts 1 and 2: Roll onto the back as Ex. 127; (3) roll onto the R side; ("3 and") move L arm to L side going through side middle. Do not swing the arm across the body as Ex. 127. With a strong pull in the side start lifting the whole torso up to its starting position. There is no circling forward over the extended leg and a minimum of successional activity. The whole torso works in one piece; and (4) return to the starting position without relaxing the tension.

Note 1: The movement of the whole phrase is smooth and firm, like drawing a long line on paper but never releasing the pressure on the pencil.

Note 2: To give a feeling of flow to the phrase, it is helpful to count one measure of eight counts.

Note 3: It is exciting to do the movement in four counts for the whole action: (1) turn; (2) slide; (3) roll on back; ("3 and") roll onto R side; (4) start the lift; and ("4 and") return to starting position.

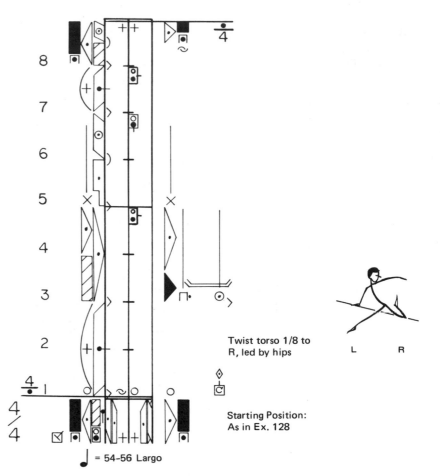

Twist torso 1/8 to R, led by hips

Starting Position: As in Ex. 128

♩ = 54-56 Largo

Performed this way, the slide becomes a fall, the recovery a whip.

Note 4: If a longer sequence is desired, an interesting combination is to do Ex. 129 twice; followed by the fast variation of Note 3 twice. Then change sides. Of course there is no law against doing one of everything either.

Note 5: This exercise could be very hard on the bent knee and the long sequence suggested in note 4 should not be attempted until the student is capable of carrying the weight in the abdominals and buttocks.

128

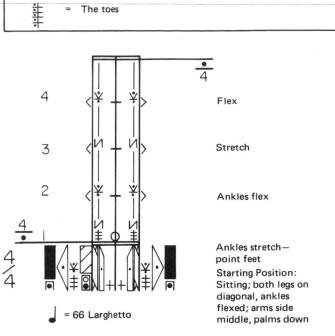

Legend

¥	=	Flexed ankle
	=	The toes

130 Ankle Stretch: Flexing and Pointing Feet

It is useful to explore the movement possibilities of the feet and ankles.

Starting Position: Sitting in the wide leg position as Ex. 123. Whole torso erect over the "sit-bones"; arms side, shoulders down; head on the plumb-line. Tighten the thighs, flex the ankles, and spread the toes. Do not take the heels off the floor. *Do not hyperextend the knees.* There is a feeling of pulling in towards the center.

Action: Simply point the feet and flex the ankle 16 times. There should always be a pressing away and pulling in on this action.

Flex

Stretch

Ankles flex

Ankles stretch—
point feet

Starting Position:
Sitting; both legs on
diagonal, ankles
flexed; arms side
middle, palms down

♩ = 66 Larghetto

131 Ankle and Toe Isolation

Sitting with the legs straight in front. The body can relax; hands on the floor back of the hips. Flex the ankle and spread the toes.

Count 1: Curl the toes over; do not move the ankle; (2) spread the toes again; do not move the ankle; (3) stretch the ankle but keep the toes spread; (4) point the toes; (5) flex the ankle but keep the toes curled; and (6) spread the toes.

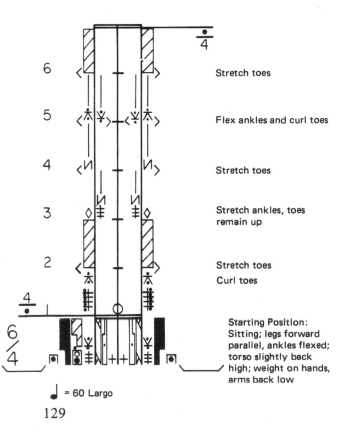

Stretch toes

Flex ankles and curl toes

Stretch toes

Stretch ankles, toes
remain up

Stretch toes

Curl toes

Starting Position:
Sitting; legs forward
parallel, ankles flexed;
torso slightly back
high; weight on hands,
arms back low

♩ = 60 Largo

129

132 Foot Circles Inward

Same body position as Ex. 131. Legs slightly separated, ankles flexed, toes spread.

Count 1: Turn the feet in until the toes touch; (2) point the feet; (3) turn the feet out; (4) return to the beginning.

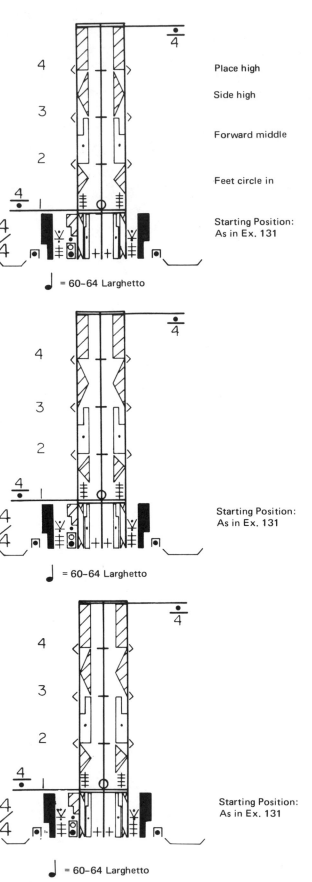

Place high

Side high

Forward middle

Feet circle in

Starting Position: As in Ex. 131

♩ = 60–64 Larghetto

133 Foot Circles Outward

Simply reverse the directions for Ex. 132 but start out instead of in.

Starting Position: As in Ex. 131

♩ = 60–64 Larghetto

134 Foot Circles Parallel

Same action, except the feet move in parallel action instead of opposition.

Parallel action is not native to the human body. The body works in opposition, this is why Ex. 134 feels funny. It feels really silly in waltz time. Try it. *The Blue Danube* provides an excellent tempo. Roll the feet four times in one direction stopping on count 1 of Measure 4. Then repeat to the opposite direction. Increase the tempo each time and improvise, stopping after two circles, then one circle, and so on. Enjoy. Enjoy.

Starting Position: As in Ex. 131

 = 60–64 Larghetto

130

135 Legs and Feet Flexing and Stretching

This is a very formal exercise for bending and straightening the legs while the body is held steady.

Starting Position: Whole torso ▯ place high, back very straight. Hands on the floor back of the hips, elbows turned back and bent, heels on the floor, ankles and knees flexed two degrees forward middle, legs parallel.

Action:

Measure 1 Keeping the back straight, straighten the legs and point the feet. Don't just flap the back of the knees into the floor, the feeling is of pressing the legs away from the center and a pulling back as the knees bend again. *Do not move the heels from their spot* ◊.

Count 1: Straighten legs; (2) bend knees; (3) straighten; (4) bend; (5) straighten; and (6) bend.

Measure 2 Alternate the bending and straightening: (1) straighten the R, hold the L; (2) bend the R, straighten the L; (3 and 4) repeat action of count 2; (5) hold the L leg straight while the R leg joins it; and (6) bend both legs, ready for the repeat.

Note: On Count 6, Measure 2, move the arms up to side middle. Hold them there for the repeat. For the third repeat, move the arms to place high. To finish, straighten both legs, point the feet and hold the position for six counts.

To release the tension, drop the body forward over the legs as in the hamstring stretch.

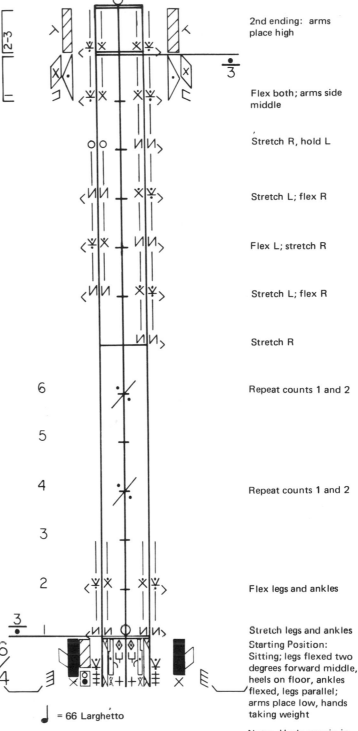

2nd ending: arms place high

Flex both; arms side middle

Stretch R, hold L

Stretch L; flex R

Flex L; stretch R

Stretch L; flex R

Stretch R

Repeat counts 1 and 2

Repeat counts 1 and 2

Flex legs and ankles

Stretch legs and ankles

Starting Position: Sitting; legs flexed two degrees forward middle, heels on floor, ankles flexed, legs parallel; arms place low, hands taking weight

Note: Heels remain in same spot throughout exercise; do not allow them to slide on floor

♩ = 66 Larghetto

131

136 Leg Stretch in Six Counts

This is by far the most demanding of the leg stretches, particularly the stretch to the back. It demands flexibility in the hips as well as strength in the back.

Starting Position: Sitting on the L hip, L leg bent in front; R leg bent to the side, sole of the foot on the floor, knee high and pulled in against the body. Body erect, hands on the floor back of the hips to keep the torso from settling back as the leg works.

Action: Count 1: With a slight pressure against the heel, slide the leg side straightening the knee and pointing the foot strongly; (2) keeping the pressure on the heel, pull the leg back to the starting position; (3) straighten the leg forward (leg will probably rest on the L foot); (4) full in again; (5) rotate the leg until the knee faces forward, the inside of the foot on the floor and with a strong thrust straighten the leg to the back. The R hand moves forward and is placed on the floor in front of the hips to prevent the body from falling forward as the leg moves back; and (6) pull the leg in again and move the hand back.

Repeat four times. On the last extension to the back, do not bring the leg in; hold the extension for count 6. (See fourth ending.) On the following measure move the R arm forward and up to ▧ place high on counts 1, 2, 3—the L hand still being used as support. On count 4 move the L arm to ◁ side middle keeping the back arched and the shoulders down. Hold for counts 5 and 6.

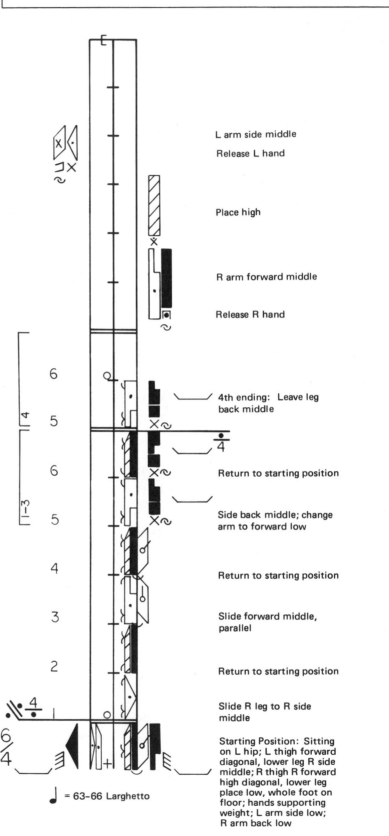

L arm side middle

Release L hand

Place high

R arm forward middle

Release R hand

4th ending: Leave leg back middle

Return to starting position

Side back middle; change arm to forward low

Return to starting position

Slide forward middle, parallel

Return to starting position

Slide R leg to R side middle

Starting Position: Sitting on L hip; L thigh forward diagonal, lower leg R side middle; R thigh R forward high diagonal, lower leg place low, whole foot on floor; hands supporting weight; L arm side low; R arm back low

♩ = 63-66 Larghetto

132

Note: During the stretch the body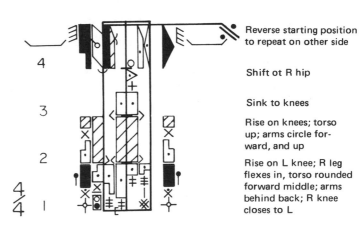
stays place high, the hips do not rotate. The working leg will probably move into a forward and back diagonal instead of side and back . The important thing is not to move the hips or the center of weight. The interesting thing about this exercise is the feeling of the leg moving side, forward, and back of the center of weight. With the center strongly established as it is, you are almost sitting on it. This is a revealing experience which can be referred to later on in the standing extensions.

137   Transition to the Other Side

Transition: Count 1: Shift the weight onto the left knee. Bring the R knee forward in line with the left.   Fold the body forward over the legs, head low, arms back. (Be sure to keep the hips low and feet pointed.) This stretches the back after the difficult contraction; (2) swing the body up, arms over the head, palms face in. The weight is now carried on both knees. (Be sure the hips move to center on this.); (3) shift the hips side and back to the R. Arms stay high; (4) move into the starting position for the L leg.

Reverse starting position
to repeat on other side

Shift ot R hip

Sink to knees

Rise on knees; torso
up; arms circle for-
ward, and up

Rise on L knee; R leg
flexes in, torso rounded
forward middle; arms
behind back; R knee
closes to L

arms and shoulders

The legs and back do brilliant and exciting things, but the expressive parts of the body are the shoulders, arms, hands, and head. The upper body declares the emotional intention of the dancer. If a dancer is to be anything more than a technician, he must learn to make his upper body speak with eloquence and style. This takes patience, sensitivity, and concentration and it demands an emotional refinement not required when training the legs and back.

In many ways it is more difficult to learn to use our hands and arms well than it is to learn to use the legs. This is because there is so much to unlearn. Most of our living is done with our hands; they are our real contact with the outside world and they must of necessity be used for the utilitarian purposes of everyday life. It sometimes seems that the legs serve only to transport our hands through all the grasping, holding, and carrying actions that are so important to our existence. During most of these actions, the arms are nearly always in front of us, with the body folded forward into a cramped position. This situation develops tension in the shoulders, neck, and pectoral muscles; a tension that is seldom relieved by any stretching or opening out of the body to the back. The rigid stoop of the elderly is partly the result of years of constant folding of the body into the forward direction without any compensating backward activity. Because our living is as close to us as our hands, it is not easy to change and use the hands, arms, or shoulders to make the silent eloquent dance gestures our culture so often denies us.

SHOULDERS

There have been several references to the shoulders in the preceding chapters but because the emphasis was on other areas, this action was not described. It is now time to state that as a general rule, unless otherwise indicated, *the shoulders must always be pressed down.* This is only slightly less important than good body alignment.

The reasons for this action are both technical and artistic and it is difficult to say which is the most important.

Artistically, pressing the shoulders down lengthens the neck. This separates the two most expressive areas of the body—the face and the upper part of the rib cage—allows for greater independence of each, and increases their expressive potential. This firmness in the shoulders allows the arms to be used with clarity and authority from their anatomical source in the shoulder girdle. But above all, this action creates the look of poise, assurance, and polish which is the mark of all good dancers.

Technically the action is of utmost importance. Pressure such as this must be made against resistance. (See definitions – Opposition). The extreme muscular tension described in Note 2, Ex. 54, Chapt. 2 would explode upward if there were no counter-tension to hold it down. Pressing the shoulders down puts a top on it. As the shoulders are pressed down there is a feeling of strings attached to the tip of the shoulder blades which run down the back and are tied to the sacrum. This pulls the shoulders down in the back allowing them to sit securely on top of the rib cage. There is a corresponding lifting up in the breast bone in front. This lift allows the abdominals to pull in under the rib cage and support it. All the great muscle groups around the waist, particularly the *latissimus dorsi,* tighten considerably and seem almost to lash the rib cage to the pelvis. This unites and stabilizes the whole torso, concentrates the energy in the middle body, and gives the firmness necessary for all disciplined dance movement.

From a practical point of view it is convenient to think that the motor muscles of the legs, situated in the lower part of the torso, and the motor muscles of the arms and shoulders, situated in the upper part of the torso meet at the waist. The meeting of the tensions here unite the whole body. Without the shoulder pressure this cannot occur.

If the shoulders are pressed down without resistance the rib cage cannot hold its position. The thrust from the legs in elevation, turns, or just walking, meeting no resistance in the middle body, causes the rib cage to shift in all directions. This destroys the plumb line, makes balance difficult, and gives the movement a blurred and fuzzy look. Obviously no clear statement can be made from this situation.

* * * * *

The simple exercises that follow do not involve big dramatic theatrical gestures. They should simply serve to introduce the student to the expressive part of his body and to suggest the enormous movement potential of the shoulder girdle, arms, and head. Most of the action is what is called *isolation,* which means moving a limited area of the body while the rest stays quiet. These exercises are simple to do and should be fun. They are often useful for relieving tension in the neck and shoulders.

Note: The hands are hardly mentioned. The reason is, it seems just one thing too much to ask of a beginner, and if the hand style is wrong, no harm—it can wait.

Note also that no word notes accompany the Labanotation in this and subsequent chapters of the book. Be sure to check starting positions carefully.

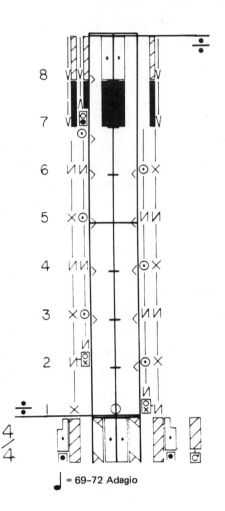
138   Rib Cage Isolation

This exercise is really a warm-up and logically should be in Chapter 1. However, because of its quality of isolation, it has been placed here.

Starting Position: Standing feet together; arms place high; face to the ceiling.

Action: There is a stretching or reaching up from the waist, first on one side, like trying to touch the ceiling—then on the other—for six counts. On counts 7 and 8 the tension is released, the body tumbles down and is immediately swung back up again to the starting position for the repeat. (See Ex. 19, Chapter 1)

Note: This exercise is like a yawn. It should feel good. Be sure to make the action start in the waist, *not* the shoulders.

♩ = 69–72 Adagio

136

SHOULDER ISOLATIONS

In all these exercises (Ex. 139 through 150), the feet are in turned-out first position; the arms hang relaxed at the sides; the rib cage and head stay steady. Notice the shoulder and head symbols.

139 Shoulder Lift and Drop

Simply pick up one shoulder and let it drop. Repeat eight times and then change sides.

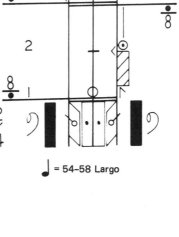

♩ = 54–58 Largo

140 Both Shoulders Lift and Drop

Same as Ex. 139, except that both shoulders move at the same time.

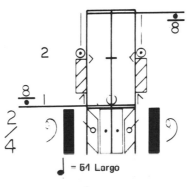

♩ = 54 Largo

137

141 Both Shoulders Lift and Drop
in Opposition: "The Paddle Wheel"

One shoulder lifts as the other drops. Here the drop becomes more of a pressing down. There is a conscious effort to create the alternation.

Note: Ex. 139 through Ex. 141: Be sure to make the directions clear. On the lift the shoulders must lift up, go to place high ▨ . A common error is to bring them forward high ▨ . The relaxed weight of the arms offers a resistance on the lift and adds to the stretch on the drop, forcing the shoulder muscles to work on the stretch rather than on the contraction.

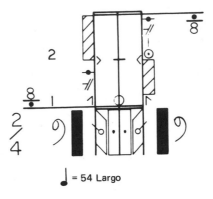

♩ = 54 Largo

142 One Shoulder Forward and Back

Move the shoulder forward as far as possible, return to center, and then move it back as far as possible and return to center. Repeat on the other side.

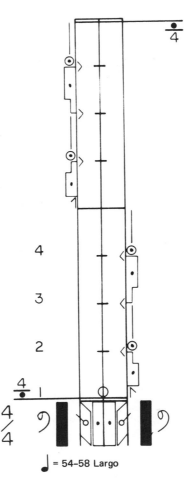

♩ = 54–58 Largo

138

143 Both Shoulders Forward and Back

Same as Ex. 142, except that both shoulders move at the same time.

Note: There is a strong stretch across the front of the chest (the pectorals) as the shoulders move back. The stretch will be felt across the shoulder blades as the shoulders move forward.

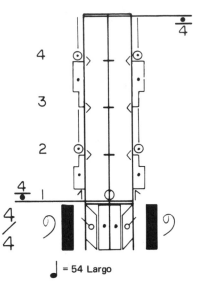

♩ = 54 Largo

144 Both Shoulders Forward and Back in Opposition

Same as Ex. 142, except that one shoulder moves forward as the other moves back, and vice versa.

Note on Ex. 142 through Ex. 144: It is almost impossible to move the shoulder forward and back without also rotating the arms somewhat. As the shoulders move backwards, the arms usually rotate until the palms face outward. As the shoulders move forward, the arms rotate again until the palms face back. This action should not be forced or emphasized. Let the arms do what they will. The important thing is to move the shoulders and let the arms follow, not the other way around.

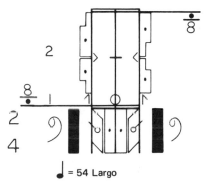

♩ = 54 Largo

139

145   Shoulder Circle Forward

This exercise combines Ex. 139 and Ex. 142.

Move the shoulder forward, lift, move it back, and drop to normal.

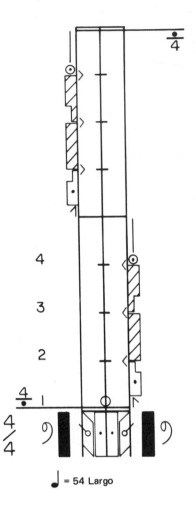

♩ = 54 Largo

146   Both Shoulders Circle Forward

Same as Ex. 145, except that both shoulders move at the same time. The shoulders just roll around on top of the rib cage.

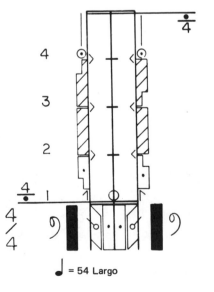

♩ = 54 Largo

147 Both Shoulders Circle Forward in Opposition

Same as Ex. 145, except that one shoulder starts the action forward.

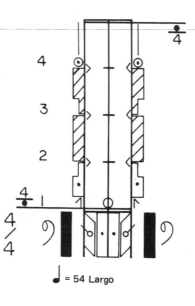

♩ = 54 Largo

148 Shoulder Circle Back

Inversion of Ex. 145. Move back first and then continue circle.

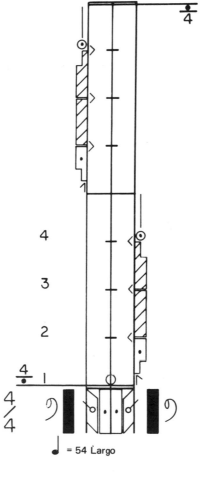

♩ = 54 Largo

141

149 Both Shoulders Circle Back

Same as Ex. 148, except that both shoulders circle back at the same time.

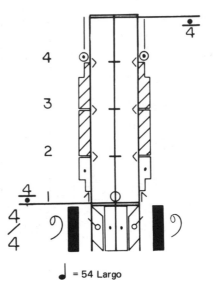

150 Both Shoulders Circle Back in Opposition

Inversion of Ex. 147.

Note on Ex. 145 through Ex. 150: These exercises have been notated in 4/4 time so that each direction is clear. Perform them as written, slowly at first, then increase the tempo, and change the meter to 3/4 to achieve a smooth continuous circle.

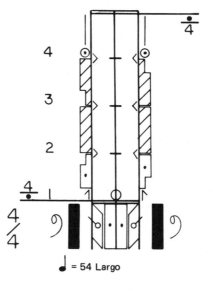

151 Head Tip Forward and Back

Same starting position as Ex. 139. Simply drop the head forward and lift it back until the face is to the ceiling. The forward drop stretches the back of the neck. The backward lift stretches the front of the neck. Notice the backward position is high which means the back of the neck is still supporting the weight of the head. The forward action is relaxed.

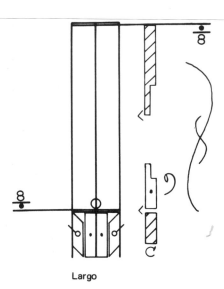

Largo

152 Head Tilt Side

With the face holding front simply tilt the head over to the side as far as possible and return to center. Repeat to the other side.

Note 1: Don't *turn* the head or allow it to drop forward. Of course as in all movement the starting position must be clear. The starting position for the head is place high. Most people carry their heads forward high. From that position a clear side movement is impossible. Half the battle in dance training is to attain the anatomically correct starting position.

Note 2: Keep shoulders steady. Do not let them lift.

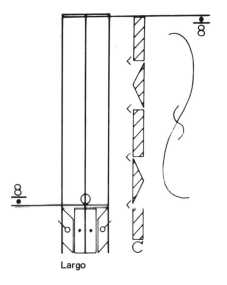

Largo

143

153 Head Circles

Similar to the shoulder circles. The head just rolls around on top of the shoulders.

Note 1: Naturally if something is going to roll there should be a firm, level surface on which to do it, otherwise gravity will have its way with a resulting loss of balance (if not of the head itself).

Note 2: Prepare the head circles as the shoulder circles (See Note on Ex. 145 through Ex. 150). Do only four circles in each direction and then change direction.

Note 3: (Nausea) See Note, Ex. 21, Chapt. 1. Our poor necks are most of the time in a state of static contraction, doomed as they are to carrying the great weight of the head usually with little or no assistance from the rest of the body. These head rotations help to release some of that tension, but the muscular moans, groans, and cries of protest that result from this kind of stretching have to be heard by the participant to be believed.

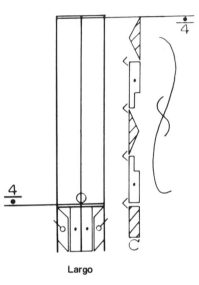

Largo

154 Head Rotations

This does not involve bending of the neck. This is just about all the head can do by itself. Every other movement of the head involves tension of the neck.

Simply turn the face to look over one shoulder and then the other. Do not lower or lift the chin. There is no change of level. Expect a tremendous stretch on the opposite side from the turn.

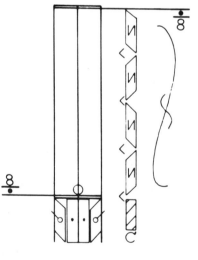

Largo

144

155 Arm Rotations

Section A. Keeping the shoulders steady, simply rotate the arm outward until the palms face out. Rotate inward, as far as possible until the palms face nearly out again. Note that the palms face in to start. Remember the shoulder is a ball-and-socket joint. It is amazing what it can do.

Section B. Repeat the rotation at shoulder level.

Section C. Repeat the rotation with the arms side high.

Section D. Repeat the rotation with the arms forward middle.

Note: These rotations pull mightily on the upper arm muscles and because of the isolation are remarkably tiring. Shake the arms a bit after performing the whole sequence.

The transition from one position to the next has four slow counts.

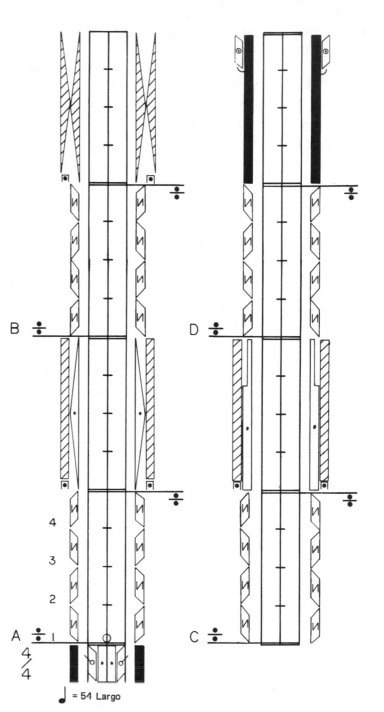

♩ = 54 Largo

156 Arm Rotations in Opposition with Side Tilt

Very similar to Ex. 155, Section B. Here one arm is rotated so the palm faces up, the other arm the palm faces down. Simply change the position of the arms.

Measure 1 An arm isolation.

Measure 2 Add a side tilt of the rib cage.

Note: The arms are slightly bent—well supported by the rib cage. There is a feeling of pressing up with one arm and down with the other, as if holding a weight. Remember, if the arm is to rotate, the upper arm does the work, not the hand. As with the legs, the rotations are from the source: in the legs the source is the hip socket; in the arm the source is the shoulder socket.

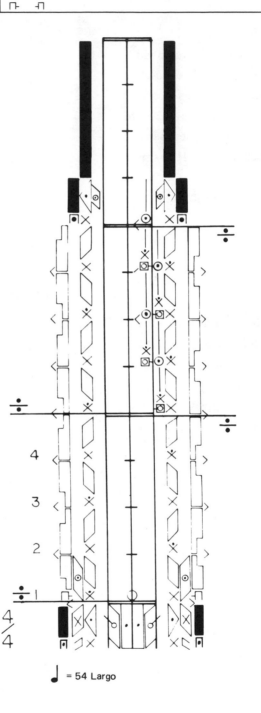

♩ = 54 Largo

146

157 Arm Rotation with Up and Down Body Swings

Here is Ex. 156 combined with Ex. 19, Chapter 1.

Starting Position: Whole torso folded forward; arms high over the back, knees bent.

Action:

Measure 1 Count 1: Swing the whole torso and arms forward and up until the body is strongly lifted and arched; (2) open the arms side, right palm up, left palm faces down. Rib cage shifts to the right as Ex. 4, Chapter 1; (3) shift left as Ex. 4, changing palm facings; (4) repeat up-reach as in count 1, palms face front; (5) swing down.

Repeat four times alternating the side tilt.

Measure 2 There are changes on counts 2, 3, and 4: (2) as the arms open, fall away with the right leg to the right; (3) shift the weight to the left bending the left knee, repeating the body action; (4) pull the right leg in to the left and straighten both legs for the body arch; and (5) is the same.

Same type of repeat, alternating direction of the fall away.

Measure 3 For the finish. Count 1 & 2: Swing up once more; (3 and 4) Center the body and face; open the arms side middle, palms up. Lower the arms to the sides, palms down.

Note: The arm and body action of Ex. 156 is used for the 3/4 Phrases in Chapter 4.

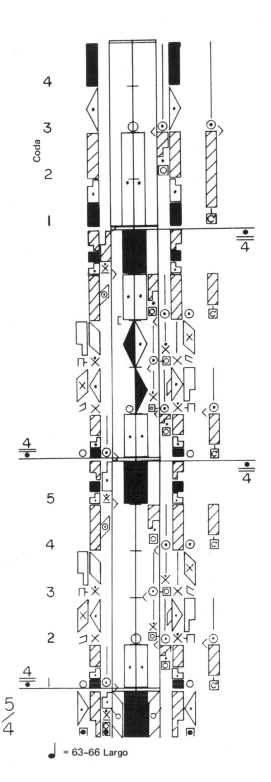

♩ = 63–66 Largo

ARM CIRCLES

In this series the whole arm describes a circle in space, like a compass, unlike the arm rotations, which simply turn the arm in the shoulder joint.

158   Arm Circle Front: One Arm

Starting Position: Standing in first with the body held as firmly as possible, the right arm is side middle, palm facing down.

Action: Count 1 and 2:   whole arm moves to place low; (3 and 4) elbow bends and starts the lift as the lower arm is brought across the body on a forward diagonal to middle level; (5 and 6) with the elbow still leading up the arm is brought to place high; and (7 and 8) lower the arm to side middle, palm up. On the "and" of count 8, rotate the arm until the palm faces down to start the Repeat.

Repeat four times and then change to the other side.

159   Arm Circle Front: Both Arms

Repeat Ex. 158 using both arms.

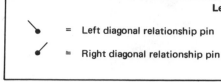

Legend

↘• = Left diagonal relationship pin

↗• = Right diagonal relationship pin

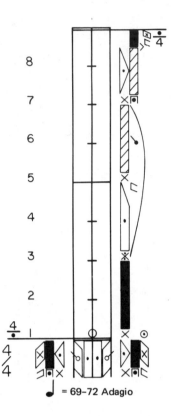

♩ = 69–72 Adagio

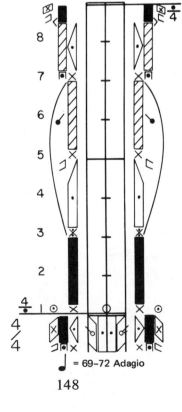

♩ = 69–72 Adagio

160 Forward Walk on the Diagonal: Both Arms Circle

This is a variation of Ex. 159. Keep the arms circling during the forward walk on the diagonal. It takes eight steps for the arms to make the full circle.

    Note: This is a very frustrating exercise. The difficulty is in the dynamic contrasts within the body. The smooth quality of the arm movement against the staccato quality of the weight change. It is like rubbing your head and patting your tummy. (See Chapter 4 for Movement Through Space.)

161 Forward Walk on the Diagonal: Alternating Arm Circles

Just like Ex. 160, but for a variation, circle one arm in four counts, then change to the other arm. There are a total of eight steps for the two complete arm circles.

    Note: There is one slight change. The arm that is not making the circle stays in a side middle position ◁ or ▷; palm ▉ facing down. It is surprising how much concentration is needed to keep the arm in that relationship to the body on the walk. Holding a position is one of the things a dancer has to learn to do well. The beginner tends to forget the non-working part of the body. In this case the forgotten arm loses energy, starts to trail behind and seems to almost drop out of sight. Holding the arm firmly in the shoulder helps keep it alive but this is not entirely a physical problem. The dancer must develop an awareness of the design his body is making in space. To this awareness must be added the will to do it, which in turn creates the energy to fulfill it.

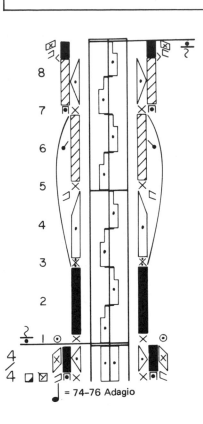

♩ = 74–76 Adagio

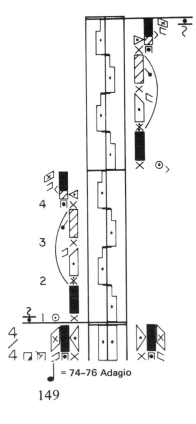

♩ = 74–76 Adagio

149

162 Side Walk on the Diagonal: Both Arms Circle

The arms are exactly as in Ex. 160. The walk is to the side. (See Ex. 178, Chapter 4, for details of side walk.) If Ex. 160 was frustrating, this is impossible. In moving the arms, it helps to think of the circle they make as though cutting a pie in quarters. It takes two counts to go down; two counts to go forward middle; two counts to go place high; two counts to return to side middle. Now repeat it and take the "jerk" out of it.

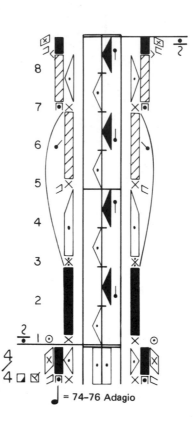

♩ = 74–76 Adagio

163 Side Walk on the Diagonal: Alternating Arm Circles

Just like Ex. 161, except the walk is side. Start stepping left, circle the right arm for four counts (steps)—the head is turned over the left shoulder.

As the left arm starts, turn the head over the right shoulder.

Note: All these walking sequences should be repeated on the opposite diagonal with the other side of the body.

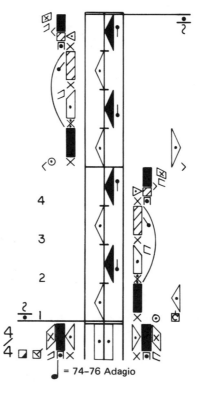

♩ = 74–76 Adagio

150

164   Phrase in Pavane Style

Here is a simple phrase, combining a forward walk and side walk, emphasizing the arm action.

Starting position: Arms side middle, palms face down, feet in first position.

Action:

Measure 1 Walk forward four steps circling the left arm. Make a 1/4 turn to the right.

Measure 2 Count 1: Step side with the left. Arms side middle; (2) Cross in front with the right leg in plié. Move the right arm, bent across the body, palm down. Keep the ball of the left foot on the floor; (3) Step back on the left, straightening the leg. Swing the right leg and arm side right; (4) Plié on the left, place the ball of the right foot on the floor back of the left. Hold the arms.

Measure 3 Counts 1 and 2: Make a 3/4 pivot turn to the right in relevé. Arms place high; (3) Move the right foot slightly downstage and complete the full turn with the hips. The body leans strongly to the left; (4) Hold. There should be a long straight line from the arms to the back heel (left, in this instance); ("4 and") Return to center and prepare for the repeat.

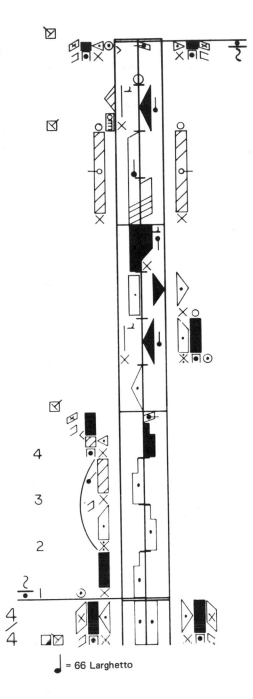

♩ = 66 Larghetto

151

165   Short Version of Pavane Phrase

Simple reduction of steps:

Take two steps forward (counts 1 and 2). The side action is unchanged (counts 3, 4, 5, and 6). The pivot turn and lean take two counts only (7 and 8). On "8 and" swing into the repeat.

Note: The style is heavy and severe. The body is held firmly erect to support the very controlled weight of the arms. Each movement should be made with great authority; yet, it is neither harsh nor pompous.

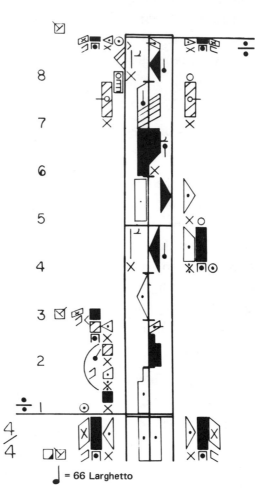

♩ = 66 Larghetto

The normal action of the body is successional. It is only with difficulty that this action is prevented, as has been demonstrated in Chapters 1 and 2. The arms are no exception. If we want to move the hand, we must move the whole arm. The same is true of the foot. The foot cannot be moved very far unless we first move the thigh. The obvious example of this is the simple successional action of the legs during the walk. If the dancer is to use his arms expressively he must understand and learn to control the similar successional action of his non-weight bearing limbs.

Upward Succession

Feet in first position, turned out, arms at the sides low, keeping the shoulder quiet. Start lifting the right elbow sideward, allowing the lower arm and hand to hang down under it. Keep moving the elbow upward as far as it will go. Then start the backward rotation of the arm as the lower arm moves forward and up followed by the wrist and hand. The whole arm ends place high ▯ , palm facing out.

Downward Succession

To start the downward succession rotate the arm in the shoulder until the palm faces in. Pulling down from the shoulder, lower the elbow, allowing the lower arm and hand to trail the action. Bring the upper arm against the side of the body, hand to the shoulder; the arm is completely folded up now. Continue the downward succession by straightening the elbow, followed by the wrist and hand to end place low ▮ . Rotate the arm again in the shoulder and start the repeat.

Repeat both successions to the other side.

Note 1: The feeling is of lifting and lowering a weight of at least five pounds. In other words, the arm moves with resistance but not so great that it cannot be easily over-come. The resistance of water as in swimming is a good guide. Moving with resistance forces the deep muscles of the torso that control the action of the arm to work strongly. Just as the legs are controlled by the great muscles of the pelvic area, the arms are controlled by the deep muscles of the upper body.

Note 2: Because of the over emphasis on push-ups in men's physical training, many men are unable to lift their arms above middle level without displacing the entire shoulder girdle upward. They have so drastically reduced their movement range that their strength is only good for very limited tasks. The effort to re-stretch such tight shoulder muscles is discouraging and only a little less painful than stretching the hamstrings. We must remember the adage, "stretch is part of your strength." In all dance training, one of the goals is to make the deep, strong muscles of the torso do as much of the work as possible and at the same time increase the range and flexibility of the extremities. Strength in the extremities unsupported by stretch and control in the middle body is of very limited value.

Note 3: This action is almost impossible to do with both arms. Try it, you'll see.

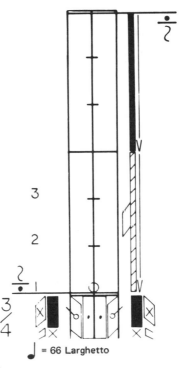

♩ = 66 Larghetto

167 Arm Succession with Body Tilt

The upward succession of the arm in this exercise is similar to Ex. 166, except that the elbow does not bend quite as much. The same is true of the downward succession. Notice that the rib cage has been added to the action. As the arm rises, it carries the rib cage with it until it is tipped to the left. The head goes with it. As the arm starts down, there is a little lift before the downward pull starts.

Repeat to the other side.

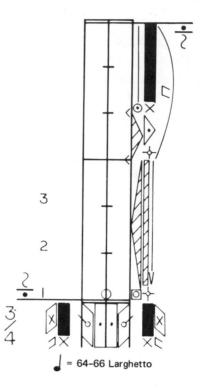

♩ = 64–66 Larghetto

168 Arm Succession with Body Tilt and Plié

Arm and body action as Ex. 167 on the lift. As the arm lowers, the downward pull is increased forcing the rib cage to tip into it and the knees to bend. Do not displace the center of weight too much.

Note: As the pressure increases on the down pull, there is a counter resistance in the legs—they are forced to bend, they do not just fold up. The same is true of the body action—there is a resistance to the up pull as well as to the down pull. This is "bound flow."

Repeat to the other side.

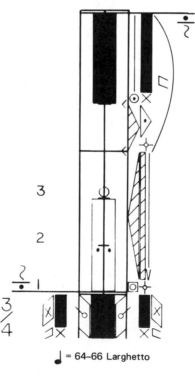

♩ = 64–66 Larghetto

169 Arm Succession with Weight Shift

Like Ex. 168, except that the up action is so strong it pulls the weight with it. The leg moves side to support the shifting pelvis. The whole body is bent strongly to the left. The stretch is on the right. The lift before the return, mentioned in Ex. 167, is emphasized— the body moves through center, place high 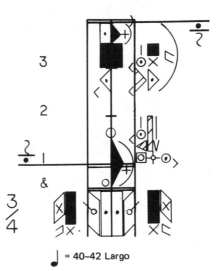, before bending to the right and pressing down into the plié.

Note 1: The left arm is held away from the body, elbow turned out, it has picked up some of the increased tension of the broader movement.

Note 2: The action starts on the upbeat. The tempo picks up a bit adding a sense of excitement to the movement.

Note 3: Exercises 167 to 169 can be performed without a break alternating sides. In this case the action to the left will start from the *right side bend, not from center*. It is fun to do this and pick up the tempo. Don't eliminate the pressure just because it is going fast. It will be lessened but it should not disappear.

Note 4: The succession to each side, alternating, makes real technical demands and gives a feeling of flight.

♩ = 40–42 Largo

155

170 Forward and Side Arm Circles:
One Arm

This exercise has some similarities to Ex. 158; the arm describes a circle in space, but now it does not cross the body. It moves forward of the shoulder to place high, rotates over the head and opens out to the side. The action is successional but is not a complete succession.

Action: Starting from place low, the arm rotates, palm facing out. Lead by the elbow, the arm moves through forward middle to the starting position. There are four counts for the whole action.

Note: Don't forget the resistance. It is like pulling the hand with a weight in it. The position is quite angular, not curved, very much like the use of the arm in Spanish dance. It is not "graceful" but it has tremendous vitality.

Repeat to the left.

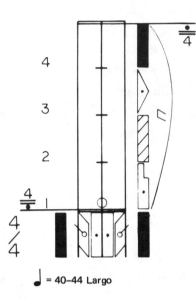

♩ = 40–44 Largo

171 Forward and Side Arm Circles:
Both Arms

Repeat Ex. 170 using both arms at the same time. Remember, keep the rib cage as steady as possible.

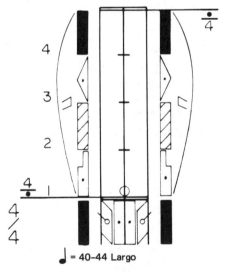

♩ = 40–44 Largo

		Legend
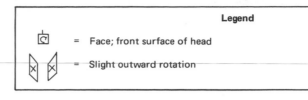	=	Face; front surface of head
	=	Slight outward rotation

172 Arm Circles with Body Action Forward

Action: Counts 1 and 2: As the arms start forward, fold the upper body forward. The arms reach beyond it and seem to be lifted into place high as the rib cage lifts to center; (3) The arms are brought quickly and firmly down to middle level; the body arches back, face to the ceiling, knees bent; (4) Hold the body position as the arms come down to place low preparing for the repeat.

Note: On the back arch, keep the pelvis center.

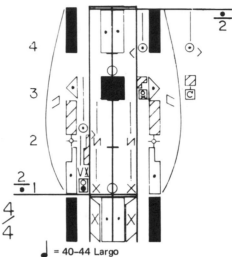

♩ = 40–44 Largo

173 Arm Circles with Body Action and Weight Shift Forward and Back

As in Ex. 168, the legs have been added to the basic arm action. Exercise 168 carried the weight to the side, here it is carried forward and back following the arm action.

Action: Step forward low with the left as the arms and body move forward. The whole body lifts as the weight is transferred back onto a straight right leg. On the back arch, both knees bend—the right turned out slightly, the left parallel, weight on the ball of the foot.

The timing is the same as Ex. 172. Come out of the plié for the repeat.

Note 1: To change sides note second ending after repeating four times.

Note 2: *Please* remember the resistance, otherwise it will look like flag waving.

♩ = 40–44 Largo

157

174   Arm Study with Body Action

Although this exercise uses the material of Ex. 171, it is shaped into a small study. This is extremely difficult to do and read.

Section A   Start with double arm succession as in Exercise 171. Repeat four times.

Section B   The forward arm succession is the same (counts 1 and 2). On count 3 the arms are brought quickly down to side middle but now the rib cage rotates as far as possible to the *right* and tilts side. The face stays front. On count 4 the body folds forward as the arms swing back, elbows bent, and *plié* in first position as in Ex. 168.

Note: *Count 4 is the beginning of the repeat to the other side.* The rib cage will rotate to the *left*.

Repeat four times.

Section C   Identical body action, with the addition of the weight shift of Ex. 169. This time the rotation slightly anticipates the weight shift (count "2 and"). Move the leg side on count 3. The resolution of the tensions is the same; on count 4 fold the body forward, arms back, pull the working leg in to first position. Repeat this section five times. On the fifth repeat, end on count 3 with the body twist to the right and hold count 4, for the coda.

Section D   The Coda: On count "4 and," pull the elbows into the hips. Straighten the right leg; shift the weight to the left bending the left leg and rotate the body to the left. The face stays front. On count 1, press the arms upward to side middle, elbows curved as if carrying a weight.

Note 1:   Repeat to the other side. Keep alternating, eight times.

Note 2:   For the finish: Count 1: Fold the body forward, arms back, feet together; (2) swing the body and arms forward and up as in Ex. 173; (3) open arms side middle, palms up; (4) arms move to place low.

Note 3:   From space reference the arms open downstage and upstage. From the body reference they open side middle. Because of the downstage bend of the body, both arms should be completely visible from the front.

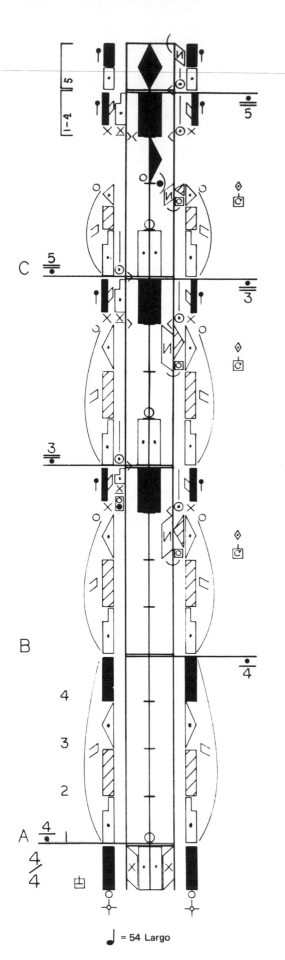

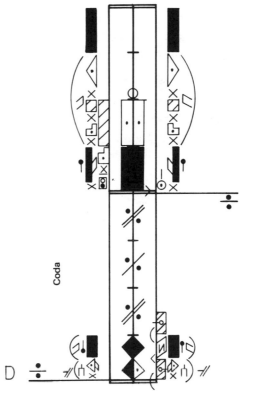

Legend

 = Led by the weight

 = Rotation bowed to the rib cage indicates simultaneous rotation and tilt for the rib cage

= Fingertips (may also mean tips of the toes when used in the leg gesture column)

♩ = 54 Largo

Coda

159

175 Arm Transition for Hops and Leaps

For most simple hops and leaps a functional relationship of arms and legs is the best for beginners. It seems wise at first to learn to use the body in its natural way before adding too much stylization.

Action: Starting from the normal place low position of the arms, swing the right arm forward middle as the left arm moves side middle. Drop to place again and reverse. The right palm faces ◁ the left palm faces ♭ . There is no rotation of the arms or hands. Notice that the arms change through place low ■ .

Note: Keep the rib cage and shoulders steady. This arm action is usually in *opposition* to the leg action. The *right arm* moves *forward* as the *left leg* moves forward.

For a more complete discussion of oppositional action, see Introduction, Chapter 1.

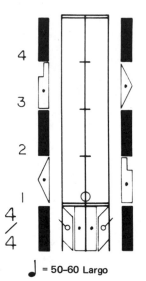

♩ = 50–60 Largo

160

chapter 4
movement through space

All the detailed concentrated work of the basic training exercises of the first three chapters is really to prepare the body for moving securely and eloquently through space. In other words, to dance. It is in movement through space that dance is most exciting; it is also the real test of the dancer.

We human beings are accustomed to thinking of ourselves as moving freely about the earth, whereas in actuality, we rarely move freely at all. We have consciously and unconsciously limited our body activity in space and in time to routine, practical tasks. In our Judeo-Christian culture, the body is conceived of as a useful tool, something to be endured, to do God's will—and God's will does not mean dancing. All the ecstasy of movement of which the body is capable and which finds its most exuberant expression in the dance has not been made part of our cultural or educational experience.

Because of this attitude toward the body, the practical discipline of the training exercises is in many ways easier than its application in movement through space. The beginner student often finds that movement without a concrete specific motivation is embarrassing to the point of being funny. He is surprised by his inability to move well and suddenly is faced with the fact that he was not being taught how to run a machine but to dance. That is the shocker!

To dance means to give in to and enjoy the controlled but precise action of the body as it plunges, leaps, and falls through space, playing games with gravity. None of this is any good unless the heart is behind it and the mind can guide it. This kind of "giving in" to the movement experience demands a commitment of the total personality. The student subconsciously knows this the moment he moves away from his spot on the floor where he did all his leg stretches. Many people find this kind of involvement almost impossible. The moment they start to move, they become self-conscious and shy. Every effort must be made by the teacher to make the student feel as completely comfortable as possible in his first free movement through space.

Note: This is not true of very young children—they are the free ones—but once in school, the cultural pressures start; it is amazing how fast the inhibitions accumulate, particularly among the boys.

Note: All these exercises should be repeated from the opposite diagonal starting with the other foot.

161

WALKS: TRANSFER OF WEIGHT—FALL AND RECOVERY

The minute we start moving away from our home base where our feet are, we have to decide how to do it. This is the least of our worries as we tumble about doing our everyday jobs, but in actuality we are performing a rather complicated maneuver. If for some reason, we want to move away from our secure spot, we simply initiate a fall, shift the weight into the desired direction, and then, in order not to crash into the floor, we move a leg to catch the weight and recover from the fall. This fall-and-recovery action goes on all the time with every step we take. After centuries of this experience, we have become fairly proficient at what is called "locomotor" movement; and an accidental, or true fall, usually receives whatever medical attention it deserves. However, there are many members of the human race who still feel very insecure about our hereditary method of moving about and find it very difficult to walk at a speed or with a length of step other than the one they have used all their lives. They feel better if they have both feet on the floor.

A dancer on the other hand, spends a great part of his dancing life standing on one leg, so one of the most important things for him to know is which leg he is on, how he got there, and how long he intends to stay.

The simplest way to move from one foot to another is by taking a step.

A step in dance terms is a complete transfer of weight from one foot to the other. If this is done very slowly, balance becomes a problem and an analysis of how to do it is in order.

Most choreographers want a walk that conforms to their stylistic concepts. The walk used in the following exercises is a very natural, unstylized way of transferring the weight from one foot to the other in all three directions: forward, side, and back.

176 Forward Walk Detail

Starting Position: Feet together, parallel, in first position. Before there is any leg action, the center of weight ● must shift slightly forward to start the fall. With a successional action starting from the hip, one leg is swung forward, knee bending, followed by the lower leg and foot. The toe touches the floor first, followed by the heel.

As the weight is transferred to that foot, the knee bends slightly. The other foot completes the weight transfer with a slight push forward from the big toe. The weight should now be supported entirely on the lead foot. The back leg is slightly back and the knee bent a little in preparation for the swing forward to make the next step.

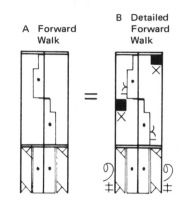

A Forward Walk   B Detailed Forward Walk

177 Back Walk Detail

Very similar to the forward walk except that the body must lean forward slightly to free the leg for the backward swing. The back walk starts with one leg reaching back from the thigh (again the succession from the hip, thigh, lower leg, foot, toe, heel) then a strong push-off from the other foot to shift the weight and a bending of that knee as the weight is transferred to that foot.

Note: In both the forward and back walk, the legs must swing under the center of weight as in the leg swings (see Ex. 63, Chapter 2). A common error is to swing all or part of the leg out to the side.

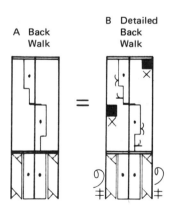

A Back Walk   B Detailed Back Walk

163

178　Side Walk Detail

In our everyday activity, we rarely walk sidewards, and if we do, we usually rotate the hips to make the crossing step. This gives the impression of a forward walk with a twist in the upper body.

Dancers, however, must make the side action as clear as possible in order to have technical variety and potential choreographic contrast. To make the side walk clearly side, the whole torso ▣ must stay facing forward. With the legs turned out from the hips, it is then possible to move sidewards with a minimum of rotation of the torso.

Starting Position: Turned-out first position.

Make a small *plié* on two feet, shift the weight to the R. Step side with the L, onto a straight leg turned out. Push off with the R, as in Ex. 89, Chapter 2. The R leg rotates until the *knee faces front*. Start a plié on the L as the R starts to turn out and cross in front of it. The whole foot slides on the floor, led by the heel. The weight should now be carried by the R, the L foot released in back. Repeat the pattern but make the crossing step in back of the L foot.

Note 1: It helps to think of leading with the toe of the stepping foot and the heel of the crossing foot.

Note 2: The side walk alternates an open and crossing step.

Note 3: Most people think the dance walk is pretentious, affected and "arty." From the point of view of everyday movement, it is true some dance styles overdo the stylization. Actually, the dance walk is functional, and very economical in its use of space and energy.

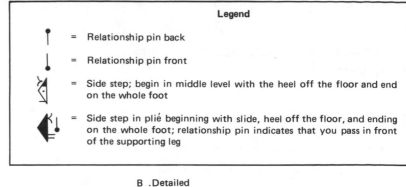

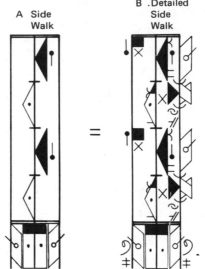

A Side Walk

B .Detailed Side Walk

WALKS IN THREE DIRECTIONS: SPACE WORK

The following exercises using the three main directions of the body are simple inventions to teach the student how to move easily and comfortably through space.

179   Forward and Back Walk

Standing in the center of the studio, feet parallel, starting with the R foot, walk forward five steps, close the feet together on count 6, and bend the knees slightly. Starting with the L foot, walk back five steps, and close the feet together. Repeat several times. The arms swing easily as in a normal walk. This is just to get the student accustomed to walking with the toes touching the floor before the heels.

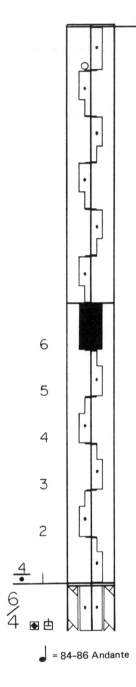

♩ = 84–86 Andante

180 Forward and Back Walk with Circle

There are six steps forward, six steps in a circle to the R, six steps back to place. Repeat to the other side.

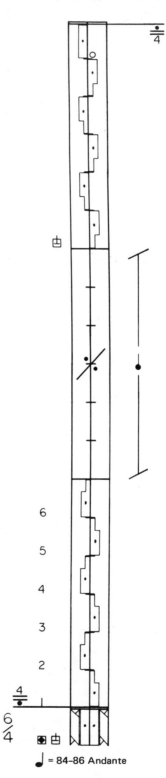

♩ = 84–86 Andante

166

181 Forward and Back with Figure Eight

In order to keep the walk going so the student has a chance to learn how to walk smoothly and the teacher has a chance to watch each individual in the class, little space patterns are fun and interesting. In this exercise there are six steps forward, six steps in a circle to the R; six steps in a circle to the L, and six steps backward. All the steps in the first three measures are in the forward direction. Measure 4 is a back walk.

Note 1: Walking in a circle (curved path) is different from walking on a straight path. As the feet walk on the circumference of the circle, they alternately turn out and in to accommodate the curve. The body leans slightly into the center of the circle. On these circles with the center alternately to the R and to the L of the dancer, the shift of focus is very strong.

Note 2: It is fun just to walk the figure eight (8) to get used to the pull of the curve and get acquainted with the many adjustments the body must make as it moves along the curved path.

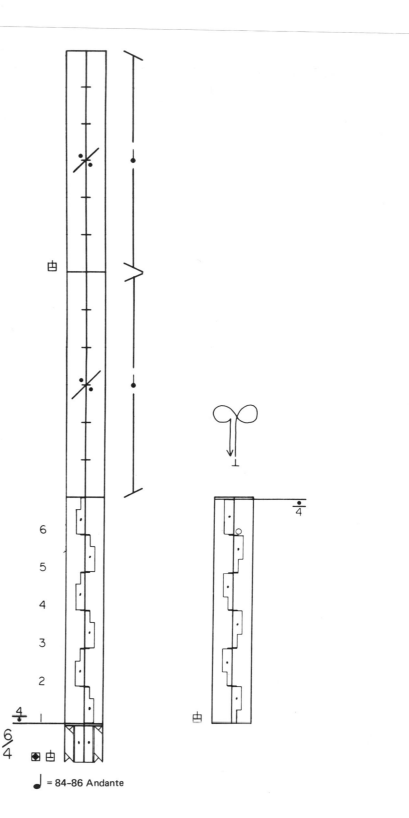

= 84–86 Andante

167

182 Side Walk

Starting Position: Standing in the center of the studio, turned-out first position.

Action: Walk side five steps, ending with the open step and hold for one count. Repeat to the other side. The arms stay side low, just off the body. From first position, make a slight *plié* and step side, R leg straight, pushing off with the L. Cross the L foot in front of the R, the whole foot sliding on the floor and *plié* on the L. Repeat the side step onto a straight leg and cross back. Step side again and hold for count 6. Repeat to the other side. (See Note 1, Ex. 178.)

Repeat this back and forth about four times and then increase the tempo.

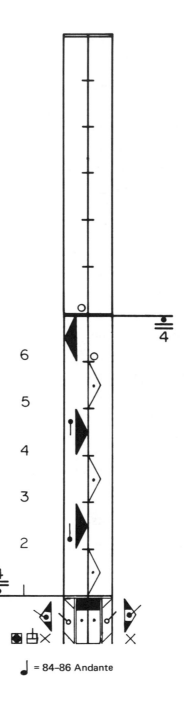

♩ = 84–86 Andante

183 Forward, Side, and Back Walk Combined

This is very similar to Ex. 199. Walk forward six steps bending the knees slightly on count six.

Walk side R as in Ex. 182.

Walk side L as in Ex. 182.

Walk back to place as in Ex. 179.

Note: The little plié on count 6 makes it easier to change direction.

All kinds of combinations are possible to keep the interest alive and the feet going until the students get the "feel" of this new way of moving.

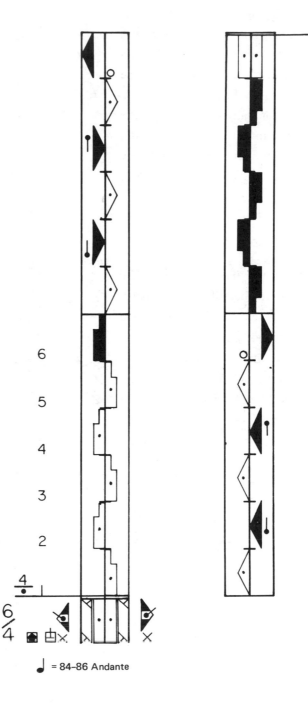

♩ = 84–86 Andante

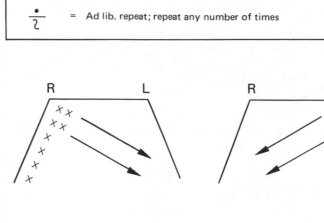

The simplest way to keep a class organized and working smoothly is the use of the diagonal. It really means the class is making a figure eight. With this procedure, the leaders are always free to lead and the rest of the class can fall in neatly behind them from their starting positions at the side of the studio. There is a minimum of congestion and jockeying for position, and all can see any demonstration clearly. It is useful to work in pairs.

184 Forward Walk

Technically this is just like Ex. 183. The difference is in the feeling of greater space. Walking on the diagonal gives the teacher a chance to check the body alignment of each student. The plumb-line is now carried forward with each step. Common errors are (1) leading with head; (2) leaning back with the rib cage; (3) locking the knee before transferring the weight.

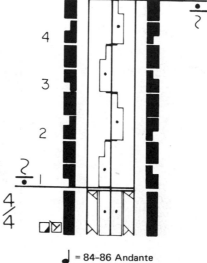

♩ = 84–86 Andante

185 Forward Walk in Relevé

This is just to give the student a feeling of walking on the half toe (progressive relevés). It is not the same as standing in one place. The emphasis is on body alignment.

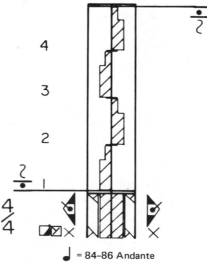

♩ = 84–86 Andante

Legend	
✳ =	Three dimensional flexion
✳ (with 3) =	Hand makes a fist

186   Forward Walk in Half Plié

Whole torso place high, legs parallel, take big strides forward. Arms are place low with the fists clenched, as if carrying a heavy weight.

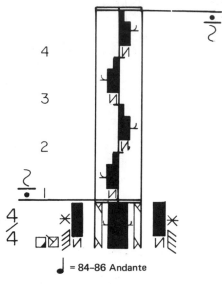

♩ = 84–86 Andante

187   Forward Walk: Half Plié and Relevé Combined in Four Counts

Combine the low walk with the high walk. Plié-relevé to give a feeling of the "spring" for future leaps and hops; four steps low; four steps high.

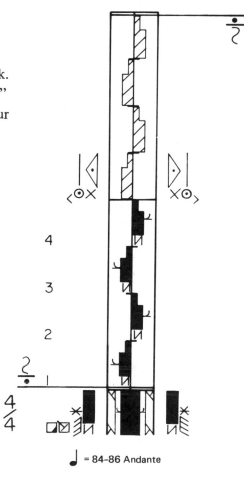

♩ = 84–86 Andante

171

188 Forward Walk: Half Plié
Relevé Combined in Two Counts

The reduction system of counting is a good way to increase the body tempo without making the students feel frantic: Two steps low, two steps high. There is a technical change: slide into the low steps, step into the high ones.

189 Forward Walk: Half Plié and
Relevé Combined in One Count

This is uncomfortable and awkward. There is no alternation of the plié or relevé—they are always on the same foot. Our normal foot pattern alternates the stress from one side to the other to avoid fatigue on one side. When this does not occur, we literally have a limp.

Note: A common error in the singles is dragging the leg that should be stepping to the high. The action here is uneven—the foot going low slides, the foot stepping high swings under the hips, knee leading. This is a technical change. The weight is then transferred directly to the ball of the foot, knee straight.

190 Forward Walk: Half Plié and
Relevé Combined in 3/4 Time

The comfortable resolution of the awkwardness of Ex. 189 is to make the stress alternate. By adding one extra high step, we have a 3/4 pattern (sometimes called a triplet). This is much easier to do than Ex. 189 because the heavy accent shifts from one side to the other. Even doubling the tempo from andante to presto doesn't present much of a problem. The students practically fly across the floor. This is a very exhilarating moment.

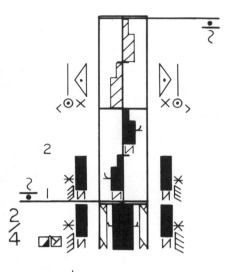

♩ = 84–86 Andante

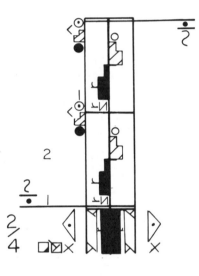

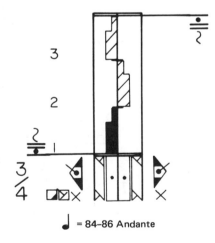

♩ = 84–86 Andante

172

191 Forward Run

Lean the body forward, let the arms swing easily and push from the back foot.

Note: Common errors are rounding the back; holding the weight back, and not pushing from the back foot. An effort must be made to straighten the back leg after the push-off.

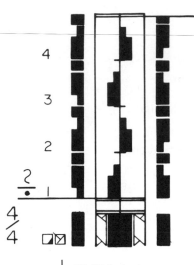

♩ = 84–86 Andante

192 Forward Walk in Straight and Curved Paths

Walk forward four steps. Walk forward in a circle four steps. Because there are only four steps, the circle is small. It almost seems to whip the body around to the starting direction.

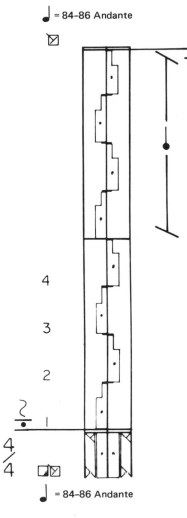

♩ = 84–86 Andante

173

193 Forward Walk with Figure Eight

This exercise is Ex. 181 without the back walk; three measures, 4/4 time.

    Note: Lean in toward the center on the circles.

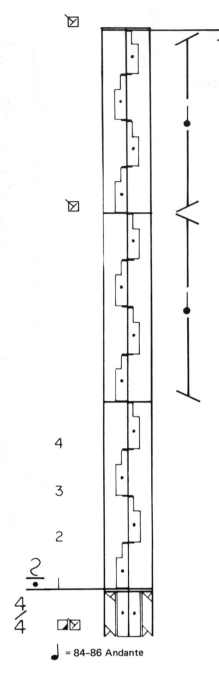

♩ = 84–86 Andante

194 Forward Run with Figure Eight

Small runs; three measures.

     Note: Take this exercise faster than Ex. 193.

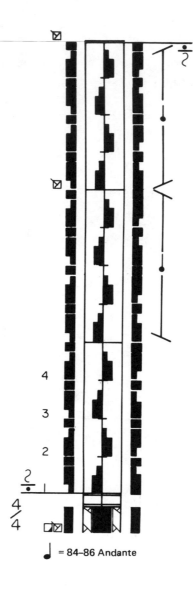

♩ = 84–86 Andante

195 Side Walk on the Diagonal

Exactly like Ex. 182, except it keeps moving in the same direction.

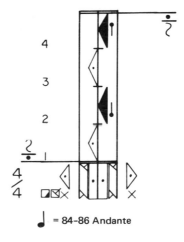

♩ = 84–86 Andante

175

196 Forward and Side Walk in Four Counts

Similar to Ex. 183 except that in order to keep moving in the same direction, a 1/4 turn has been introduced before the side walk starts and again as it finishes.

Action: Walk four steps forward, make a 1/4 turn to the R; walk four steps side, make a 1/4 turn to the L, and repeat.

Note: Arms are added.

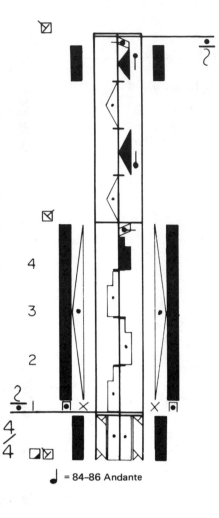

♩ = 84–86 Andante

197 Forward and Side Walk in Two Counts

With two steps in each direction the side walk crosses in front only, in this sequence.

Note: Remember, a step in Modern Dance means a transfer of weight from one foot to the other, unlike the folk and social dance terminology which means a pattern of weight transfers; e.g., polka step, waltz step. Therefore, the side walk has a pattern—open step, crossing step, with the crossing step alternating front and back. The side walk with two steps has only the front crossing.

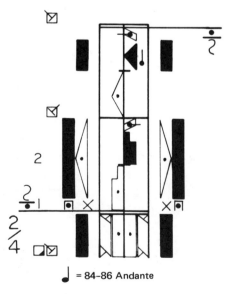

♩ = 84–86 Andante

198 Forward and Side Walk with Balance

This is a more formal use of the forward and side walk with a piece of technique from Chapter 2. It has the stately feeling of the Sarabande (see Ex. 83, Chapter 2).

Action:

Measure 1 Walk forward four steps; turn.

Measure 2 Walk side four steps; turn.

Measure 3 Step forward. Tip the body forward, back arched, R leg bent in back.

Measure 4 Lift out of the *plié*, make a 1/4 turn to the R. Step side with the R on a straight leg, pointing the L foot and prepare for the repeat.

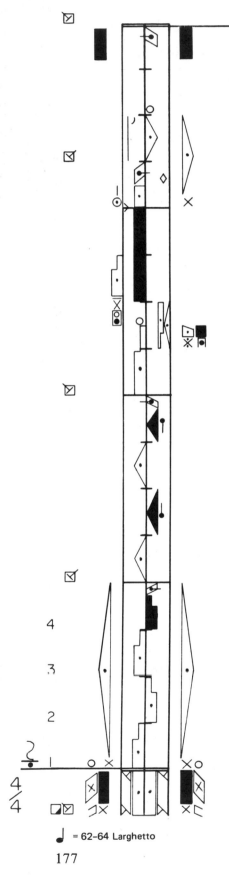

= 62–64 Larghetto

199 Back Walk

Lean the body forward and reach back with the leg. The arms should swing in opposition. The back must be straight, the working leg parallel, the eyes focused on a point straight in front. As in rowing a boat the focus is on a point you are leaving.

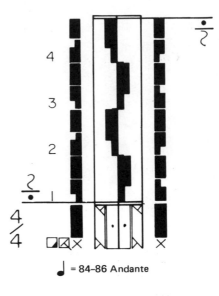

♩ = 84–86 Andante

200 Walks in Three Directions: Four-Measure Phrase in Four Counts

Measure 1 Walk forward four steps; 1/4 turn R.

Measure 2 Walk side four steps; 1/4 turn R.

Measure 3 Walk back four steps; 1/4 turn L.

Measure 4 Walk side four steps; 1/4 turn L.

Repeat.

Note: Watch for the changes in level. The back walk is low, the side walk goes from middle to low, giving an up-down feeling.

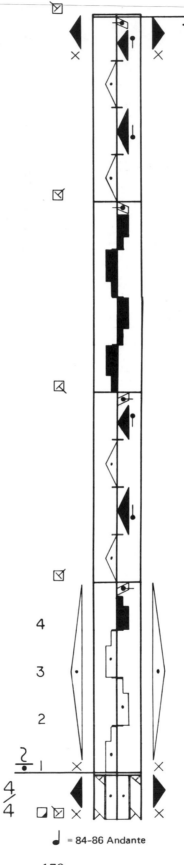

♩ = 84-86 Andante

201 Walks in Three Directions: Two-Measure Phrase in Two Counts

Like Ex. 200 but with two steps in each direction. The up-down of the side walk seems more obvious.

Measure 1 Counts 1 and 2: Walk forward two steps; 1/4 turn to the right; and (3 and 4) walk side two steps; 1/4 turn to the right.

Measure 2 Counts 1 and 2: Walk back two steps, 1/4 turn to the left; and (3 and 4) walk side two steps, 1/4 turn to the left.

This feels better if it is counted as a total of eight counts.

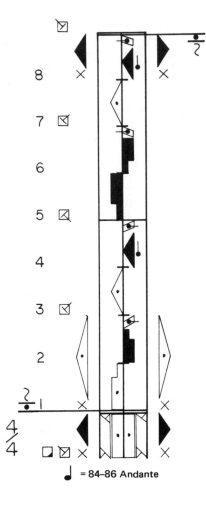

♩ = 84–86 Andante

202 Walks in Three Directions: One-Measure Phrase in One Count

For this pattern start with the downstage leg.

Slide forward low, step side high, step back low, step side high. The up-down feeling is really emphasized now. This should be done with the arms side middle, rib cage and head facing front. The hips rotate. Watch for the space hold on the rib cage symbol and the rotations in the support column. The side step has been raised to high and becomes little more than a transition from the forward to the back step. This is a jazzy number, start slowly and speed it up as fast as possible.

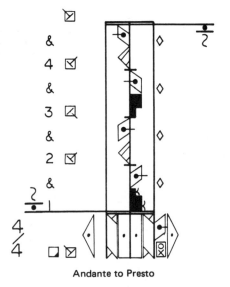

Andante to Presto

203 Walks in Three Directions:
Three-Measure Phrase in Four Counts

A more challenging variation is the three-measure phrase obtained by omitting the second side step. This gives a half turn at the end of the back walk in order to start the repeat. Carry the arms side low to get them out of the way.

Measures 1, 2, and 3 as Ex. 200. On count "4 and" of Measure 3, make half turn to the left and start the repeat. This alternates the starting leg and direction of the turn.

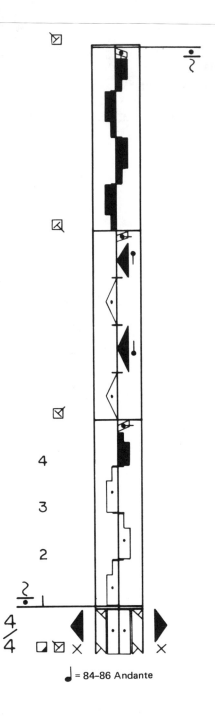

♩ = 84–86 Andante

204 Walks in Three Directions: Three-Measure Phrase in Two Counts

The two-count variation is the same as Ex. 201. Count a total of six instead of eight.

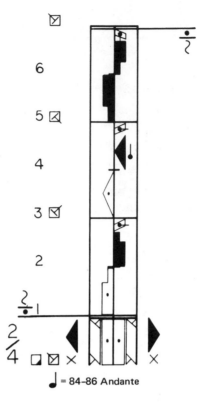

205 Walks in Three Directions: One-Measure Phrase in One Count

The one-count version makes the greatest demands.

Count 1: Slide forward L, low; ("1 and" 1/4 turn L; (2) step side R, high; ("2 and") 1/4 turn L (face starting corner); (3) step back L, high; and ("3 and") 1/2 turn L. The R leg is now ready to slide forward to start the Repeat to the other side.

Note: This pattern has now become a pivot turn alternating the directions of the turn. As with Ex. 203, start slowly and then speed it up.

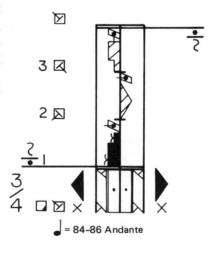

182

Here is a series of phrases based on the two-measure 3/4 pattern suggested earlier. They incorporate much of the basic technique already described in Chapters 2 and 3. Start with the two-measure pattern moving forward, with the variations or additions beginning on Measure 3. The directions of the body, forward, side, back, diagonal, circulate are our constant companions in what is really a choreographic problem, not a technical one. The two-measure introduction is just to get people out of the corner and moving—to overcome the static of the beginner.

206 Basic 3/4 Pattern Forward

See Ex. 190. Watch for the arm action. See Ex. 156, Chapter 3.

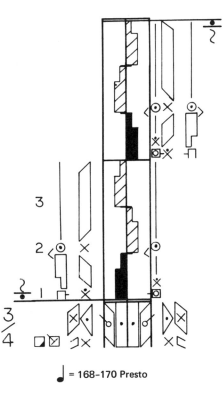

♩ = 168–170 Presto

207 Third Measure Side High Variation of Basic 3/4 Pattern

Same two-measure introduction as in Ex. 206.

Measure 3 Step forward high; step side high right; and step side high left.

Repeat entire pattern to the other side.

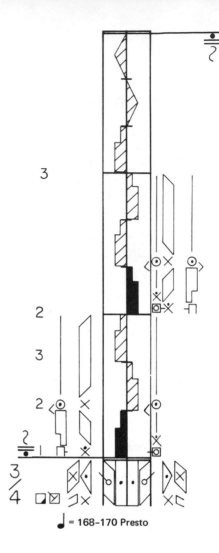

♩ = 168–170 Presto

208 Third Measure Side High with Turn Variation of Basic 3/4 Pattern

Same two-measure introduction as in Ex. 206. This is a step turn as in Ex. 95, Chapter 2.

Measure 3 Count 1: Step forward high, make 1/4 turn to the left on the left foot; (2) step side high, make 1/2 turn to the left on the right foot; and (3) step side high with the left. Make 1/4 turn to the left on the left foot.

Repeat entire pattern to the other side.

Note 1: This phase alternates the starting foot and the direction of the turns. Every step is in the line of direction. There is no retreating on or moving away from the diagonal.

Note 2: In order to get the feel of the "pull" of the direction, it is a good idea to practice the whole phrase at half the set tempo before speeding it up again.

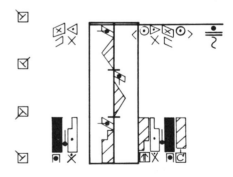

184

209 Third Measure Forward and Back
      Variation of Basic 3/4 Pattern

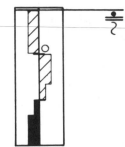

Same two-measure introduction as in Ex. 206.

Measure 3 Count 1: Step forward low;
(2) step back high; (3) close feet together
(place).

     Repeat entire pattern to the other side.
See Ex. 92, Chapter 2.

210 Three-Count Leap Variation
      of Basic 3/4 Pattern

Same two-measure introduction as in Ex. 206.

Measure 3 Count 1: Step forward low;
(2) leap—legs straight in the air; (3) land in
plié.

Measure 4 Repeat the leap on the same side.

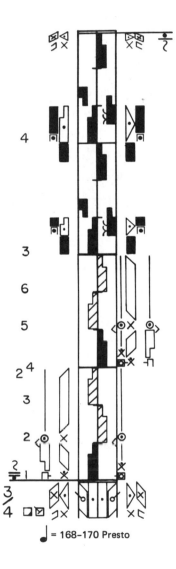

♩ = 168–170 Presto

185

211 Rhythmic Variation of Basic 3/4 Pattern

Same two-measure introduction as in Ex. 206.

Measure 3 Count 1: Step forward high; (2) swing leg forward low; (3) step forward high.

Measure 4 Count 1: Swing leg forward low; (2) step forward high; (3) swing leg forward low.

Repeat to the other side. The alternation is automatic.

Note: It is easier to count this phrase as two measures of 6/4. In the first measure of 6/4 the accents would be on counts 1 and 4— 6/4 ♩ ♩ ♩ ♩ ♩ ♩ . In the second measure of 6/4 the accents would fall on counts 1, 3, and 5—6/4 ♩ ♩ ♩ ♩ ♩ ♩ . This adds rhythmic and dynamic interest to the phrase, and helps develop the musicianship of the student. It also suggests that all dance problems need not be technical. The real intellectual challenge often comes from the musical side of the training.

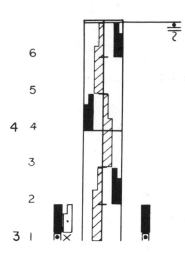

212 Rhythmic Variation and Turn of Basic 3/4 Pattern

Same two-measure introduction as in Ex. 206. The weight change and rhythm are identical to Ex. 211. The only additions are the rotations on counts 2 and 6 of Measures 3 and 4.

Measures 3 & 4 Count 1: Step forward high; (2) hold the weight on the forward foot and make 1/2 turn in the opposite direction from the support. (This is called a reverse turn—in ballet, inside turn.); (3) step forward high on the forward foot; (4) swing the back leg forward; (5) step forward on that foot; (6) hold the weight on that foot and make a 1/2 reverse turn to face the line of direction again. This Exercise alternates on the repeat.

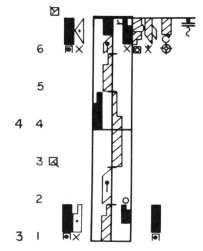

186

213   3/4 Pattern Side

This is a simple variation of the 3/4 pattern using the side direction.

Start in first position, facing downstage right.

Measure 1   Count 1: Slide side low with the left foot, keeping the right foot in its place; rise on lift; (2) bring the right foot to place just behind the left; and (3) step side high with the left.

Measure 2   Count 1: Cross the right foot in front of the left with the right leg in plié; (2) step side high left; and (3) bring the right foot to place high in back of the left (see count 2, Measure 1).

Repeat.

Note 1: Start by carrying the arms side middle. Then add the rotation of the arms when the action becomes more familiar. The difficulty is in keeping the weight between the feet while sliding to second position.

Note 2: Errors are made by holding the weight on the back leg or sliding too far toward the leading leg.

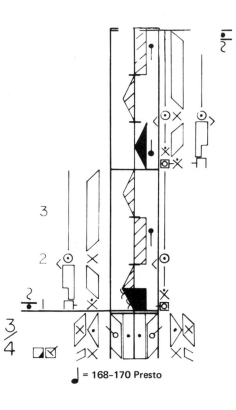

♩ = 168–170 Presto

214 3/4 Pattern Forward and Side

As with the forward and side walk, the transition from one direction to the other is made with a 1/4 turn. There are two measures in each direction. The arms are the same for both directions.

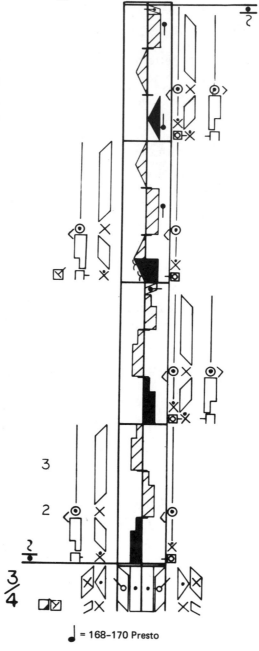

♩ = 168–170 Presto

215 3/4 Pattern Forward, Side, and Back with Back Extension

The first four measures are as in Ex. 214. There is a change in the foot pattern in Measure 5 when the movement is to the back. Instead of the low, high, high—it is like walking up a hill, low, middle, high—holding in relevé on both feet, one in front of the other on Measure 6. A flourish has been added on Measures 7 and 8. The forward leg is brushed back, the body tips forward middle as Ex. 82, Chapter 2.

Measure 8 is a half turn bending the knee in front and rising to the ball of the supporting foot, as in Ex. 86, Chapter 2. Watch for the arm change, the L arm moves diagonal high. The weight keeps moving forward to prepare for the repeat. The rib cage rotates in the direction of the turn.

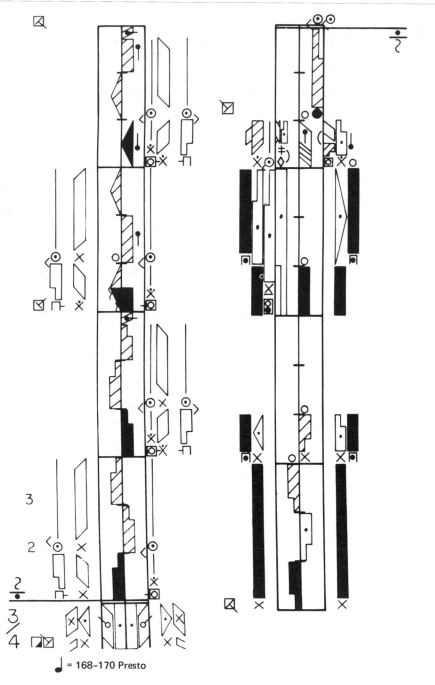

♩ = 168–170 Presto

216 3/4 Pattern Forward and Side with Pivot Turn and Weight Shift

This is a variation of Ex. 209, but the side shift of Ex. 89, Chapter 2, has been added along with a pivot turn and extension.

Measures 1, 2, 3 as in Ex. 208 plus a 1/4 turn to the R on count "3 and" of Measure 3.

Measure 4 Count 1: Step side low with the R facing downstage right; and (2 and 3) lift the L leg and arms side middle; the face turns over the L shoulder.

Measure 5 Count 1: Holding the plié, bring the L foot across and in front; the ball of the R foot on the floor; and (2 and 3) make a 3/4 pivot turn to the R, straightening both legs and rising to the half toe. End the turn facing the line of direction. On count "3 and," make another 1/4 turn to the right.

Measure 6 Count 1: Step side and extend again as in Measure 4, facing downstage diagonal; and (2) step side L in relevé, make 1/4 turn L, and close the feet together, place high; arms come down to the sides as the body arches slightly.

Note: On the turns the torso does not have to stay center. Side bends, forward bends, tipping the head—almost anything the dancer wants to do is acceptable as long as it is not so wild that it detracts from the base pattern.

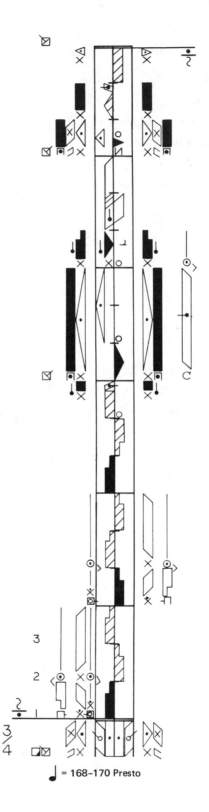

♩ = 168–170 Presto

190

3/4 Pattern with Extensions and Balance

This is by far the most difficult of all the variations. It is really for the advanced student but is included here to show how basic technique can be used in the space phase.

The beginning is as in Ex. 208, except that the step turn is only a 3/4 turn. End facing downstage right.

Measure 4 Count 1: Step across the L foot with the R, in plié; and (2 and 3) straighten the R leg, lift the L leg side high, body straight and facing front, arms just above shoulder level, elbows lifted.

Measure 5 Counts 1 through 5: Shift the weight quickly to the L, stepping onto the ball of the foot. The R leg is lifted quickly as high as possible to the side, the body is center but arches back high, the face to the ceiling; the arms press down just below shoulder level. Hold through Measure 5 and count 2 of Measure 6.

Measure 6 Count 3: Drop the R leg quickly, in front of the L in plié. Hold the weight on the R. On "3 and" make a 1/4 turn to the L, and prepare for the repeat.

Note 1: Common errors are allowing the body to lean to the L side in Measures 5 and 6. Also, the R extension on count 1 of Measure 5 must have the knee facing up. Many students lift the leg with the knee facing forward. In this particular action, the leg moves slightly forward to a diagonal and rotates on the lift.

Note 2: This phase is broad and ecstatic and should feel like wind on an open beach. It is sometimes good to finish it with three-count leaps in a half circle around the studio.

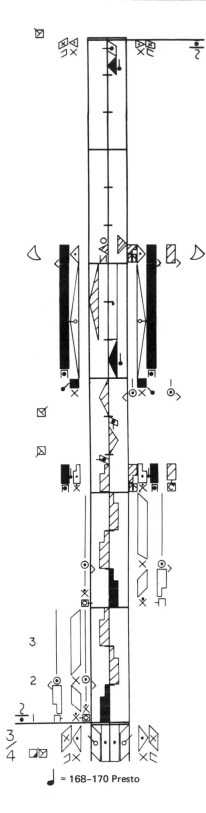

♩ = 168–170 Presto

191

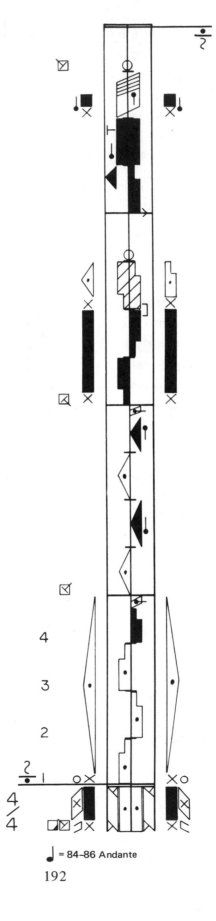

WALKS AND RUNS DEVELOPING INTO HOPS AND LEAPS

Legend

= Half turn to the right on both feet ending in relevé

218 Forward, Side, and Back Walks

The material is again very simple. The tempo is deliberate and only the little turn adds a flourish.

Basic pattern:

Measure 1 Walk forward four steps.

Measure 2 Walk to the side four steps.

Measure 3 Walk back three steps and hold in relevé, one foot forward of the other, for count 4.

Measure 4 Shift the weight to the forward foot, cross the other foot over it as in Ex. 216, Measure 5, and make one half turn ending in relevé.

♩ = 84–86 Andante

**219 Short Version of Forward, Side,
and Back Walks**

This is the same as Ex. 218 with the reduction of counts in Measure 1.

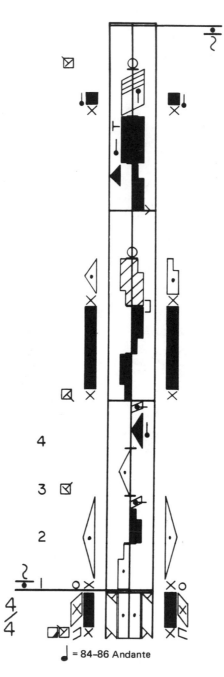

♩ = 84–86 Andante

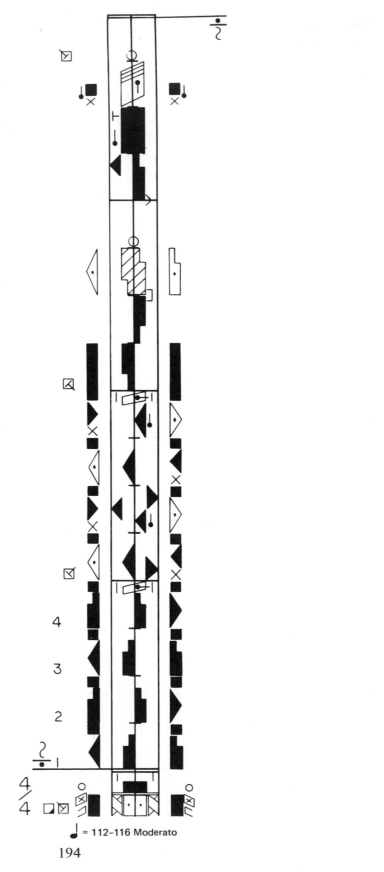
220 Forward, Side, and Back Runs

Same as Ex. 218, except it is taken at a running tempo (four Measures).

Picking up the tempo changes the character of the phrase. The forward runs seem now only to prepare for the two side leaps. The back steps are taken low, rising quickly to the hold, place high on the 3rd count (3) of Measure 3. The pivot turn whips around, allowing for some freedom of action in the torso as Ex. 216.

Note 1: In the side leaps of Ex. 220 and Ex. 221 the crossing foot is always in front. This makes for a smooth transition into the back direction. Watch for the arm action on the side leaps; they go "with" the leap.

Note 2: When the "flow" finally gets into the phrase, it is good to emphasize the side leap and the pivot turn, and broaden the beat in both those areas. The chief characteristics of the phrase are (1) the change of facing directions; (2) the big side leap; and (3) the fast pivot with its resultant suspension.

♩ = 112–116 Moderato

194

221 Short Version of Forward, Side, and Back Runs

Like Ex. 218, but reduced to two counts for Measure 1. One leap forward, one leap side.

Measure 2 Has been reduced from three steps back to one step back with a hop, one leg bending in front, arms in opposition, but ending with the same holding positions as in all the other sequences 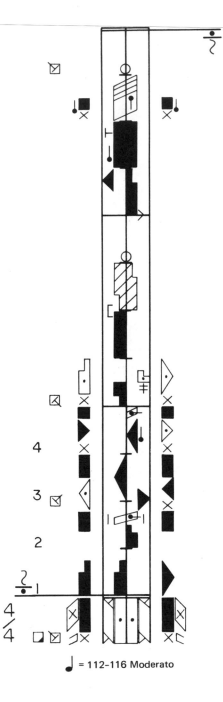.

Measures 2 and 3 are still four counts each.

♩ = 112–116 Moderato

BREAKDOWN OF TAKE-OFF
AND LANDINGS

222 Plié-Relevé Brushes Forward

This is a simple analysis of how to transfer the weight from one foot to the other in preparation for the leap. It has a jazzy feeling.

Action: Step forward on the L foot. Brush the R foot forward under the center of weight until the toe leaves the floor. Straighten the supporting knee and rise to the half toe. From this position fall forward onto the other foot with the usual procedure—toe, heel, plié—and release the weight from the back foot. The arms swing in a gentle opposition. Keep the body steady. The action is up and down, there is no twist. The body positions must be maintained, center of weight over the supporting arch and the parts of the body centered around the plumb-line. The feeling is of carrying the plumb-line with you and bouncing it up and down.

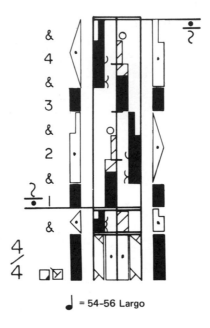

♩ = 54–56 Largo

223 Plié-Relevé Brushes Side

Very similar to Ex. 215 except that the push-off from the back foot is emphasized and the crossing leg rotates from a parallel position on the push-off to a strong turn-out on the crossing. The crossing is in front of the support, the arms work in a parallel movement with the emphasis on the swing over the open position of the legs.

Note: There should be a minimum of rotation of the pelvis. The parallel lifting of the crossing leg prevents the lurch of the hips that usually occurs when the leg is turned out on the push-off. It also makes for a very smooth transfer of weight emphasizing a long low curve in space.

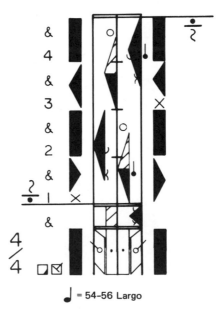

♩ = 54–56 Largo

224 Brush Leaps Forward

All that is added here is a little spring off the floor. The quality and size is like the little jumps of Ex. 101, Chapter 2. Watch for the tempo change.

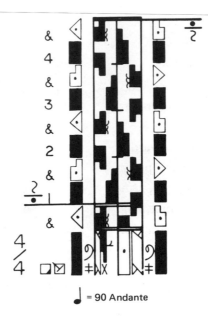

♩ = 90 Andante

225 Brush Leaps Side

Same as Ex. 224, moving sideward.

Note: These little "springs" are just small leaps. Enlarging the range of movement makes a true leap, which has a larger "up" curve and covers more ground. Remember: the higher the leap, the slower the tempo.

Note: Arms same as Ex. 223.

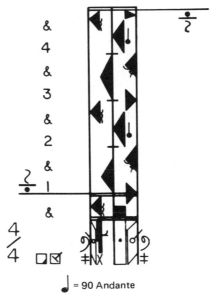

♩ = 90 Andante

197

226   Brush Leaps with Jump

This exercise combines Ex. 222 with Ex. 105, Chapter 2. There are two little leaps forward followed by two jumps in first position.

    Action: Count 1: Brush leap forward R and (2) brush leap forward L, arms in opposition; (3) jump in first; (4) jump in first, arms side low; and ("4 and") jump from first, land on L in plié, R leg bent in back; R arm forward, L arm side middle.

    Repeat.

    Note: The brush is on the upbeat, the landings are *on* the beat. Therefore Ex. 222 is the preparation for this exercise.

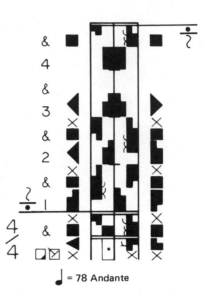

♩ = 78 Andante

227   Brush Leaps with Jump and Air Turn

A variation of Ex. 226. There is a turn in the air with the feet together in first, after the first jump. A run, run, leap can be added to lengthen the phrase.

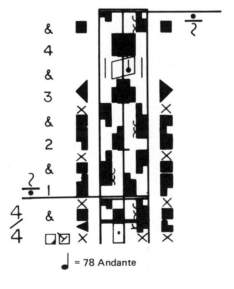

♩ = 78 Andante

A leap has very definite characteristics. It consists of three parts: a take-off, an air space, and a landing. The take-off is on one foot, and the landing is on the other. This exercise is a true leap.

Action: Count 1: Step forward on the L foot; (2) brush the R leg forward low, knee straight, and push off with the L foot. The L leg straightens in the air after the push-off. (Note that both legs are straight during count 2—the air-space—one leg is forward low, the other back low. The arms are in opposition—the L arm forward middle, the R arm side middle, the body is center between the legs, shoulders pressed down.); and (3) the R foot comes to the floor as in Ex. 76, Chapter 2 and the plié starts immediately.

Note 1: There is a lifting up in the body to overcome the downward pull of gravity and to prevent the torso from collapsing from the shock of the landing. The back leg stays straight through count 3. The feet are pointed in the air, of course.

Note 2: For the repeat—stay in the plié of the landing, swing the back leg forward under the center of weight, step forward low and repeat the spring. This leap does not alternate sides.

Note 3: Runs, leaps, and hops are really only extensions of the walk. Instead of transferring the weight by falling from one foot to the other, the leap takes the long way around and goes into the air before transferring the weight to the other foot. The hop takes-off and lands on the same foot before transferring the weight. In all elevation the normal fall and recovery of the walk is reversed—you fall *up* before you fall *down*. In order to do this, both feet have to be off the floor at the same time, of course. It is a most sophisticated way of moving through space.

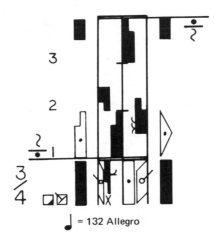

♩ = 132 Allegro

199

229 Three-Count Leap Side

A simple variation to the side. Mechanically similar to Ex. 223.

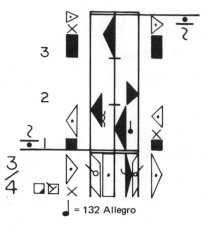

♩ = 132 Allegro

230 Three-Count Leap Forward and Side

Notice the 1/4 turn as in the walks and runs, to change the directions.

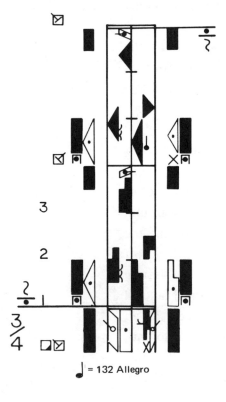

♩ = 132 Allegro

In this sequence the hop goes straight up and down. Ideally, the landing should be in the same spot as the take-off, with no air curve but rather a high air space. Space is covered as the weight is transferred forward in the run, after the landing from the hop. This action sets up an uneven rhythmic pattern. The hop take-off is on count 1; "1 and" and count 2 are in the air, and the landing is on count "2 and," while the weight transfers on count 3.

In this exercise, the knee is lifted forward middle, the arms are in opposition as for the leaps as in Ex. 175, Chapter 3. This exercise does not alternate feet.

Note 1: The lifted leg holds its position through the landing and is then quickly lowered for the forward step. Also, when repeating, try to stay in the plié on count 3, and step forward low for the next hop.

Note 2: The key leg action for these repetitious hops and leaps is the two lows (half pliés) on counts 1 and 3. When the measures are strung together, a 3-1 rhythm is set up—even for the leap, broken for the hops.

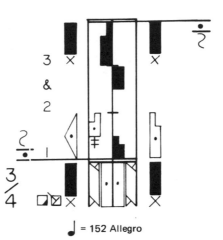

♩ = 152 Allegro

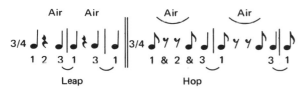

The two lows (pliés) on those counts are a preparation for the spring into the air.

Note 3: Many students keep popping up to a straight leg on count 3, or stepping onto a straight leg for the take-off (wrong way). This action makes excessive demands on the foot and usually limits the height of the elevation. The plié and relevé action is the beginning and end of all elevation.

232   Hops and Leaps in 3/4 Time

Use the arms in opposition, changing through place low. This exercise does not alternate feet. The difficulty is the vertical hop followed by the forward thrust of the leap. It has a stop-and-go sort of feeling.

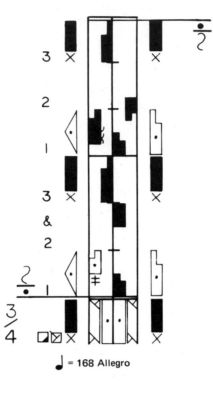

♩ = 168 Allegro

233 Hop, Leap, and Runs Combined

This exercise is Ex. 232, followed by four runs and a leap.

Note: This is easier to count in 6. The hop counts are 1, 2, 3; the leap 4, 5, 6; followed by run (1), run (2), run (3), run (4) (take-off), (5) air space, (6) land. The leaps alternate feet.

The hop has the leg bent in front, both leaps have the legs straight in the air. The leaps alternate.

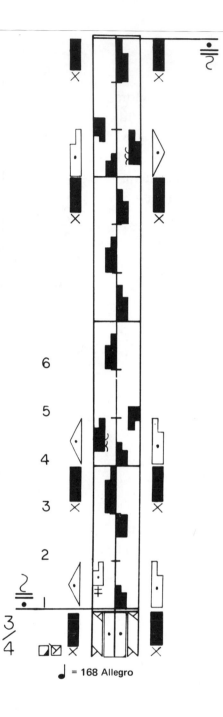

= 168 Allegro

234 Run, Run, Hop in 4/4 Time

This is a lively sequence with two runs before the take-off; the hop itself is the same. With the take-off on count 3 and the landing on count "4 and," the transfer step is on count 1 of the next Measure. This sets up the alternation of feet and adds momentum to the action. Hold the arms during the run and swing to the opposition on the take-off—count 3 (see Chapter 3, Ex. 175).

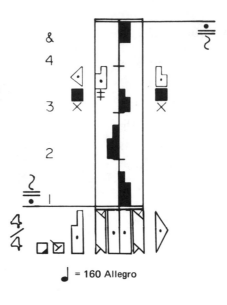

♩ = 160 Allegro

235 Leaps with a Run Preparation in 4/4 Time

As in Ex. 234, the take-off is on count 3; the air space on count 4, and the landing on count 1 of the following Measure.

The arms are as in Ex. 234.

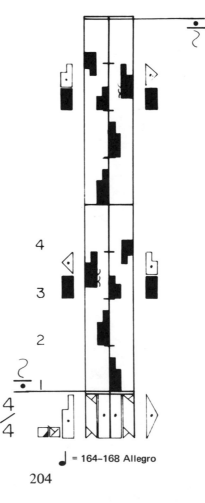

♩ = 164–168 Allegro

236   Hops and Leaps in 4/4 Time

Here is a dynamic change from the vertical hop to the horizontal leap. This can be inverted too (combine Ex. 234 and Ex. 235). It is more satisfying to put the leap before the hop because of the greater involvement in space in the leap. The greater effort is thereby reserved for the leap.

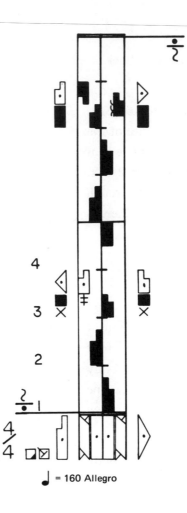

♩ = 160 Allegro

237 Brush Runs Forward, Side, and Back with Tilting Body

This is another way of preparing the feet for landing from leaps and jumps. Because of the spring and weight change, it is a run. The foot action is like the brushes of Chapter 2, Ex. 193, but with a quick change of feet through place, as if cutting the weight away. There is considerable body change in this exercise.

Starting Position: Standing on R foot, L foot pointed in back; arms side middle.

Action:

Measure 1 Counts 1 to 4: Cut the R foot forward low with the L and point the foot strongly just clearing the floor. The body leans on a back tilt. The feeling is of one straight line running through the body from the ear to the toe. Alternate legs.

Measure 2 Counts 1 to 4: Center the body and continue the cutting action to the side.

Measure 3 Counts 1 to 4: Lean the body forward and continue the cutting to the back. This feels like a scissor-kick.

Note: The toes should glide across the floor and release the contact only at the last possible moment. The ankle is fully extended on the spring. The knee bends as the foot takes weight and straightens immediately for the spring. The movement of the legs is very tight and very small; the thighs scarcely separate. The space curve made by the head is quite large. It is really a tipping plumb-line.

This exercise may be reduced to a two-count phrase and a one-count phrase (in 3/4 time).

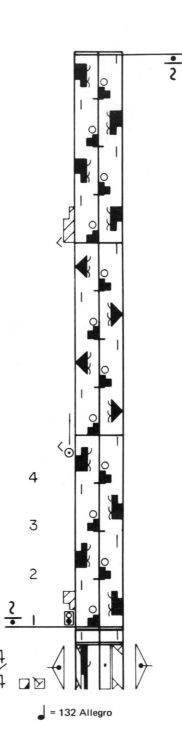

♩ = 132 Allegro

206

238   Walk in Sarabande Style

A very formal step pattern, suggesting a Sarabande, has been added to the floor plan of
Ex. 193. The whole torso is place high. One
arm gesture has been added for style.

Action: Count 1, step forward R. Count
2, forward L. As the plié starts, pull the back
foot forward to touch the heel of the forward
foot. Toe stays on the floor. Slide the same
foot back, transfer the weight back, push off
with the forward foot and point the toe. Repeat to the other side.

Walk in a circle to the right. Walk in a
circle to the left.

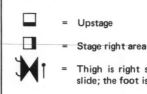

Legend		
□	=	Upstage
▣	=	Stage right area
⋈	=	Thigh is right side low, the lower leg is left side low, and the toes slide; the foot is in back of the support leg.

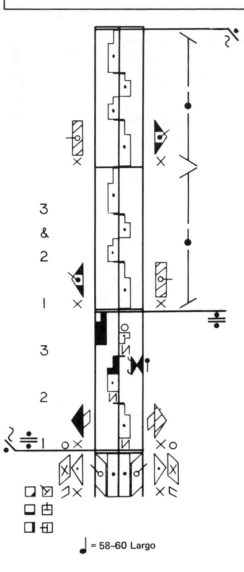

♩ = 58–60 Largo

239 Back, Side, and Forward Walks in Four Counts

By using simple choreographic devices, a walk can be manipulated into many interesting patterns, which in turn could be developed into complete compositions.

Here is a walk in the three principal directions of the body; forward, side, and back. This exercise starts with the back walk; there is the 1/4 turn to prepare for the side walk. The forward walk is taken in a circle. This is followed by two steps backward and two steps forward. Watch for the arm positions and the half turn to prepare for the repeat.

Note: There is a 1/4 turn to start the circle. At this point the center of the circle is on your left.

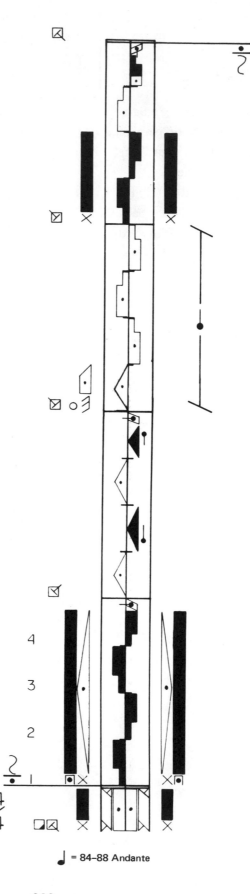

♩ = 84–88 Andante

240 Back, Side, and Forward Walks in Two Counts

This is the same as Ex. 239, but with the usual reduction of counts and steps the whole character of the phrase changes.

Counts 1 and 2: There are two steps backward, 1/4 turn; (3 and 4) two steps side, crossing front with the crossing knee bent; ("4 and") 1/2 turn to the left, holding the weight on the R; this faces upstage left; (5) step side; (6) cross the R foot over the L; ("6 and") made 3/4 pivot turn to face the line of direction; (7) take one step back; (8) one step forward; ("8 and") make the 1/2 turn; and repeat.

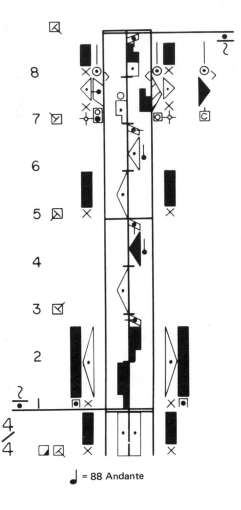

♩ = 88 Andante

209

241 Can-Can

This is very similar to Ex. 237. However, the emphasis here is on a quick picking up of the legs. The body positions are the same in relation to the legs. Because of the Can-Can quality, the side direction has been eliminated. So there are four leg lifts forward and four back. This is then reduced to two in each direction.

Note: This is fun to do with the girls swinging an imaginary skirt over the lifting leg and keeping the face turned downstage. When the legs kick up in back, shake the skirt in the back.

If there are boys, a top hat or an imaginary cane works wonders for creating the mood. Almost any choreographic invention is good at this point. Boys come at the end of the line, legs lifting in front. Girls leaning forward, legs kicking in back. Notice the tempo marking—it should be bright.

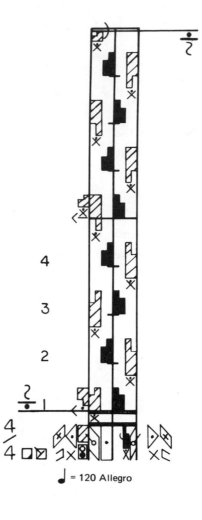

♩ = 120 Allegro

242 Two-Count Variation of Can-Can

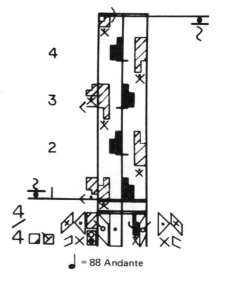

♩ = 88 Andante

210

243 One-Count Variation of Can-Can

With the reduction to one count in each direction, the character seems to change and the action becomes a "galloping leap." The body is held center as the legs and hips rock.

Note: Watch for the starting position. R leg lifted forward high, knee bent, the body back. On the downbeat, cut the L leg sharply to the back, knee bent, and repeat the cut forward with the L. This feels like a see-saw and looks like riding a horse. It is fun to hold both arms forward middle, elbows bent and held against the waist, fingers curled as if holding the reins, palms face down. Performed dead-pan, this can be very funny.

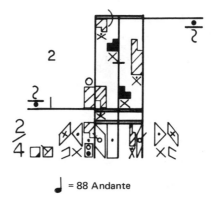

♩ = 88 Andante

211

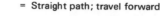

Legend

𝖔	= Front surface
𝖔	= Front surface of lower leg
	= Straight path; travel forward

244 Highland Phrase

Here again is another way to train the feet and legs for quick, precise action. This time the style is borrowed from the Scottish dance.

In the Highland or Scottish dance, the placing of the body is superb and the remarkable precision of the footwork makes it an ideal source for dance training.

Most Highland dances take place in a rather confined area, the emphasis being on the hop and jump rather than movement through space. In this exercise an attempt has been made to keep the precision of the footwork but move the phrase on the diagonal.

Starting Position: Standing in turned-out position, facing forward on the diagonal, body place high and strong. Hands on the hips, with knuckles touching the hips, fingers turned back, wrists straight, elbows turned out. The whole position suggests prickly vitality. (Don't forget the national flower of Scotland is the thistle.)

Action:

Measure 1 With a little spring forward, cut the L foot forward low with the R, bending the knee and brushing sharply with the toe as the leg straightens. At the same time lift the L arm to place high and hold it strongly with the shoulder. Hop again on the R, hold the L. Repeat to the other side.

Measure 2 Change arms on count 1. The leg and foot action is like Ex. 237, alternating, but the body stays center. Emphasize the bounce and move forward with each step. Make 1/4 turn to the right to face downstage.

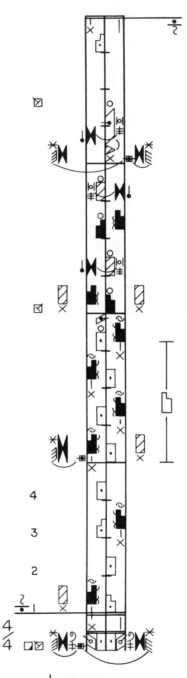

♩ = 96-100 Andante

Measure 3 Both arms swing over the head. Brush the foot forward and plié on the supporting leg. Quickly relevé on the support and pull the working leg in sharply, turning it out and bending the knee. Place the ankle on the front of the R leg midway between the ankle and knee. Repeat to the other side. *Do not jump this.*

Measure 4 On count 1 step side high with the R directly on the ball of the foot. Quickly bring the ankle of the L foot to the mid-calf of the R leg. The arms come down to their starting position. Make a 3/4 spin turn to the R on counts 2 and 3, ending facing the line of direction. On count 4, cut the R foot forward with the L, pointing the foot strongly and bending the L knee as it takes weight. Repeat the phrase. It does not alternate.

Note: Although the foot-and-arm action is extremely precise, it is not fussy or precious. There is no tilting of the head to either side, the neck is straight and strong. The phrase should be performed with a sense of strength and pride.

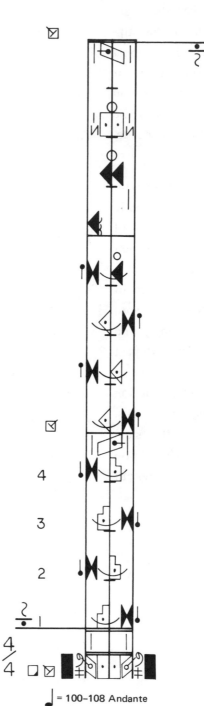
245 Basque Phrase

Again a phrase for training the feet and legs. This time borrowed from another mountain people, the Basques. The characteristics are vertical movement, precise footwork, and strong straight backs.

The Basques use more space than the Highlanders, but the arms are glued to the sides most of the time. The head and neck are held strongly center and the eyes focused straight ahead. Although there is a feeling of strength, it is not as martial as the Highland dance. We must remember the Highland dances were originally performed only by the men before battle or to celebrate a victory after battle. The Basque dance was a more social affair performed by both men and women.

Starting Position: Facing forward on the diagonal. Turned out first position, arms at the sides.

Action:

Measure 1 Take off from both feet, and on count 1 land on the L foot, R foot touching the L ankle, R knee turned out. Alternate feet, repeating four times in all. Make 1/4 turn to R on fourth hop.

Measure 2 Continue the quick picking up of the feet. On count 4 hold the plié on the R, L foot touching the back of the R ankle.

Measure 3 Brush the L leg out to the side, jump off the R. Move toward the lifting left leg and land on both feet in plié on count 2. Straighten both legs on count 3, and hold for half of count 4. On the "and" of 4, prepare for the repeat with a little spring into the air. Repeat.

♩ = 100–108 Andante

Note: Don't smile; but there is an inner giggle.

214

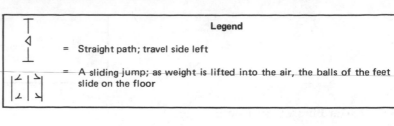
All people have wonderful dances that celebrate their national characteristics, and they always speak of strength. Not only are these dances excellent sources for technical training, but they also take the dance student around the world, introducing him to different people and to different concepts of strength. As will be seen by these phrases, strength doesn't mean the same thing to everyone.

Here is a phrase with a slightly Slavic flavor. The feeling is of a cavalry charge, sabers flashing, and shields held high to protect the body. Technically, it is a simple plié and relevé in second position moving on the diagonal.

246 Tartar Phrase: Section A

Starting Position: Almost full plié in second position. R arm high, hand makes a fist, as if holding a sword. L arm bent across the body, hand makes a fist as if holding a shield. Face is turned over the L shoulder, eyes focused straight ahead. Body center and strong.

Action: Keeping the legs in a wide second position, alternately move the L and then the R, traveling to the left. The rhythm is "1 and," "2 and." Continue through count 4, stopping on count 4. On count 5 slide the legs together to place high as the R arm makes a complete circle opening to the side and swinging across the body ending in the starting position. On count 6 with a sliding spring, like a chassé, return to second position. Repeat.

Note: The feeling on count 5 is of a saber cut, intended to shock and wound.

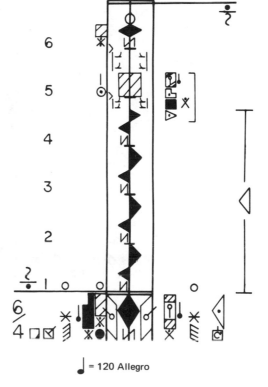

♩ = 120 Allegro

215

247   Tartar Phrase: Section B

Starting from the second position of Section A:

Count 1: With the R step across in front of the L. Lean the body side R, carrying the bent arm with it. Lift the L leg side, knee bent and turned out, ankle flexed; (2) sharply straighten the L leg with a kick as high as possible, keeping the ankle flexed, like kicking a man in the chest; (3) swing the body strongly to the opposite side, L, with a feeling of stabbing with the R arm. Bend the R knee. The L leg bends quickly, the L ankle is placed over the R knee. Hold for count 4. The face stays turned over the shoulder, body facing downstage right; and (5 and 6) fall side low with the L foot; step across low with the R— almost a run.

Repeat to the other side.

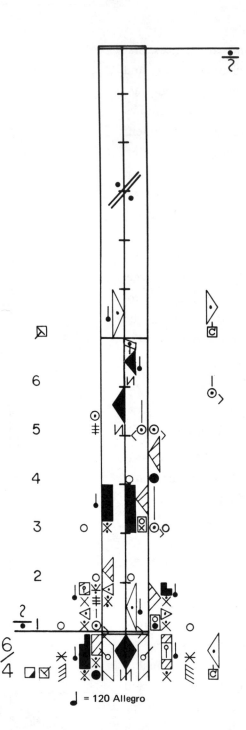

♩ = 120 Allegro

216

248 Tartar Phrase: Section C

Count 1: Step forward low with the L;
(2) push off the L foot, lifting the R leg followed by the L. Both legs are bent in the air.
Both arms swing up over the head. Make a
3/4 turn in the air; (3) land on the R foot,
arms side. Make a 1/4 turn to the left;
(4). Step forward low, tip the whole torso
forward middle, head up, eyes still on the
target, R leg bent back, foot above the knee.
With a strong thrust, the R arm shoots forward like running the enemy through with the
sword. The L arm is side middle for balance;
(5) hold; (6) fall forward low onto the R foot
keeping the body position; and ("6 and") lift
the body up to the starting position and
prepare for the repeat. Repeat on the other
side, from the opposite diagonal.

Note 1: Sections A, B, and C should
be performed as one Phrase. Here they have
been presented separately for teaching convenience.

Note 2: This is a nice bloody phrase.
Students love to do it.

Note 3: The girls should not be allowed
to soften the body lines of the neck or rib
cage. It is not that kind of attack! Once the
phrase starts moving, there are usually shouts
for punctuation on the jumps.

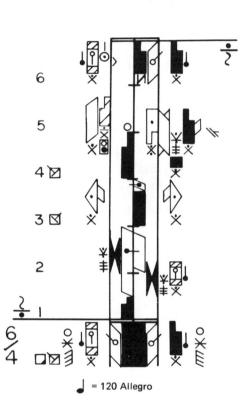

♩ = 120 Allegro

217

249 Israeli Phrase: Basic Step in Place

The simple weight change which is the basis of this study is common to people of the Plains where the ground is level and there is space to move into. Circle or serpentine dances are common, and men and women frequently dance together. This first step is common to women's dances.

Starting Position: Arms at the sides, feet together.

Action: Count 1: Step on the R bending the knee; ("1 and") step on the L, but take the weight on the ball of foot, knee straight; repeat only "2 and" and "3 and"; and ("4 and") simply tap with the ball of the L foot, without shifting the weight. On count 1 repeat the pattern on the other side.

Note: Stay in one place until the pattern is learned. Then make it travel forward.

250 Israeli Phrase: Basic Step Turning in Place

Exactly like Ex. 249 but turn to the R four steps, and then repeat to the L. Make a complete rotation with each four steps. The arms and body can be added to give a "dancey" feeling. The arms are middle level, one bent in front. The body leans slightly to the side in the direction of the turn.

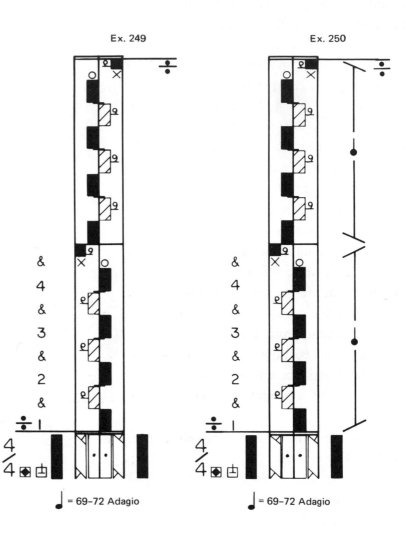

Ex. 249 Ex. 250

♩ = 69–72 Adagio   ♩ = 69–72 Adagio

251   Israeli Phrase: Basic Step Side

Move the step pattern to the side with an open
and closing action of the feet.

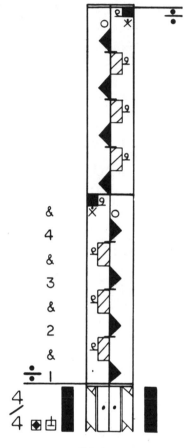

Adagio

252   Israeli Phrase: Basic Step Forward

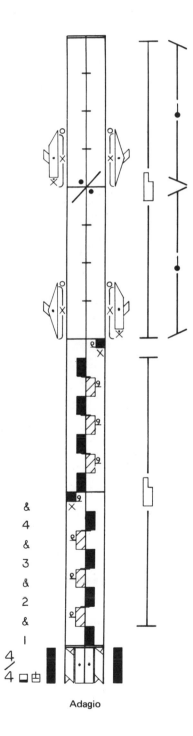

Adagio

219

253 Israeli Phrase: Basic Step Forward in Straight and Circular Paths

Ex. 249 and Ex. 252, moving on the diagonal. Three Measures: Add the arms and body on the circles, as in Ex. 252. For arms on the forward action, slowly bring them up sideward to side high, palms up, elbows bent slightly.

Note: Be sure the arm gestures have a feeling of carrying weight—like carrying water jugs or rugs for weaving or something. Don't let it look like a praying gesture. The body, although bending and arching must be used strongly to support a weight.

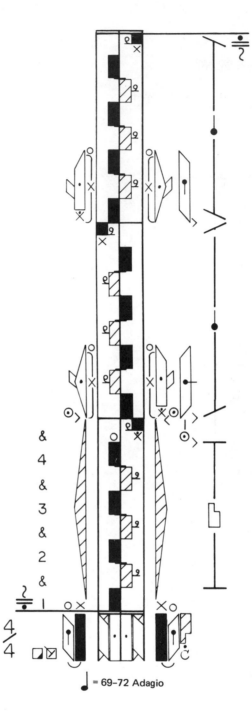

♩ = 69–72 Adagio

254 **Israeli Phrase: Basic Step Side in Straight and Circular Paths**

255 **Israeli Phrase: Basic Forward and Side Steps Combined in Straight and Circular Paths**

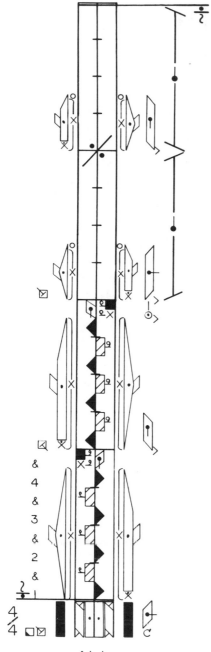

Adagio

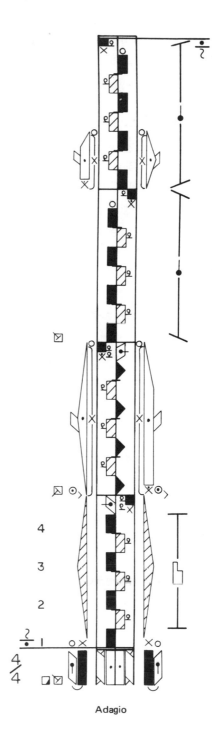

Adagio

256 Israeli Phrase: Men's Forward Variation

This is a strong aggressive movement, directly contrasting to the women's step.

Starting Position: Body held high and strong, feet parallel, knees bent slightly. Arms side middle, elbows bent, hands in fists, palms facing front. Feeling of holding heavy swords or torches.

Action: Count 1: Step forward low with the L; (2) step forward low with the R; (3) step forward low with the L, and make a strong accent with the heel as the R leg swings forward, knee straight, foot extended strongly; and (4) hold the leg position but keep the weight shifting forward as if being pulled by the toe. Repeat to the other side.

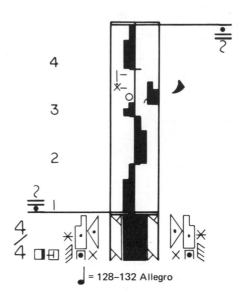

♩ = 128–132 Allegro

257 Israeli Phrase: Men's Diagonal Variation

Same body position but zig-zag the step. Step to side low with the L, cross in front with the R. Repeat side step L. Make the heel accent and brush the R leg across to a forward L diagonal. *Keep the body facing forward.* Repeat to the other side.

Note 1: For the repeat to the other side, watch for the action of the crossing leg. From the diagonal brush to the L. The R leg must move to second position, *going through place.* A common error is to step into the forward diagonal after the brush. Obviously the pattern cannot be started this way and all is confusion.

Note 2: This step looks better if it moves straight across the studio rather than on a diagonal.

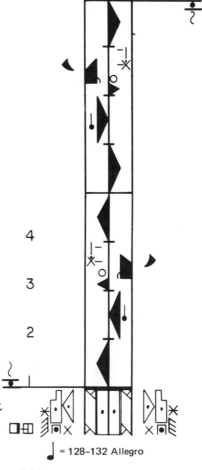

♩ = 128–132 Allegro

222

258 Serpentine Dance

This is a quiet step designed to move continuously in one direction. It is for a large number of dancers following one after the other,
holding hands. The dancer in the front leads
the line through many circular patterns.

Starting with the feet together, step side
with the L leg straight, plié and cross back
with the R, bending the body to the R. Repeat the side step, body center, make 1/4
turn to the L, leg straight, and close the feet
together. Repeat the side and crossing step,
the 1/4 turn L, but add a slight spring off the
L to the R, bending the knees, and close the
feet together. Watch for the rhythmic change.

Note: The emphasis is on the change of
front and the little spring at the end of Measure 2. This has an unhurried charm about it.

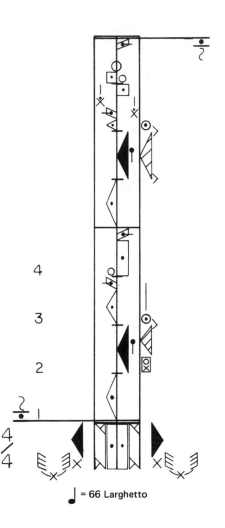

♩ = 66 Larghetto

223

259 Cowboy Phrase: Basic Step in 2/4 Time

Lean the body *forward* high, with the back straight. Step on the R foot, lift the L leg side middle, knee bent and directly side of the hip. Pull the weight slightly to the L, keeping the whole foot on the floor. Release the heel slightly. In Measure 2, step on the L in second, lift the R leg and pull to the R. Keep repeating. The counts are "1 and," "2 and," etc. The arms swing parallel across the body, the face stays front. It is easier to learn this in the center of the studio.

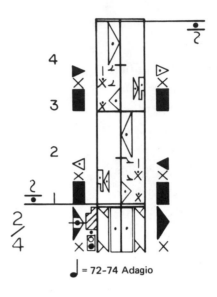

♩ = 72–74 Adagio

260 Cowboy Phrase: Basic Step on the Diagonal in 3/4 Time

Almost the same step as Ex. 259, moving on a diagonal. It is in 3/4 time. Step across on R count 1, slide on "and" of 1, and count 2, step to left side on count 3. Repeat. Body and arms are as in Ex. 259.

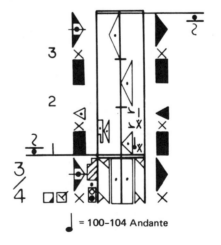

♩ = 100–104 Andante

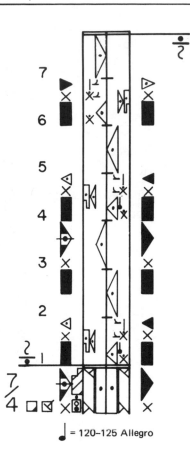
261 Cowboy Phrase: Basic Step on the Diagonal in 7/4 Time

Counts 1, 2, and 3: Slide step as in Ex. 260; (4 and 5) slide step as in Ex. 259; and (6 and 7) step in left and pull to the right as in Ex. 259.

Repeat.

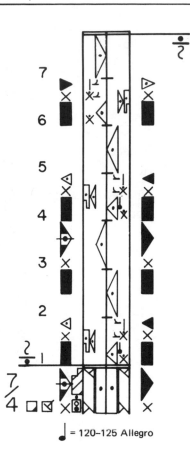

♩ = 120–125 Allegro

262 Cowboy Phrase: Hitch Kick

Very much like the Can-Can but with a different beginning.

Starting Position: Both arms place high. Stand on the R. L foot back, ball of foot on the floor.

Action: Step forward on the L, kick the R leg in back, knee bent; arms come down to place low. Jump off the L, change legs in the air, and land on the R. For a transition, step forward with the L on the ball of the foot, bend the R leg in front, and swing the arms up again to place high. Step forward on the R on count 6. Repeat. This does not alternate. On counts 1, 2, and 3, Hitch kick; (4 and 5) hold on the toe; and (6) step forward with the R.

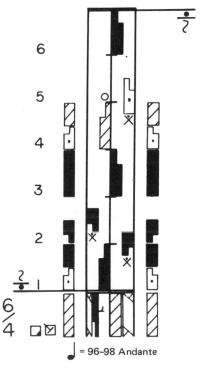

♩ = 96–98 Andante

225

263   Cowboy Phrase: Hitch Kick in 7/4 Time

After the Hitch kick (counts 1, 2, 3), step forward on the left (4), hop (5), bringing the right leg under the body, ankle flexed; hop (6); (7) plié on the L, and dig the right heel into the floor. The arms move back low on the Hitch kick, reach forward middle on the hop, and pull in close to the body, elbows touching the waist like reining in a horse.

Repeat.

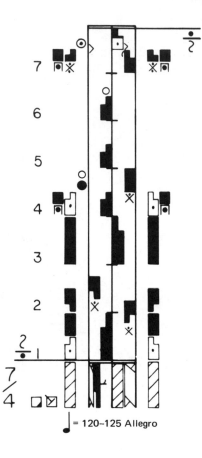

♩ = 120–125 Allegro

**264 Cowboy Phrase: Basic Step on the
Diagonal and Hitch Kick in 7/4 Time**

Combine Ex. 261 and Ex. 263. It's pure corn
but fun.

Note: To go into the Hitch kick, make
a 1/4 turn to the L so that on the downbeat
of Ex. 263 you are facing the line of direction.

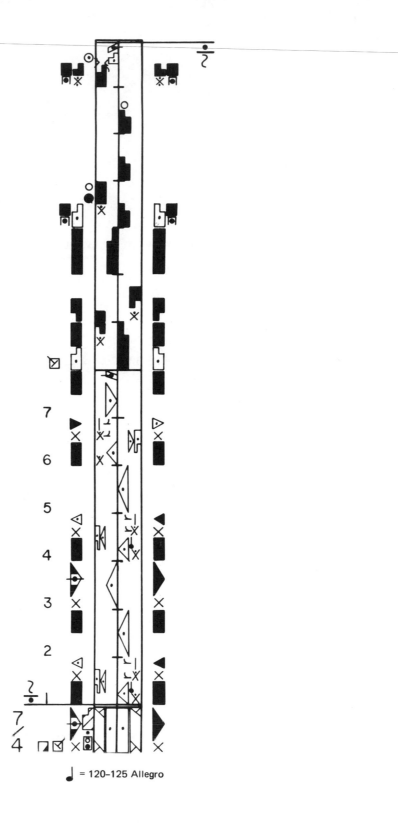

♩ = 120–125 Allegro

**Forward Successions with Body Rotations
and Arms: Beginners' Warm-up
(Ex. 265 and Ex. 266)**

These are Ex. 1, Chapter 1 with an added
rotation of the rib cage as in Ex. 165 and the
arms as in Ex. 266.

Ex. 265 Forward Succession with
Body Rotations: Beginners' Warm-up

Ex. 266 Forward Succession with
Body Rotations and Arms: Beginners'
Warm-up

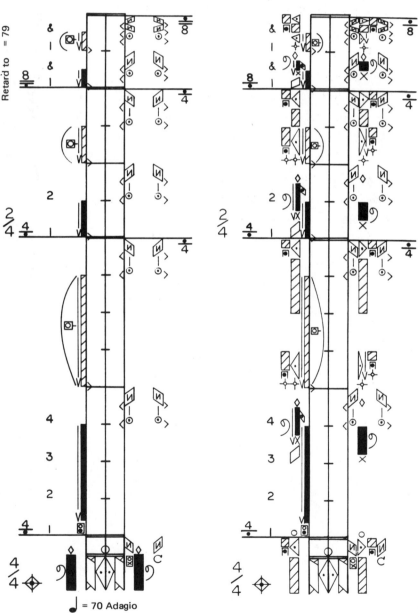

♩ = 70 Adagio

228

BODY BENDS SERIES:
ADVANCED WARM-UP

267 through 272   With Arm Swings and
                          Leg Action

Variations of Charles Weidman's Body Bends, Section A. The arms swing into their positions moving through place low and carrying the rib cage with them. Watch for the dynamic markings. The up swing is strongly accented, like a slash. The return is heavy and firm, like squeezing. With each variation something new is added:

Ex. 268 Var. I: Half plié in turned-out second position.

Ex. 269 Var. II: Half plié to relevé in turned-out second.

Ex. 270 Var. III: Half plié to relevé sliding to first.

Ex. 271 Var. IV: Half plié on two feet, shifting to one foot, leg straight with leg extensions.

Ex. 272 Var. V: Same as Ex. 271 but rising to relevé.

To finish the study, repeat Var. V once in each direction. End on both feet, legs straight, arms move to place low.

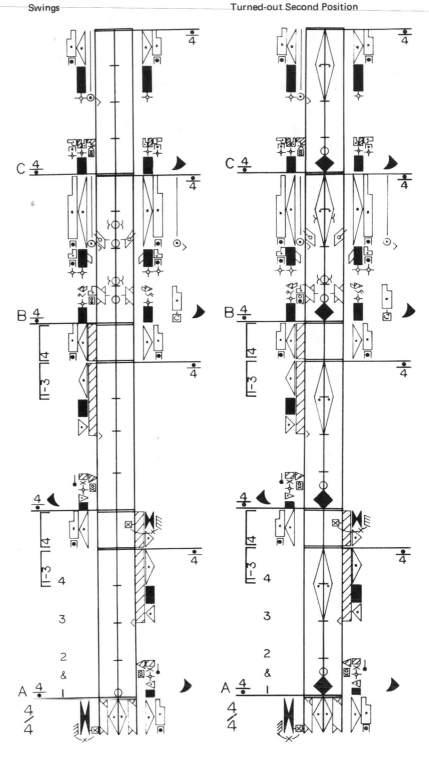

Ex. 269 Body Bends: Half Plié to Relevé in Turned-out Second Position

Ex. 270 Body Bends with Half Plié and Relevé Sliding to First Position

Ex. 271 Body Bends in Half Plié with Leg Extension

Ex. 272 Body Bends: Half Plié to Relevé with Leg Extension

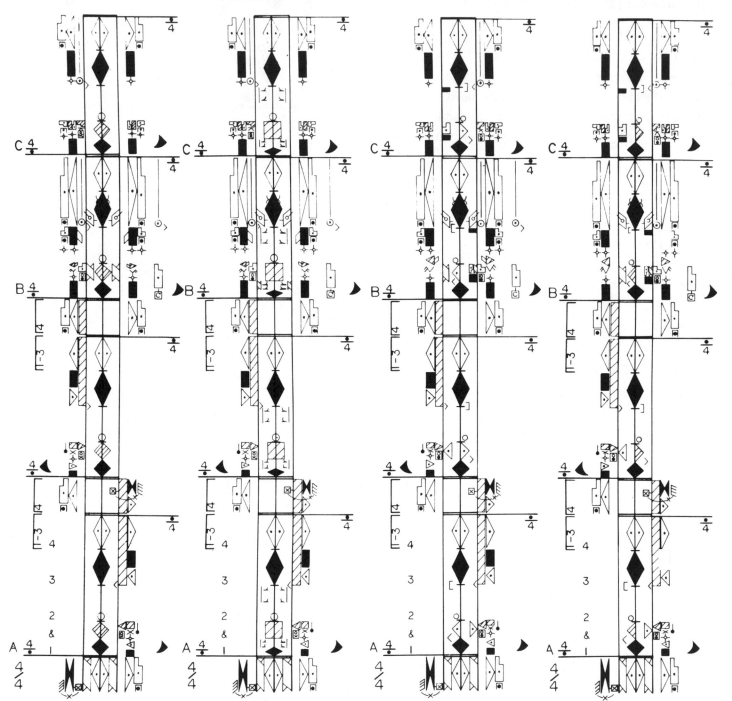

Back Arch—Standing: Advanced Warm-Up (Ex. 273 through Ex. 276)

Ex. 273: Hip shift forward (see Ex. 17, Chapter 2). Here the hips shift forward carrying the upper body back.

Ex. 274: As Ex. 273; arch back on count 2 and return to normal.

Ex. 275: Forward and back swings in 4/4 time.

Ex. 276: Forward and back swings in 3/4 time.

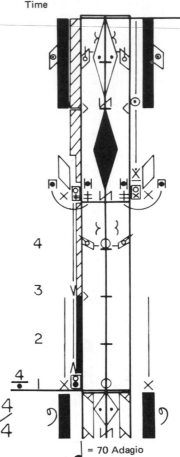

♩ = 70 Adagio

Ex. 273 Hip Shift Forward: Standing

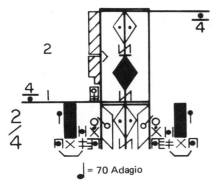

♩ = 70 Adagio

Ex. 276 Forward and Back Swings with Hip Shift in 3/4 Time

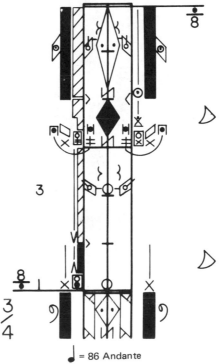

♩ = 86 Andante

Ex. 274 Hip Shift with Back Arch: Standing

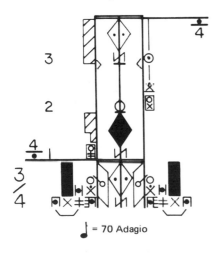

♩ = 70 Adagio

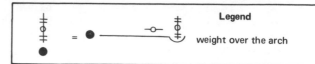
277 Pliés and Relevés

"The Eleven 4's": Advanced Sequence, Eleven measures of 4/4 time. This includes half pliés, relevés, and full pliés.

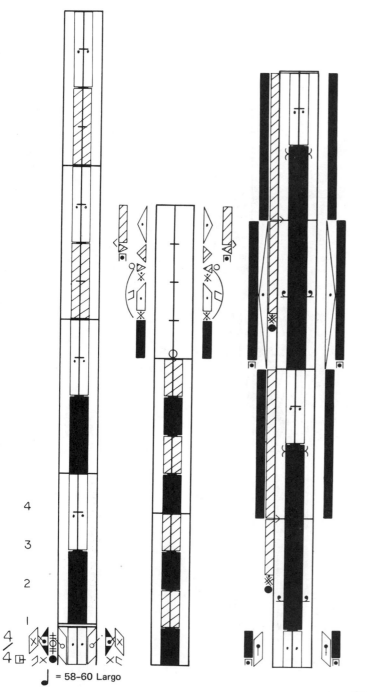

♩ = 58–60 Largo

Transitions for the Feet for Ex. 277 (Ex. 278 through Ex. 281).

Ex. 278: Turned-out first to second position.

Ex. 279: Second position to fourth position (right foot in front).

Ex. 280: Fourth position to fourth position (left foot in front).

Ex. 281: Fourth position to parallel first position.

Ex. 279 Transition: Second Position to Fourth Position

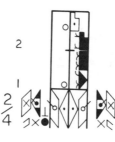

Ex. 281 Transition: Fourth Position to Parallel First Position

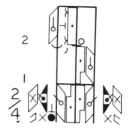

Ex. 278 Transition: Turned-out First to Second Position

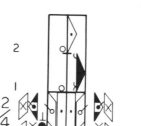

Ex. 280 Transition: Fourth Position to Fourth Position

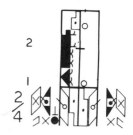

This includes many of the exercises of Chapter 1. The arrangement is, however, very formal and this is what makes it difficult.

For class work, divide the class into two groups. One group completes the whole sequence while the second group rests, and vice versa.

Repeat the whole sequence with two counts to each measure and again with one count for each. Attach the coda to the end of the fast sequence.

Ex. 282   Study for the Middle Body: "The Agony"

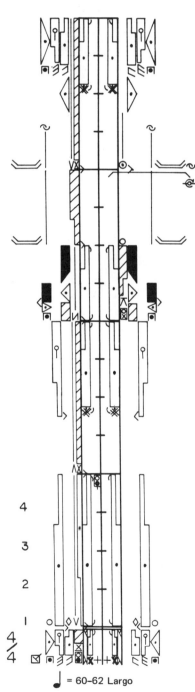

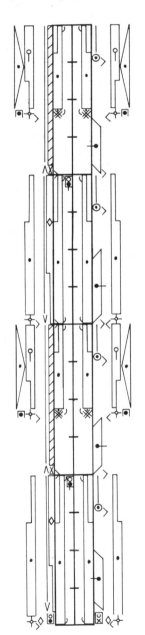

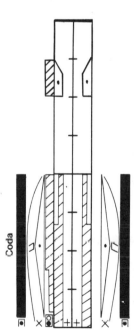

♩ = 60–62 Largo

233

283 Advanced Hamstring Stretch

Bound-flow action with a heavy reach of the body and arms over the legs.

Ex. 283 Advanced Hamstring Stretch

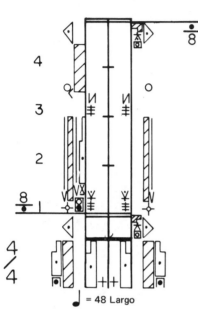

♩ = 48 Largo

284 Foot-and-Leg Stretch in Six: Sitting

Variation of Ex. 135, Chapter 2. This includes the outward rotation of the legs with an outward succession to rest the back.

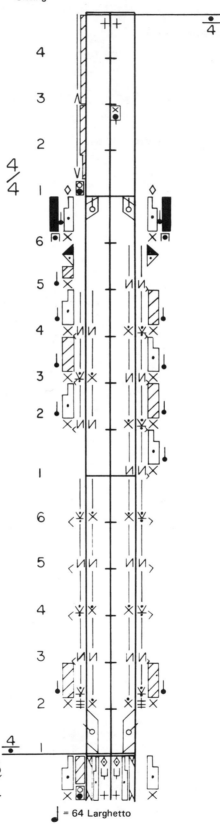

♩ = 64 Larghetto

234

285   Leg Stretch on Floor in 3/4 Time

An accumulation of all the leg stretches in Chapter 2, arranged in two very formal phrases of unequal length; section A, a seven measure phrase, section B, a five measure phrase.

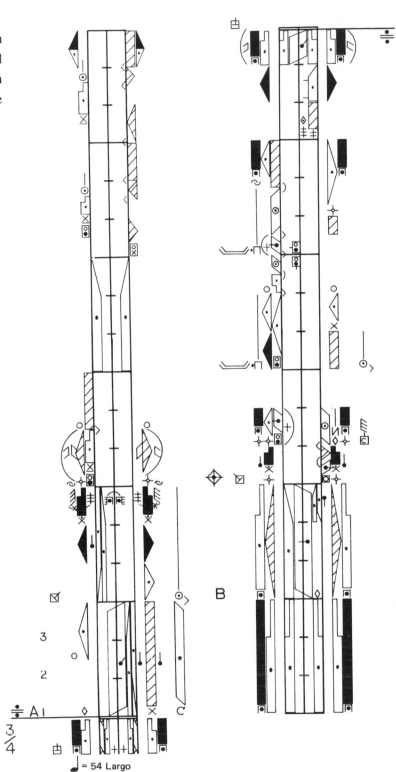

235

CLASSIC STUDY FOR FEET AND LEGS

Ex. 286 through Ex. 294

This study suggests the conventional way of using the feet and legs in Western European (American) theatrical dance.

   This is a long study for the feet and legs incorporating similar material to that used in the ballet barre sequences; pointing feet with and without weight, legs in air, elevation, etc. In such a long sequence, it is wise to use the two-group form for class work until their endurance is built up.

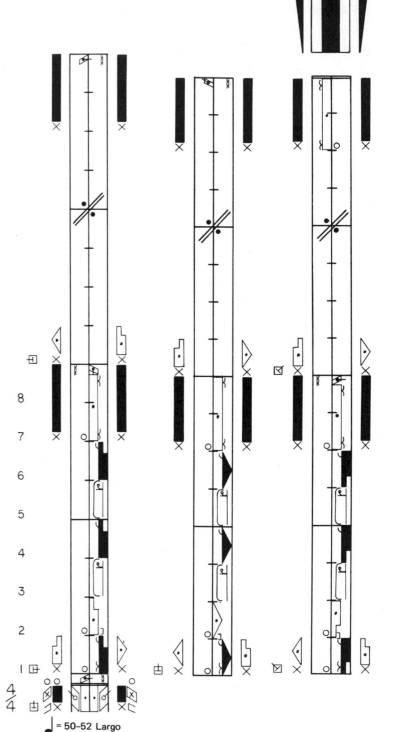

♩ = 50–52 Largo

236

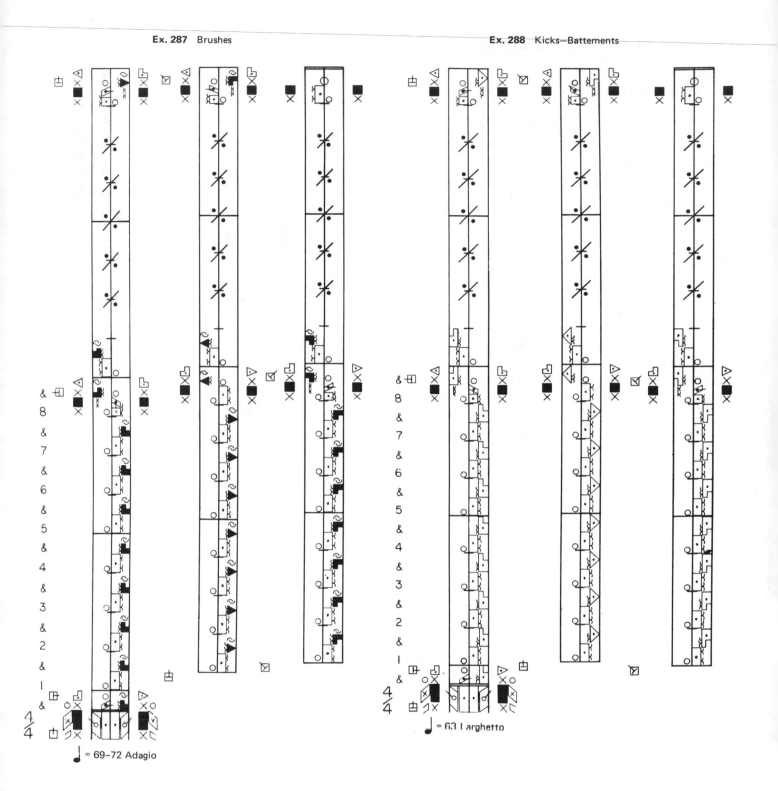

$\frac{4}{4}$ ♩ = 69–72 Adagio

$\frac{4}{4}$ ♩ = 63 Larghetto

Ex. 289 Leg Circles and Balance

Ex. 290 Leg Extensions

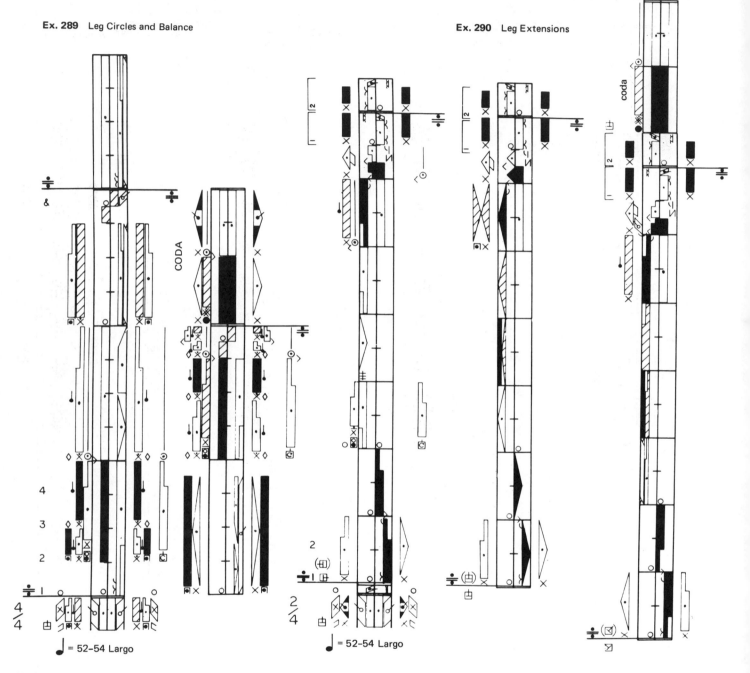

CODA

coda

4

3

2

$\frac{4}{4}$

♩ = 52–54 Largo

2

$\frac{2}{4}$

♩ = 52–54 Largo

Note: This sequence is also done with 2 counts for
each movement resulting in 2/4 time and 1 count for
each movement resulting in 3/4 time.

Ex. 291 Preparation for Jumps

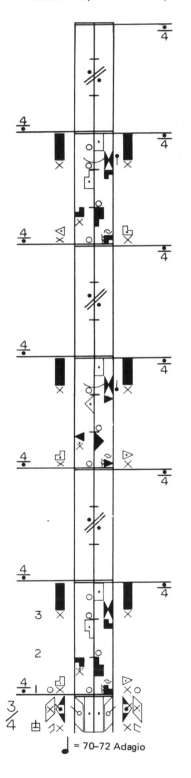

♩ = 70–72 Adagio

Ex. 292 Jumps in Turned-out
First Position

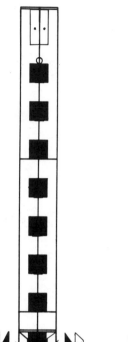

♩ = 72–74 Adagio

Ex. 293 Jumps with Straight
and Bent Legs Combined

♩ = 72–74 Adagio

Ex. 294 Jumps with Bent Legs

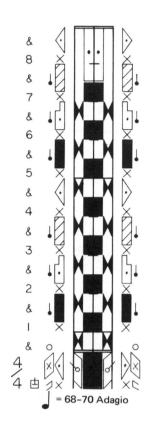

♩ = 68–70 Adagio

239

Jumps With Air Turns (Ex. 295 and Ex. 296)

This sequence includes jumping from second position and closing in first in the air with half turns and full turns.

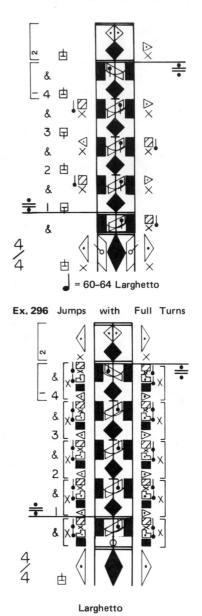

Ex. 295 Jumps   with   Half   Turns

♩ = 60–64 Larghetto

Ex. 296 Jumps   with   Full   Turns

Larghetto

297 Elbow Drop

(From Doris Humphrey's "With My Red Fires")
Much like Charles Weidman's back bends, but by increasing the knee bend and adding a rotation of the rib cage, the elbow can be placed on the floor back of the heels. This is not for beginners. *This should be taken very slowly at first, alternate sides.*

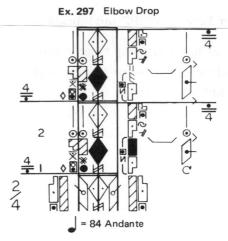

♩ = 84 Andante

298 Knee Fall from Standing

This is very much like the elbow drop, but with symmetrical action as the knees are placed on the floor. The recovery is a variation of the hip lift.

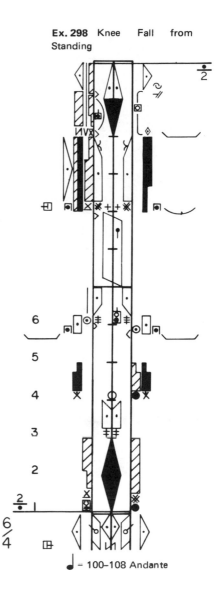

Ex. 298 Knee   Fall   from Standing

♩ = 100–108 Andante

(Ex. 299 and Ex. 300) Variations of Charles Weidman's Jumps

Jumps traveling, changing foot positions. For endurance for boys or the very advanced student.

Use the studio space from upstage to downstage and have the class work in lines of four or six, depending on the size of the class. To keep things orderly, the lines can split to left and right of center and feed in from both sides at the back.

Ex. 299 Variations of Charles Weidman's Jumps: Second Position Moving Forward

Ex. 300 Variations of Charles Weidman's Jumps: First Position Moving Forward

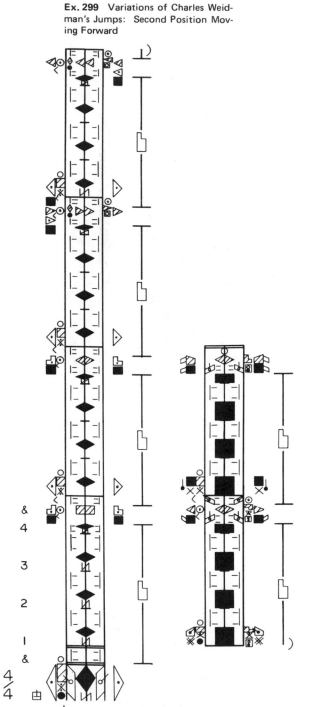

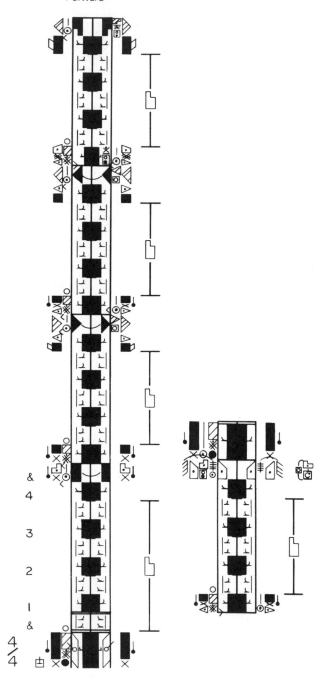

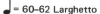= 60–62 Larghetto

The weight is held on the same leg most of the time. Therefore, this sequence is very demanding.

Because it moves so slowly, it is wise to have the class move straight across the studio in lines of three or four depending on the amount of space available. This does not alternate.

302 Back, Forward, and Side Extensions through Space

Similar to Ex. 301, but with a leg whip on Measure 4.

Ex. 302. Back, Forward, and Side Extensions through Space

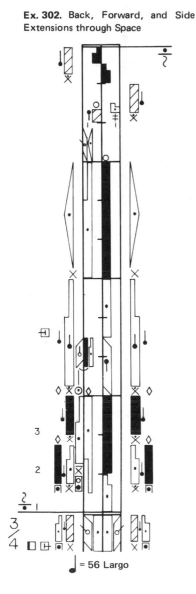

♩ = 56 Largo

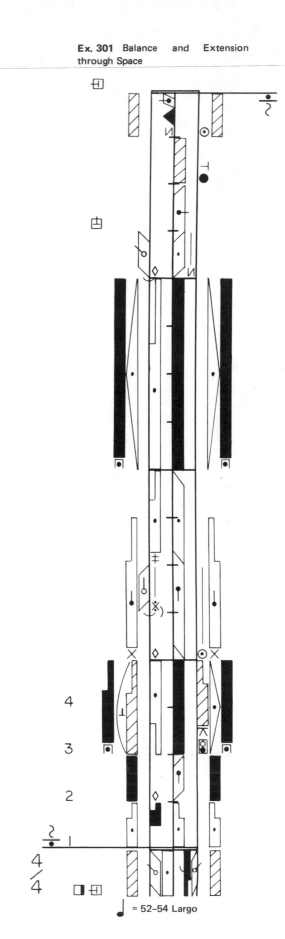

♩ = 52–54 Largo

Ex. 303. Spanish Step Forward.

Ex. 305 Spanish Step Forward with Arms

Ex. 306 Spanish Step Side with Arms

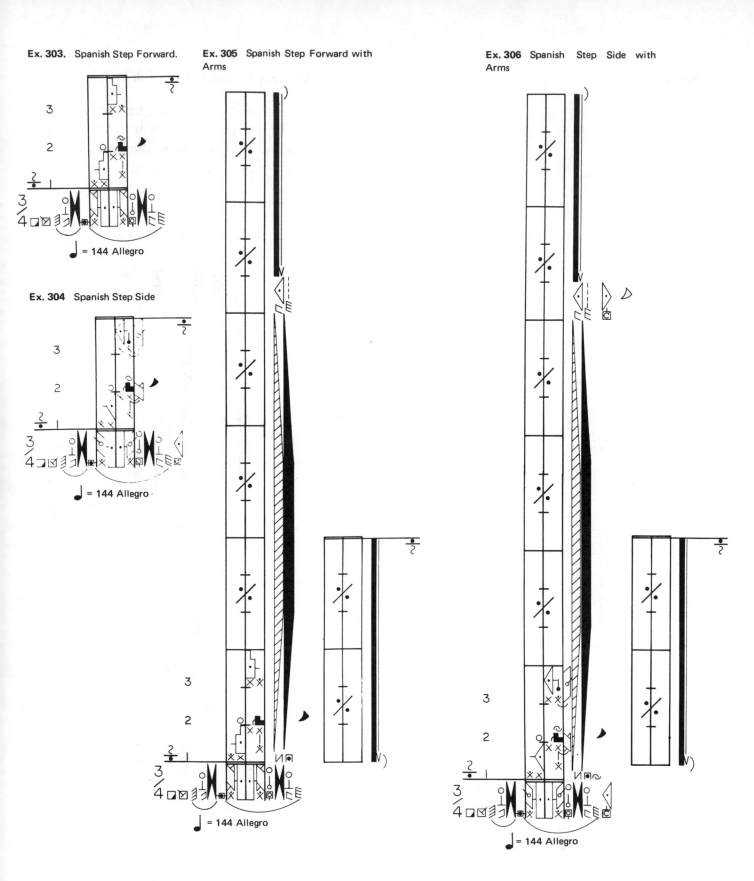

♩ = 144 Allegro

Ex. 304 Spanish Step Side

♩ = 144 Allegro

♩ = 144 Allegro

♩ = 144 Allegro

This phrase is a combination of Ex. 305 and Ex. 306 adding a run and a back arch with a turn.

Ex. 307 Spanish Phrase

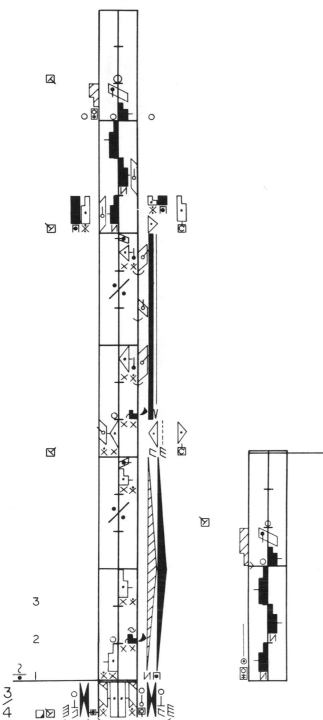

♩ = 142–144 Allegro

Variation of Ex. 212, Chapter 4.

By making an accent with the heel in Measure 1 and changing the dynamics and arm action, a Spanish flavor is suggested.

Ex. 308 3/4 Variation in Spanish Style

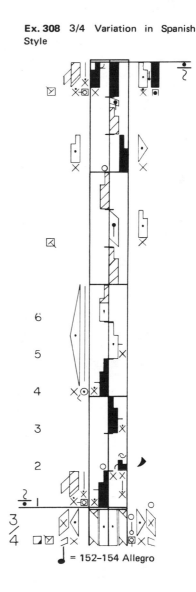

♩ = 152–154 Allegro

309 Pavane

The 16th century court dance was stately and severe in style. This sequence uses the style to suggest the precise pointing of the feet and the clean transfer of weight.

Ex. 309 Pavane

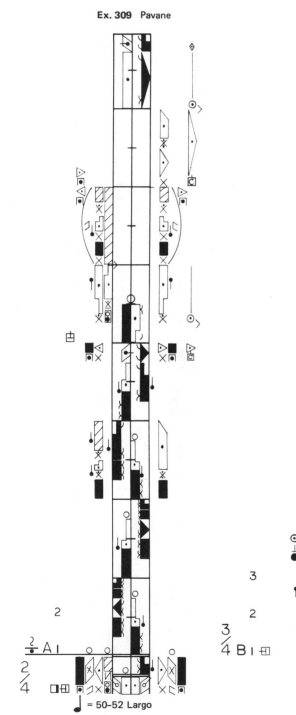

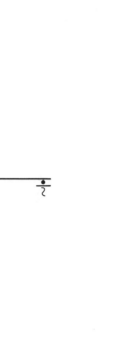

310 Tartar Phrase

Ex. 310 Tartar Phrase

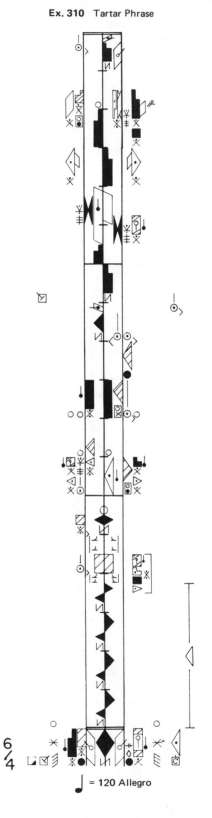

246

311 Jazz Step

Foot action from Ex. 88, Chapter 2 with a jump and a pivot turn.

312 Jazz Run with Air Tune

Long, low run with a "lay-out" tour jeté.

Ex. 312 Jazz Run with Air Tune

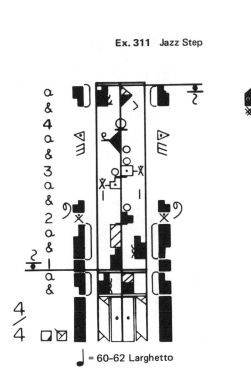

Ex. 311 Jazz Step

♩ = 60–62 Larghetto

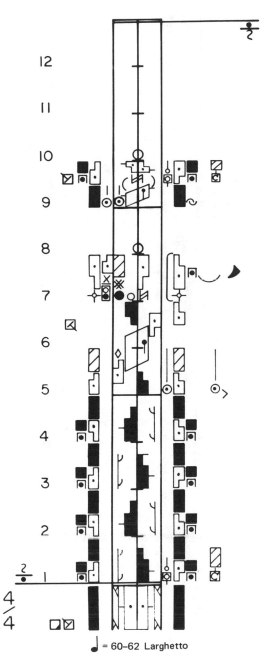

♩ = 60–62 Larghetto

313 Cowboy Phrase

This is Ex. 264 with a C Section added. This is a "bell" jump. The heels click together in the air. On the landing the free leg extends side, ankle flexed.

Ex. 313 Cowboy Phrase

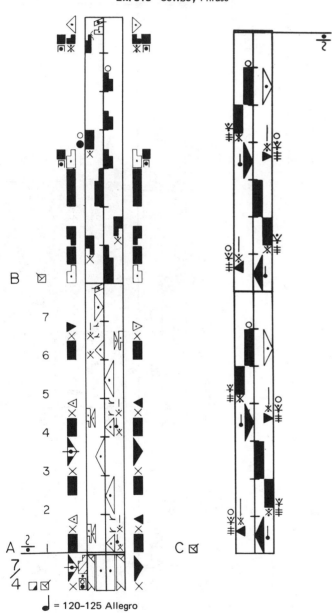

♩ = 120–125 Allegro

314 Forward Fall Preparation

Doris Humphrey's forward fall with the slide on the hands is too difficult for beginners. This exercise is designed to prepare the student to do that fall. In the meantime, this helps to develop strength in the arms and pectorals.

Ex. 314 Forward Fall Preparation

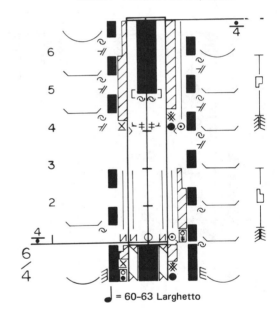

♩ = 60–63 Larghetto

315   Charles Weidman's Body Bends: Section A

This series of bends is the model for all the warm-up exercises in this book.   It is an absolute gem and deserves technical and choreographic study.   The author is deeply indebted to Charles Weidman for the technical and choreographic concepts involved in this sequence.   The simple device of count reduction has been an invaluable teaching tool over the years.   See Ex. 3, Ex. 4, and Ex. 17 Chapter 1, and Ex. 203, Ex. 204, and Ex. 205 Chapter 4.

Ex. 315   Charles Weidman's Body Bends: Section A

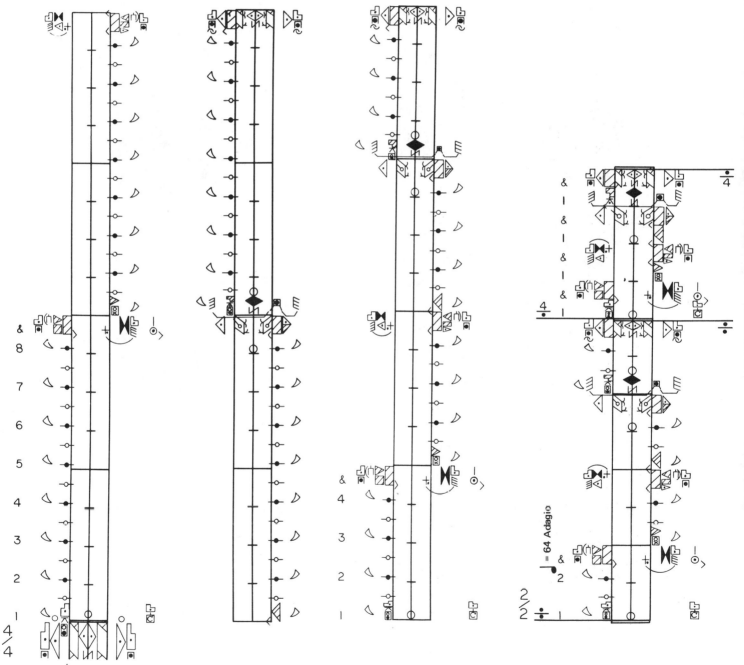

316 Back Fall and Recovery from Doris Humphrey's First Series of Falls

Ex. 316 Back Fall and Recovery from Doris Humphrey's First Series of Falls

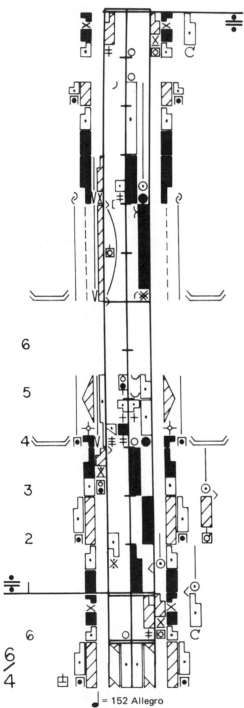

317 Side Fall and Recovery from Doris Humphrey's First Series of Falls

Ex. 317 Side Fall and Recovery from Doris Humphrey's First Series of Falls

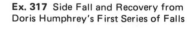
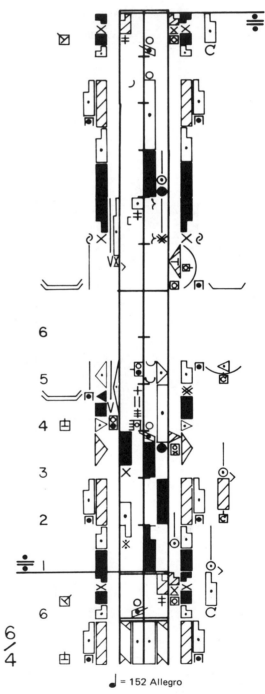

318 Doris Humphrey's Succession at the Barre

A beautiful example of a complete successional folding and unfolding of the body in the forward and backward directions.

This is also done with two counts and one count for each section. The one count becomes a whip. There is a fast drop and opening out to the back with a slight retard and suspension as the movement reaches the top of the curve preparing for the repeat.

This repeats on the other side.

319 Doris Humphrey's Succession Away from the Barre (from "Water Study")

Very similar to the succession at the barre. Notice that both arms move forward on the going down and back on the back arch. Because of this symmetry, there is no rotation of the rib cage.

This exercise is extremely difficult and demands tremendous strength in the legs, middle body, and buttocks.

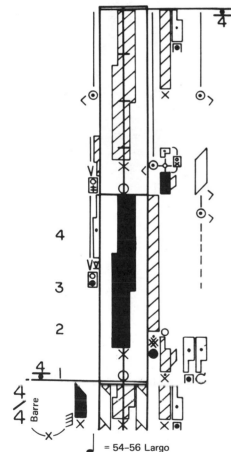

Ex. 318 Doris Humphrey's Succession at the Barre.

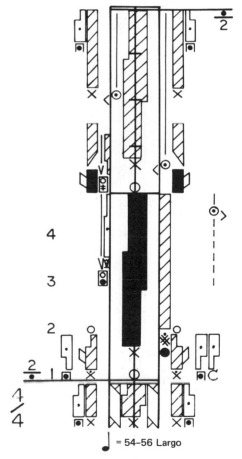

Ex. 319 Doris Humphrey's Succession away from the Barre.

320 Doris Humphrey's Succession on the Knees (from "Water Study")

Successional action starting from a folded position on the knees. The hands hold the heels throughout.

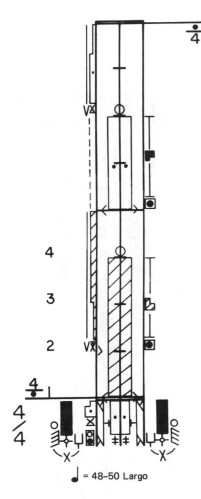

Ex. 320 Doris Humphrey's Succession on the Knees

321 Doris Humphrey's Side Succession

Application of the principle of succession into the sideward direction.

Ex. 321 Doris Humphrey's Side Succession

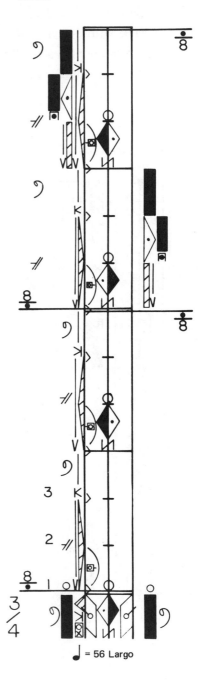

322   Charles Weidman's Knee Fall

Successional action from a sitting position suggesting Doris Humphrey's succession on the knees, or the Hip Lift of Chapter 1. Here the succession is continued into a forward fall ending face down on the floor.

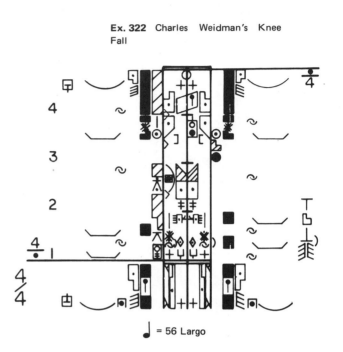

Ex. 322   Charles   Weidman's   Knee Fall

♩ = 56 Largo

253

part III
organizing material for class use

". . . we are in the long line," was a statement Doris Humphrey often used concerning her dance and that of Charles Weidman. This was Doris' way of describing the history of dance as well as the story of man as he has made his long journey through the ages.

Just as myths and legends have come down to us today, a few preserved in print but many yet passed on by the ancient methods, so also has the dance been brought through time. Just as the teller of stories embellished his tale, adding episodes here and omiting others there as he passed his narration on, so has the dancer of dances learned his craft, adding personal gesture and ornamentation as he commented upon his times, and then, once again, returning dance to the long line.

Just as the printing of a legend or myth captures forever that one particular version of man's mystical past, so will this book, with one particular version of the craft preserved in notation, more readily enable students of the dance to study, analyze, and interpret a part of man's non-verbal expression. And, with the craft securely learned and the body trained and aware, so then may new dancers of dances add their improvisations and embellishments to the art, and once again return dance to the long line.

Sharon Leigh Clark

chapter 6
organization of technique

Perhaps the most frustrating problem facing a beginning dance teacher is how to organize materials pertinent to his or her unique teaching situation efficiently. What to include in a specific dance course cannot be dictated by persons unfamiliar with that special situation. Such factors as age level, background of students, the institutional situation, and the amount of time and space available for instruction will all be considerations in determining what each teacher will include. However, some suggestions for the organization of technique classes may be helpful.

Aims and Objectives

A word about the purposes of aims and objectives is in order. General aims and objectives serve as the guidelines to help the teacher decide what to include in the dance course. They are of particular value in planning a long-range dance program for an entire school system involving Grades 1–12. If what has been taught in preceding class is known, it then becomes possible to base the content of the present dance course on the actual background and experiences of the students. In any case, the real purpose of any aim and objective is to provide a means to get from here to there and to make meaningful what happens in between.

General Technical Aims

General technical aims for students at the end of a first course in dance might be to understand tempo, to be able to move on the beat; to be able to learn a technique sequence quickly and to perform it with some degree of confidence; to be aware enough of body alignment and basic anatomical positions so as to avoid injury; to develop a spatial awareness of being in the right place at the right time; and to be sensitive to good body line and the design the body makes in space.

257

General Improvisational Aims

General improvisational aims for students at the end of a first course in dance might be to be able to transfer the principles learned in technique to another situation not bound by the specific exercise or learned pattern; to be able to understand that the elements of dance (time, space, effort, and content) are not isolated elements but that they are inherent in all technical and improvisational work; to be able to see the possibilities in any movement as a part of or the basis for improvisation; to be able to perform simple improvisation with style and confidence; to be able to develop small improvisational sketches.

What to Include in a Typical Dance Class

A typical dance class should include: (1) A general warm-up, including large body movements such as body swings and successions; (2) a more formal contrasting section emphasizing body alignment, and pliés and relevés; (3) exercises for the upper body, head, shoulders, and arms; (4) exercises for the middle body from lying, sitting, and kneeling positions on the floor; (5) work for the legs and feet that includes stretches, brushes, kicks, extensions, and balance; (6) ending the technique session with movement through space including walks, leaps, turns, and combinations; and (7) improvisations.

Specific Examples

The choice of technical exercises and the decision of how much time is spent on each section is the responsibility of the individual instructor. It is almost hopeless to attempt to design specific content when all the conditions of the teaching situation are not known. However, the following section contains four specific situations with suggestions for organizing and pacing different types of class. Too much rather than too little is undoubtedly included, but it is easier to leave out exercises than to bring in unrelated material on the spur of the moment.

The ending of any class is very important. Students should be able to leave with a feeling of both exhilaration and success. A slightly formal ending of class also gives a sense of security. This can be achieved by having students return to the center of the floor for a series of jumps in First and Second Positions; or the instructor may use a spirited combination on the diagonal such as the Brush Leaps with Jump (Ex. 226) or the Hop in 3/4 Time (Ex. 231) combination.

It is suggested, especially for beginners students, that a small assignment be made at the end of the class. This may take the form of improving an exercise from the technique or of perfecting a movement from the improvisation. For dance majors, learning the technique and the notation together, the instructor could assign specific exercises to work out. The object of an assignment is to give students something specific to work on between classes, and also something to do when they arrive in the studio for the next class. This adds both challenge and continuity to a dance unit.

The exercises offered here are arranged in a sequential pattern that will serve as a structure for the beginning instructor. The size of the class and the amount of individual help given to each student will of course affect the number of exercises covered. It is hoped that rather than deleting one entire section of technique, the instructor will drop one or two from the end of each grouping.

Ex. 1   Forward Succession from Standing
Ex. 2   Breakdown of Forward Succession from Standing
Ex. 3   Forward Body Tip with Straight Back and Body Drop and Lift
Ex. 4   Side Bend of Rib Cage and Head
Ex. 5   Side Bounce with One Arm
Ex. 6   Transition from Ex. 5 to Ex. 7
Ex. 7   Side Bend with Both Arms
Ex. 8   Coda for Ex. 7

Ex. 151   Head Tip Forward and Back
Ex. 152   Head Tilt Side
Ex. 153   Head Circles

Ex. 27   Body Bends from Sitting Position: Side
Ex. 28   Body Bends from Sitting Position: Forward
Ex. 29   Body Bends from Sitting Position: Side and Forward
Ex. 30   Body Bends from Sitting Position: Forward and Side
Ex. 26   Inward Succession from Lying Position

Ex. 52   Leg Rotations: Parallel First Position
Ex. 53   Leg Rotations: Turned-out First Position
Ex. 54   Half Plié: Turned-out First Position
Ex. 55   Relevé: Turned-out First Position
Ex. 63   Leg Swings Forward and Back
Ex. 64   Transition to the Other Side
Ex. 88   Exercises for the Feet with Weight Shift Forward
Ex. 89   Exercises for the Feet with Weight Shift Side

Ex. 179   Forward and Back Walk
Ex. 185   Forward Walk in Relevé
Ex. 186   Forward Walk in Half Plié
Ex. 187   Forward Walk: Half Plié and Relevé Combined in Four Counts
Ex. 193   Forward Walk with Figure Eight
Ex. 191   Forward Run
Ex. 194   Forward Run with Figure Eight

Ex. 101   Little Jumps in Parallel First Position
Ex. 102   Little Jumps in Turned-out First Position

The techniques offered here are designed to offer suggestions as to how variations can progress from techniques offered in the preceding sample lesson.

Ex. 1   Forward Succession from Standing
Ex. 3   Forward Body Tip with Straight Back and Body Drop and Lift
Ex. 12   Side Bends with Both Arms and Leg Action
Ex. 13   Body Circle with Leg Action
Ex. 14   Half Circle of Body with Leg Action
Ex. 15   Coda for Ex. 9 through Ex. 13
Ex. 16   Ex. 12 and Ex. 13 Combined
Ex. 19   Body Swings: Up and Down

Ex. 151 Head Tip Forward and Back
Ex. 152 Head Tilt Side
Ex. 153 Head Circles
Ex. 143 Both Shoulders Forward and Back
Ex. 144 Both Shoulders Forward and Back in Opposition
Ex. 146 Both Shoulders Circle Forward
Ex. 149 Both Shoulders Circle Back
Ex. 159 Arm Circle Front: Both Arms
Ex. 167 Arm Succession with Body Tilt
Ex. 172 Arm Circles with Body Action Forward

Ex. 30   Body Bends from Sitting Position: Forward and Side
Ex. 31   Body Bends from Sitting Position with Slide to Floor
Ex. 40   Hip Roll from Lying Position
Ex. 22   Pelvic Tilt to the Back from Sitting Position
Ex. 23   Body Curl from Lying Position
Ex. 37   Rib Cage Lift from Lying Position
Ex. 130 Ankle Stretch: Flexing and Pointing Feet
Ex. 135 Legs and Feet Flexing and Stretching
Ex. 111 Single Leg Stretch with Body Bounces
Ex. 113 Double Leg Stretch: Bouncing Both Knees
Ex. 121 Hamstring Stretch with Bounces
Ex. 124 Wide Leg Stretch with Body Bounces

Ex. 62   Plié and Relevé Combination
Ex. 63   Leg Swings Forward and Back
Ex. 65   Leg Swings Side
Ex. 76   Brushes and Kicks Forward
Ex. 77   Brushes and Kicks Side
Ex. 78   Brushes and Kicks Back
Ex. 94   Weight Shift Forward, Back, and Side Changing Feet
Ex. 100 "Slow Treading": Spring from Foot to Foot

Ex. 192 Forward Walk in Straight and Curved Paths
Ex. 200 Walks in Three Directions: Four-measure Phrase in Four Counts

One-hour Class for Beginning Students

Ex. 121   Hamstring Stretch with Bounces
Ex. 320   As Preparation for Transition to Standing Use Ex. 320—Doris Humphrey's Succession on the Knees (from "Water Study").

Ex. 52   Leg Rotations: Parallel First Position
Ex. 53   Leg Rotation: Turned-out First Position
Ex. 54   Half Plié: Turned-out First Position
Ex. 55   Relevé: Turned-out First Position
Ex. 67   Free Kicks Forward
Ex. 70   Free Kicks Side
Ex. 73   Free Kicks Back
Ex. 88   Exercises for the Feet with Weight Shift Forward
Ex. 90   Exercises for the Feet with Weight Shift Back
Ex. 92   Weight Shift Forward and Back Changing Feet
Ex. 97   Ankle and Toe Isolation
Ex. 98   Quick Push-off
Ex. 99   Preparation for Landings
Ex. 100   "Slow Treading": Spring from Foot to Foot

Ex. 176   Forward Walk Detail
Ex. 177   Back Walk Detail
Ex. 179   Forward and Back Walk
Ex. 190   Forward Walk: Half Plié and Relevé Combined in 3/4 Time
Ex. 222   Plié–Relevé Brushes Forward
Ex. 224   Brush Leaps Forward
Ex. 226   Brush Leaps with Jump
Ex. 228   Three-Count Leap Forward
Final Ex. Improvisation on Walk: How can you characterize a basic walk to change the style and shape?

One-and-half-hour Class for Advanced Beginners

Ex. 1   Forward Succession from Standing
Ex. 265   Forward Succession with Body Rotations: Beginners' Warm-up
Ex. 266   Forward Succession with Body Rotations and Arms
Ex. 3   Forward Body Tip with Straight Back and Body Drop and Lift
Ex. 5   Side Bounce with One Arm
Ex. 7   Side Bend with Both Arms
Ex. 12   Side Bends with Both Arms and Leg Action
Ex. 16   Ex. 12 and Ex. 13 Combined
Ex. 17   Back Succession from Standing
Ex. 267   Body Bends with Arm Swings

Ex. 151   Head Tip Forward and Back
Ex. 152   Head Tilt Side
Ex. 153   Head Circles
Ex. 154   Head Rotations
Ex. 139   Shoulder Lift and Drop
Ex. 140   Both Shoulders Lift and Drop

chapter 7
developing improvisation
from a technical exercise

In recent years, much emphasis has been placed on creativity as an important part of the educational process. Dance educators have often been criticized as forsaking technique and surrendering to creativity in the form of unstructured improvisation. On the other hand, professional dancers have frequently been accused of stringing a series of technical movements together to form a dance. Combining aspects of these two critical extremes—sound technique and guided improvisation—is one of the purposes of this book.

A great deal of the joy and excitement that improvisation provides, lies in creating something artistically satisfying and choreographically sound. Therefore, good improvisation must be as carefully planned and paced as technique. The problems in learning to do this well are twofold. Many beginning teachers do not know where and how to begin, and most beginning students when faced with a demand to create feel uncomfortable and insecure. The purpose of this chapter is to illustrate the use of technical material as a basis for improvisation. This allows the student to organize familiar material from a new point of view using sound choreographic devices; and it prepares beginners to develop their own patterns of movement in a well-organized manner. For the teacher, it suggests a method of structuring small studies, each emphasizing one or more of the elements of dance, and each relating to the one preceding it. This can culminate in a class presentation of a series of improvisational sketches that may later be developed for formal performance.

Use of Artistic Devices

The elements of dance—time, space, effort, and content—are artistic devices that can be used to change and vary dance movements. Without variety, dance is vulnerable, for it can

265

quickly lose vitality and become stale, both for the participant and for the audience. The controlled manipulation of variations is a basic way to provide excitement. This brings a sense of satisfaction to the performer as well as to the audience.

One of the most basic artistic devices available to a dancer is theme and variation, $A \, A^1 \, A^2 \, A^3$. The theme, A, is a simple statement, a movement or series of movements that are related. The variations, A^1, A^2, etc., modify and change the appearance and design of the original statement. Dancers use the elements of time, space, effort, and content as material for variations. Here are some examples of variations:

Space   Change of direction
         Change of front
         Contrasting levels
         Changing floor patterns
         Use of focus
         Change of dimension
         Varying shape or contour

Time   Variation in tempo
         Adding or changing accents
         Varying rhythmic patterns (even and uneven)

Effort   Varying flow (bound and free)
         Dynamic changes
         Use of movement quality (sustained, vibratory, swinging, percussive)

Content Use of various styles
         Thematic material
         Sequential patterns

There are other variations not mentioned above. It is wise to remember that the use of variations appropriate to the choice of theme is often a matter of much trial and error. It is also wise to note that multiplication of variations for their own sake does not necessarily result in good dance design. Developing exciting improvisation usually means trying many variations and discarding inappropriate ones while keeping those that seem to relate to the theme.

With that in mind, the following section suggests several ways in which a simple phrase from the technique may be varied. Although these variations have been informally designed to follow in sequence, not all may be appropriate for every situation. It is up to the instructor to help students select those variations most relevant to the particular improvisation or to suggest others not specifically referred to in this section.

Class Organization

For clear understanding of the space or area of dance, students should note the following locations:

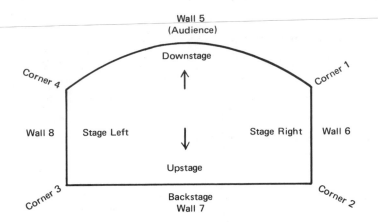

This method of organizing space gives everyone the same points of reference for starting positions; and as students move through space, they can be more secure in their directional paths.

For presentation of new material, or even for familiar material presented in a new way, start with the entire class working together facing front, Wall 5. Each person should have space to move freely in all directions. If this is the beginning of improvisation, every student will have to learn an awareness of his own working area. This kind of spatial orientation is necessary from an aesthetic point of view in order for students to relate well to his or her performing space. It is also very necessary for practical purposes as well. One has to learn to avoid running into other people! Teachers with especially large classes will find this virtually the only method possible. It keeps each student in his or her place, allows everyone a spot in which to work, and provides opportunity for clear presentation of material.

Selection of Theme

Any technique in Chapter 1 through Chapter 5 may be a point of departure; that is to say, a theme for improvisation. For this discussion, a simple walking combination will be the basic theme used for developing improvisation. The technical example, Ex. 239, Chapter 4, stresses change of direction and change of front. In the variations that are used, students should be reminded that what often distinguishes a dancer from one who merely dances is the clear understanding and use of these two choreographic tools.

Basic Improvisational Theme (Eight Measures—32 Counts)

This theme is taken from Ex. 239, Chapter 4. However, for improvisational work, it has been slightly changed from the original technical pattern. Watch for a change of facing pin in Measure 2. Also, note that it repeats, but because of the change in Measure 2, the floor path becomes a square rather than continuing across the diagonal as presented in Chapter 4.

267

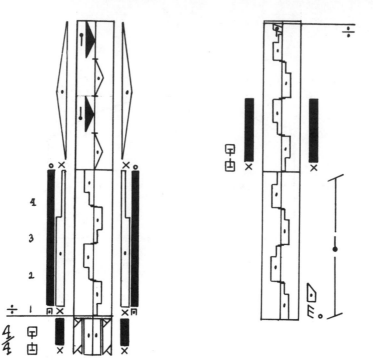

Arm Gestures and Points of Focus

Beginners often dance with their heads down, their eyes fixed firmly on the floor. One of the technical devices for lifting the head is the use of specific eye focal points. This gives dancers practice in the use of the eye as an important part of performance.

Learning to use the arms in coordination with other moving body parts is also often frustrating for beginners. Start as early as possible to design movements for the arms. In this embellishment of the theme, both the arms and the eyes are added to the original movement through space.

Students like to be challenged. Because one of the major premises of this book is the learning and immediate application of notated technique, the instructor may suggest to students that they choose arm gestures from Chapter 3. In Ex. 239, the technical presentation of the basic theme, students will find the notated arm gestures for the original exercise. They may, of course, use these. However, they may be adventurous and try others. When they work out the arm gestures, ask them to direct the eyes to follow the arm and hand, or both if it is possible, as the gestures move through space. This lifts the head and adds to the importance of the movement.

Selection of Variations

Simple Variations in Space

Change of starting foot. As students move across the diagonal, they learn to start the exercises with the upstage leg. This means that they must alternate feet. Learning to move equally well with either foot is necessary in dance and can often be surprisingly difficult at first.

Have students perform the complete theme, including their arm gestures and eye focus, starting with the other foot, in this case, the left foot. However, the directions and the facing pins remain the same. Watch for technical changes. In Measure 2, for instance, the first step will be across rather than open. Although the basic pattern is the same, this pattern looks and feels distinctly different.

Change of front. A change of front occurs within the basic pattern in Measures 3, 4, 7, and 8. To increase awareness of where they are in space, have students perform the phrase starting with the right foot, but facing the corners rather than the walls. On a proscenium stage, this change of front increases the feeling of depth or third dimension of the moving figure, rather than the two-dimensional or flat feeling that occurs when a dancer constantly turns his face or back to the audience. Repeat this variation with a change of starting foot.

Simple Variations in Time

Increasing body tempo. The underlying tempo of the theme is MM 70 (adagio). Without changing the underlying tempo of the accompaniment, have students take two steps for each count. To challenge the students and to help them acquire an understanding of what they are experiencing, have students count the basic underlying beat while they are doubling the tempo of their body movements.

This variation provides a change of pace for students. The first results may be a bit frantic and directional lines tend to completely dissolve. However, practice, coupled with stressing of clear directions of the body, will soon help to clear up the fuzziness of the movements.

The instructor might point out that other changes are taking place as well. One of the results of this variation is a decrease in the size of the movements. As the body tempo increases, the range or dimension of movements is diminished. A dynamic change will also be noticed. To perform quick movements with precision and clarity seems to require more effort than when doing slower ones. Both these change factors affect movement and give it different character.

Decreasing body tempo. This variation uses two counts for each step while the tempo MM 70 (adagio) remains the same as in the basic theme. Performance of this variation is much slower and consequently it requires a more controlled release of the energy. Students should count this aloud at first, two counts for each movement. Stress sustained movement and have students concentrate on the firm muscle control, balance, and secure body alignment that are required of them in this variation.

For either of the above variations, it is possible to increase or decrease the musical tempo to MM 170 (presto) or MM 60 (largo). Students will only have to follow the underlying beat in this case. Add arm gestures and eye focus on both variations just as soon as students acquire a basic confidence in the performance of the exercise.

For the beginning dance student full and complete projection of movement is often difficult. This is due in part to technical limitations and in part to inexperience and inhibitions. Dance gestures must be more clear, precise, accurate, and exaggerated than ordinary movements. Adopting a specific style of performing is an interesting way to experiment with projection of movement and to learn how movements become effective.

The following sections have been designed as a unit. Each section relates to each other section. The unit culminates in a combination of the sections and may be expanded for class presentation or more formal presentation.

Many styles of movement may be used. The five suggested here are ones that students have responded to with enthusiasm. They are Tribal, Baroque, Martial, Roaring Twenties, and Electronic. These five also provide a small but important contact with the history of dance.

Tribal style. The tribal type of society is a stage of development through which most cultures have passed. Although each tribal culture or even each village within the larger culture may develop unique ways of moving, most tribal dances have common movement characteristics. Generally, the distinguishing features of tribal dance are the use of the full bare foot flat on the ground, the knees bent in plié, and rhythmic contractions of either the pelvis or the rib cage and shoulders, or both. The primary feeling conveyed is of a closeness with the earth.

The accompaniment used may be a drum, clapping or chanting, or a combination of these.

Baroque style. During the European Baroque period, roughly from 1500 to 1750, ladies wore extremely heavy dresses and gentlemen wore tight breeches, waist coats, and knee stockings; and both wore high heels. In such restricting costumes, dances were usually slow, elegant, and stately. Patterns of movement were very formal, reflecting the formal social structure of the time. The dances used many sustained movements, although the mood of the dancers was frequently gay and coquettish. In dance history, this period is called Pre-Classic. The Allemande, the Pavane, the Sarabande, the Courante, the Gigue—and later—the Minuet were some of the important dances.

For improvisation in this style, try using the music of Bach, Couperin, Scarlatti, or Vivaldi, or a slow drumbeat, MM 60 (lento).

Martial Style. A marching type of society, like the tribal type of society, seems also to be a stage in the cultural development of peoples, at least in Western societies. In the historical context, marching appears to be associated with war/patriotism. In the theater or recreational sense, as is stressed in this improvisational sketch, examples such as drum majorettes, bands, or drill teams may be suggested.

Marches are clipped and precise with much emphasis on the use of the legs, arms, and feet. The feet are almost always picked up and returned to the ground in a strong manner. Marches are usually brisk, with accents that are strong, very evenly spaced and easily anticipated.

Accompaniment may be a drumbeat MM 104 (andante) or a march record.

Roaring Twenties style. The decade between the end of World War I and the Great Depression is remembered as the Roaring Twenties. The life style of the stereotypical "Flapper" epitomized the flaunting freedom of the era. Clothing designs allowed great freedom of movement. Music was loud, syncopated, and exciting—the early days of Jazz.

Dances involved the whole body in wild swinging movements, emphasizing a complete body response to the rhythms of the "new" music. Even today, the Charleston, a favorite dance of its time, retains it popularity.

Accompaniment for this improvisation may be a drumbeat MM 112 (moderato) with syncopation, if possible, or a typical Dixieland recording.

Electronic style. The electronic age surrounds people with gadgets and computers, push buttons and planned obsolescence. The frantic pace of advanced technocracy has man, the creature, in conflict and competition with man, the machine maker. Electric amplification of musical instruments, the invention and production of the Moog and other sophisticated devices for recording and producing sounds have led to an entire spectrum of new sounds in music, reflecting the advances of the times.

Expanding borders of man's space limitations beyond the demands of earth's gravity and the establishing of new dimensions in time—such as immediate, simultaneous, and global television viewing of an event—have created whole new dimensions for human beings. In dance, a kind of awareness of total body parts and a subsequent reaction to the mechanical quality of life are reflected in the movements. Rhythm is less predictable, more random. This allows the dancer enormous freedom, but it also makes enormous demands. It means that dancers must *know* where they are in space and time without the help of a strong underlying beat.

Accompaniment for this may be a drumbeat, random sounds, a wide collection of percussive instruments (homemade or otherwise), or electronic recordings—such as those of Nikolais, Subotnick, Stockhausen, or others.

Problems in Structuring an Improvisation

Organization of the Class

Divide the class into five groups. Assign one of the five specific styles of movement to each group. It is possible, if the class is small enough, for students to choose the style with which they wish to work. However, for large numbers of students, this is somewhat impractical.

Divide the working space into five parts. Each style of movement will have a separate area in which all students of the same style will be working together.

Problem One: Phrase A (Eight Measures—32 Counts)

The original theme, Ex. 239, is still used for this complete section. Have each student adapt the style of performance he or she is working with to this original theme. At the beginning of this problem, each student is working alone, but within the assigned area.

As soon as each individual has practiced the phrase enough to be familiar with it, ask all the students working on the same style to develop the basic theme as a group pattern.

This assignment necessitates cooperation and involvement among group members, a not inconsiderable task. Learning what other people are doing, learning where each is in space, deciding how they should relate to each other, weaving together the different movement patterns of each one, relating them to a general floor plan, and finally, determining how they would like their work to appear to an audience are all very important parts of learning to compose a dance.

Because group endeavor is difficult, the instructor should be prepared to help with the organization and to make suggestions. If groups are really groping for an idea, at first suggest the use of geometric space patterns such as the square, the circle, or the triangle. One new element such as this may serve as an impetus to get students started, and they often come up with even more exciting ideas.

Other suggestions for group work might be unison movement, duet/trio (depending on the number in each group), solo with ground bass, combinations of these, or others.

After a short practice time, have each group perform its material while the other groups act as audience. Working with a new idea for such a short time will not produce stunning dances. Performance of this small section at this time will prepare students to perform later. It also gives students a basis for comparing different styles of presentation, all of which have basically the same floor pattern and fundamental movements. And last, but by no means least, it gives groups who have not had much success with the assignment some ideas for their own works. Follow the performances of Phrase A with a short session of comments and constructive criticism, and then let the groups return to their areas to polish their sketches.

Problem Two: Phrase A^1 (Eight Measures—32 Counts)

Use the same style of movement called for in Phrase A, but ask students to compose a second phrase of the same length, Phrase A^1. This phrase will be structurally contrasting and the material for varying it may be chosen from any of the exercises in Chapter 1 through Chapter 4. Encourage any appropriate use of the artistic devices of choreography such as change of level, tempo, direction, floor pattern, dynamics, etc.

As soon as the groups have worked out a satisfactory pattern for Phrase A^1, have them combine Phrases A and A^1 so that the main phrase is followed by the variation. The transition from one phrase to the next will not be given any extra counts so that the major problem in combining the two phrases lies in readjusting the ending of A to be in position to begin A^1 or readjusting the beginning of A^1.

The students may perform this section if the instructor and the groups wish. However, it may be more satisfying if they go on to problem three before performing.

Problem Three: Phrases A, A^1, A (24 Measures)

The third section of the study merely means returning to the first phrase, A, to complete the series. The transition between A^1 and A will be the only part that needs work. After the students practice, have each group perform their complete study as a unit for critical suggestions.

This manner of structuring improvisation, sometimes called sequential form, may be continued (i.e., A, A^1, A, A^2, A) or students may go on to problem four.

Problem Four: Phrase B (Choice of Length)

Using the same methods assigned in Phrase A^1, and keeping the same style, ask students to now add another section that relates to the theme but has marked contrasts. The dynamics may be changed, the group pattern varied, the level and focus may be inverted or reversed, or changes may be introduced by adding new movements.

When students have completed this assignment, ask them to combine the theme, A, with A^1 and phrase B. Since they have the choice of duration of the phrase in B, suggest that it be last.

Transitions

Performing suggestions. Beginning dancers often have a tendency to project their movements fairly well during the actual performance of the phrases. Then the feeling of the dance style is dropped when they change to another phrase. As the students prepare to complete their sketches, ask them to pay special attention to the transitions. Between A^1 and B, because they have freedom in the count, a transition requiring additional counts may be added.

Beginnings and Endings

For the final assignment in this study, have students add a beginning and an ending. This may take the form of stage positions, entrances, or exits, or possibly even a coda. This addition of beginnings and endings places a patina of professionalism on a related series of movements and adds to the satisfaction of having completed a work.

Presentations

Costumes. For final presentations to the class, a feeling of performance can be established by having students supply bits of costume. These do not need to be elaborate. Students seem to be able to do wonders with crepe paper, tinfoil, paper sacks, bits of cloth, adhesive tape, string, glue, and scissors.

Non-performing students. The instructor will be wise to remember that not every student likes to, or needs to perform. Most reluctant students eventually enjoy the experience, especially if the situation is congenial and non-threatening. However, forcing a shy, inhibited youngster into a performing situation may alienate him from dance. If a student really reacts strongly against performing, assignment of such roles as costumes-collector, accompanist, technical director, or engineer—running the recording device—may allow him to feel a part of the production without the accompanying fears.

Stage fright. Stage fright, in one form or another, is common with most people. Beginning dancers, especially when performing for their peer groups, are often affected by this. Usually a dress rehearsal or even the opportunity to perform twice helps most beginners over the nervousness preceding a showing.

Learning to be an audience. To complete the performance experience, encourage constructive criticism by class members. This is an excellent teaching technique. Draw out valid criticism. "I liked it" or "I thought it was awful" are not helpful to either critic or performer. Students should be able to say *why* a particular movement or group of movements succeeded or failed. Before the performance, prime the students to ask such questions as: were the directional lines clear? Have the dancers fulfilled their ideas? Were the variations both in keeping with the style and exciting to watch? Were the transitions smooth and a part of the dance? Was there unity of style? Were the variations recognizable? Was there contrast? Were they really variations of the given material? What could you suggest to improve the presentation?

On the basis of good criticisms, it is possible for the students to rework their dances and to improve them. If the students' response to their performances is general approval or satisfaction, they may move on to the next improvisation.

Summary

The preceding development of a simple technical exercise into five improvisational sketches and presentations illustrates that devising improvisations need not be terribly involved, difficult, or traumatic. It is just a matter of organizing and structuring so that the methods are workable and the results meaningful. Almost any exercise from the technical material, or for that matter, any movements may be used as a point of departure for an improvisation.

The particular studies in Chapter 4 and Chapter 5, the Sarabande, Tarter Phrase, Cowboy, Highland, Israeli, or Pavane already have the basic style and floor pattern inherent in the space pattern. Reworking these into a sequential form for presentation or self-satisfaction is very easy.

Any sketches developed (with much practice by the dancers) make very handy offerings for such events as Sports Nights, Parents' Nights and all programs dear to the hearts of parents, principals, and PTAs.

appendix—definitions

Accent   The beat or beats with greater stress than the surrounding beats. For example, in 6/8 time there may be one strong and one weak accent 1–2–3–4̄–5–6–, or one strong and two weak accents, 1̂–2–3̄–4–5̄–6–.

Ad lib.   Musical term to indicate performance as the performer wishes.

Beat   Pulse; counts of music or dance.

Bound flow   Action or movement that is controlled for its entire duration; pulling or pressing, for example.

Center of weight   The center of the body mass; located in the area of the pelvis.

Change of front   Change of facing of the body.

Choreography   The art of making dances. Dance composition.

Coda   A passage added to a composition for the purpose of bringing it to a complete close.

Content   The meaning of a dance as opposed to the structure or specific movement.

Cut   In Ballet a "coupé". One foot replaces the other as a support very quickly.

Diagonal   Direction between forward and side; diagonal line of a studio or dance area—from one corner to the opposite corner obliquely across from it; often used during a dance class for movement through space.

Dimension   Size or range of movement or gesture.

Direction   In dance the directions are forward, back, side, diagonal, circular.

Downbeat The first beat of a measure; usually the most heavily accented.

Duration Element of time: statement of relative length; how long a movement or sound lasts.

Dynamics The amount of strength or force given to a movement.

Effort The amount of energy given to a movement.

Elevation When the whole body is in the air; as in jumps, leaps, etc.

First position of the feet—Turned-out A closed position of the legs rotated outward at the hips; feet under the center of weight, heels touching, toes and knees pointed sideward; the weight evenly balanced on both feet.

First position of the feet—Parallel A closed position of the legs; feet side by side and parallel under the hip bones; toes and knees face forward; weight evenly balanced on both feet.

Floor pattern The design or path made by the dancer while performing steps across and around the stage or dance area.

Focus Center of activity or attention. **Spotting** is a highly stylized form of focus.

Form Overall shape or structure of a dance which gives it identity.

Free flow The movement is initiated and then allowed its freedom; the opposite of bound flow. Example: swings.

Full plié (grand plié) Bending the knees until the heels are lifted off the floor and the hips lowered until they are level with the knees; when in second position, the heels stay on the floor.

Gesture *Technical:* In notation the term means the movement of a limb which does not carry weight. *Artistic:* Any movement made by the human being such as social gestures of greeting or farewell, or emotional gestures of grief, joy or confusion, and work movements of all kinds.

Half plié (demi-plié) Bending the knees but keeping the soles of the feet on the floor.

Half toe The ball of the foot and the toes.

Hyper-extension When a joint is pushed or extended beyond the anatomically correct position, such as sway-back, saber-legs, and sway-back knees.

Inversion   Turned upside down; starting at the end of a phrase and moving to the beginning.

Inward Succession   Movement originating in the extremities and flowing in to the center of the body; folding the body parts in orderly sequence.

Level   Usually refers to up and down—the vertical aspect of space.

Measure   In music notation, notes are grouped into measures which are separated by bar lines.

Meter   The basic pattern of accented notes or beats in a piece of music usually indicated by a time signature.

Middle body   Lumber area in the back and the abdominal area in the front.

Moog   An electronic synthesizer.

Movement   Activity of the total body or parts of the body, in time and in space, which produces visual results.

Note   Musical notation of a beat; note values to show durations are

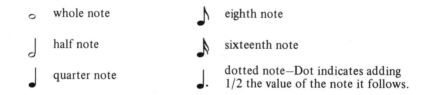

Opposition   One part of the body moving against another part in direction or level; e.g., in walking, the right leg moves *forward* as the right arm moves *back* in opposition.

Outward Succession   Movement originating in the center of the body and flowing outward to the extremities; unfolding the body parts in orderly sequence.

Parallel   Any action where different parts of the body go in the same direction at the same time.

Pavane   A slow stately dance that originated in Spain in the sixteenth century.

Pelvis   Hip area of the body defined by the hip bones; area of the sacrum.

Percussive quality   A sharp, broken energy pattern. Percussive movement has no follow-through.

278

Phrase A sequence of movement or music expressing a single thought; a movement sentence.

Plié Bend the knees; from the French meaning to bend, to fold up.

Plumb-line (gravity line) Imaginary line running through the body from the head to the feet and around which the parts of the body are balanced.

Proscenium stage A traditional stage, usually enclosed on three sides with the audience placed opposite the fourth and open side.

Relevé Rising onto the balls of the feet with the knees straight; rising onto half toe.

Rest Musical notation used to indicate duration of a pause, as follows:

$\quad$ — $\quad$ whole rest

$\quad$ — $\quad$ half rest

$\quad$ 𝄽 $\quad$ quarter rest

$\quad$ 𝄾 $\quad$ eighth rest

$\quad$ 𝄿 $\quad$ sixteenth rest

Rhythm Pattern of strong and weak accents recurring more or less regularly. These patterns can be termed even or uneven depending on whether the accents fall far apart and occur at regular intervals or close together and occur at irregular intervals.

Rib cage The chest; the thoracic cavity.

Second position of the feet—Turned-out Open position of the legs rotated outward at the hips; feet either side of the center line of the body; weight evenly balanced on both feet with the center of weight suspended between them.

Sequential form Specific arrangement of sections in dance and music such as A B, A B C, A B A C A; A, A^1, A^2, etc.

Shape The contour and line the body makes in space.

Space As opposed to Time. (Dance exists in Time and Space). Dancers usually conceive of space in geometrical terms—three dimensional—limited to the dance or playing area.

Spatial emphasis Movement made by the dancer emphasizing the spacial aspects rather than the time aspects of the movement.

Stage areas (from performers' point of view)

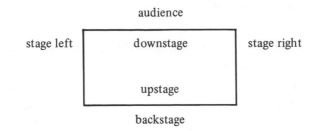

Style A specific manner of moving: national styles of dance or personal style, for example, Humphrey style, Ballet style, Tribal style.

Succession Action that starts in one area of the body and flows in orderly sequence to another part.

Sustained quality A steady, even flow of energy—more bound than free.

Swinging quality A free flow of energy which uses the force of gravity.

Syncopation An accent on a weak beat or the omission of an accent on a normally strong beat.

Tempo Rate of speed of music or dance, designated in various ways:

Italian	Metronome Markings
Largo	40–60
Larghetto	60–66
Adagio	66–76
Andante	76–108
Moderato	108–120
Allegro	120–168
Presto	168–200
Prestissimo	200–208

Texture Element of dynamics; for example, rough, light, and smooth.

Time As opposed to Space. Used here in the Newtonian sense as Time flowing by. (Cent. Dic.) Musical terms, such as Pulse, Beat, Tempo, Rhythm, Accent and so on are used to indicate how that flow is organized for teaching or artistic purposes.

Time signature Used in music notation to indicate groupings of notes into measures. They look like fractions, the most common ones are, 2/4, 3/4, 4/4, 6/8. The top number says how many, the bottom number what kind of note has the value of one beat.

Torso The trunk of the body, including the shoulders and hips.

Turn out (of the legs) The legs are rotated outward from the hips. The outward rotations of the leg includes the thighs, knees, and feet; the knees and feet point sideward.

Underlying beat The steady continuing pulse of the piece.

Upbeat The beat before the downbeat; the preparation for the downbeat.

Variation Slight altering of a movement to add interest or variety.

Vibratory quality A shaking release of energy, usually rapid.

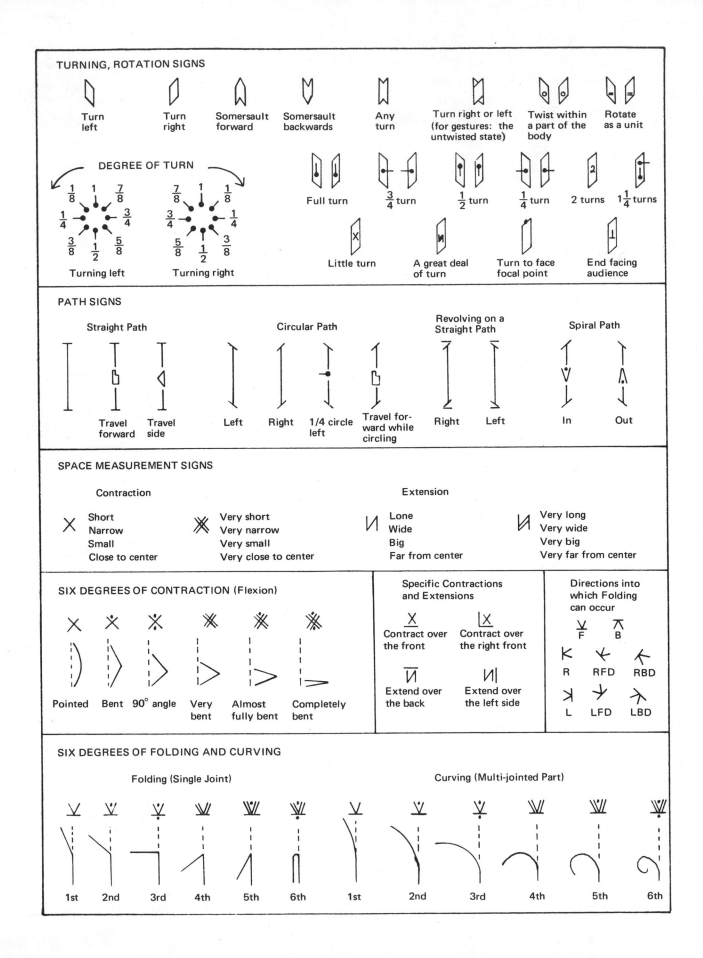

Principles of Services Marketing

Sixth Edition